ゲーム&アニメ
キャラクターデザインブック
Heroes & Heroines
Japanese Video Game+Animation Illustration

Heroes & Heroines
Japanese Video Game + Animation Illustration

©2011 PIE International/PIE BOOKS

All rights reserved. No part of this publication
may be reproduced in any form or by any means,
graphic, electronic or mechanical, including
photocopying and recording by an information storage
and retrievalsystem, without prior permission
in writing from the publisher.

PIE International

2-32-4, Minami-Otsuka,Toshima-ku, Tokyo 170-0005 JAPAN
Tel:+81-3-3944-3981 Fax: +81-3-5395-4830
e-mail:sales@pie.co.jp

ISBN978-4-7562-4169-6 C0079
Printed in Japan

ジャケットデザイン　草野剛（草野剛デザイン事務所）
ジャケット・扉　イラスト　『キャサリン』副島成記
©ATLUS CO.,LTD. 2010

収録作家インデックス

あ

蒼樹うめ —— 166
『魔法少女まどか☆マギカ』

足立慎吾 —— 188
『WORKING!!』シリーズ

碇谷敦 —— 146
『Fate/Zero』

石黒正数 —— 106
『それでも町は廻っている』

石野聡 —— 122
『NO.6』

いとうのいぢ —— 072
『シャイニング・フォース』シリーズ

伊東伸高 —— 174
『四畳半神話大系』

岩元辰郎 —— 038
『逆転検事』シリーズ

うし —— 070
『剣と魔法と学園モノ。Final ～新入生はお姫様！～』

羽海野チカ —— 138
『東のエデン』

エナミカツミ —— 102
『戦律のストラタス』

円居雄一郎 —— 036
『ガチトラ！ ～暴れん坊教師 in High School ～』

織田広之 —— 034
『俺の妹がこんなに可愛いわけがない』

CONTENTS

収録作家インデックス ……………… 0(
Artist's name INDEX ……………… 0(

【デザイナーインタビュー1】
『キャサリン』『ペルソナ3 ポータブル』『ペルソナ4』シリーズ
キャラクターデザイナー
副島成記 ……………………………… 01

ゲーム&アニメ
キャラクターデザインブック ……… 01

【デザイナーインタビュー2】
『REZELCROSS』キャラクターデザイナー
金田榮路 ……………………………… 190

作品インデックス ……………………… 196

か

風間雷太 ……………………………… 160
『ボーダーブレイク エアバースト』

加藤裕美 ……………………………… 058
『ギルティクラウン』

金田榮路 ……………………………… 176
『REZEL CROSS』

岸田隆宏 ……………………………… 166
『魔法少女まどか☆マギカ』

岸田メル ……………………………… 130
『花咲くいろは』

きゆづきさとこ ……………………… 066
『グングニル -魔槍の軍神と英雄戦争-』

ギンカ ………………………………… 140
『BEYOND THE FUTURE - FIX THE TIME ARROWS -』

黒裃 …………………………………… 068
『月華繚乱ROMANCE』

コザキユースケ ……………………… 128
『NO MORE HEROES 2 DESPERATE STRUGGLE』

こにしひろし ………………………… 064
『グロリア・ユニオン -Twin fates in blue ocean-』

小松崎類 ……………………………… 108
『ダンガンロンパ 希望の学園と絶望の高校生』

さ

佐々木啓悟 …………………………… 094
『閃光のナイトレイド』『青の祓魔師』

佐々木政勝 …………………………… 026
『Aチャンネル』

島崎麻里 ……………………………… 156
『BAYONETTA』

島田フミカネ ………………………… 148
『武装神姫 BATTLE MASTERS Mk.2』

新川洋司 ……………………………… 170
『METAL GEAR SOLID PEACE WALKER HD EDITION』

鈴平ひろ ……………………………… 144
『ファントムブレイカー』

須藤友徳 ……………………………… 146
『Fate/Zero』

関口可奈味 …………………………… 130
『花咲くいろは』

副島成記 ……………………………… 044
『キャサリン』『ペルソナ3 ポータブル』『ペルソナ4』シリーズ

た

竹安佐和記 ——— 028
『エルシャダイ』

田中将賀 ——— 020
『あの日見た花の名前を僕達はまだ知らない。』

tanu ——— 018
『AKIBA'S TRIP』

為重英子 ——— 064
『グロリア・ユニオン -Twin fates in blue ocean- 』

千葉崇洋 ——— 086
『世紀末オカルト学院』

津路参汰 ——— 104
『ソニコミ』

土林誠 ——— 100
『戦国BASARA3』

つなこ ——— 110
『超次元ゲイム ネプテューヌmk2』

toi8 ——— 122
『NO.6』

な

中澤一登 ——— 168
『宮本武蔵―双剣に馳せる夢―』

中村佑介 ——— 174
『四畳半神話大系』

長浜めぐみ ——— 118
『DUNAMIS15』

西村キヌ ——— 056
『極限脱出 9時間9人9の扉』

猫将軍 ——— 186
『ロリポップチェーンソー』

は

pako ——— 072
『シャイニング・フォース』シリーズ

左 ——— 150
『フラクタル』

日向悠二 ——— 088
『世界樹の迷宮』シリーズ・『ノーラと刻の工房 霧の森の魔女』

福田知則 ——— 184
『ROBOTICS;NOTES』

huke ——— 082
『STEINS;GATE』シリーズ

ま

前田浩孝 ———— 178
『Lucian Bee's』シリーズ

松原秀典 ———— 120
『とある飛空士への追憶』

三輪士郎 ———— 092
『セブンスドラゴン 2020』

ミノ☆タロー ———— 126
『NEWラブプラス』

森川聡子 ———— 138
『東のエデン』

森井しづき ———— 172
『メモリーズオフ ゆびきりの記憶』

森田和明 ———— 054
TVアニメ『ペルソナ 4』

や

ヤスダスズヒト ———— 112
『デビルサバイバー』シリーズ

病 ———— 070
『剣と魔法と学園モノ。Final ～新入生はお姫様！～』

山川宏治 ———— 098
『戦国乙女～桃色パラドックス～』

山村洋貴 ———— 106
『それでも町は廻っている』

ユウヤ ———— 134
『華ヤカ哉、我ガ一族』

吉崎観音 ———— 032
『オトメディウスX（エクセレント！）』

ら

redjuice ———— 058
『ギルティクラウン』

わ

wagi ———— 162
『真剣で私に恋しなさい！』シリーズ

渡辺明夫 ———— 136
『バレットソウル -弾魂-』

渡辺真由美 ———— 164
TVアニメ『真剣で私に恋しなさい!!』

Artist's name INDEX

ABCDEFG...

Adachi Shingo — 188

aokiume — 166

Chiba Takahiro — 086

Enami Katsumi — 102

Enkyo Yuichiro — 036

Fukuda Tomonori — 184

Ginka — 140

HIJKLMN...

Hidari	150		Kiyuduki Satoko	066
Himukai Yuji	088		Komatsuzaki Rui	108
huke	082		Konishi Hiroshi	064
Ikariya Atsushi	146		Kozaki Yusuke	128
Ishiguro Masakazu	106		Kuroyuki	068
Ishino Satoshi	122		Maeda Hirotaka	178
Ito Nobutake	174		Matsubara Hidenori	120
Ito Noizi	072		Mino☆Taro	126
Iwamoto Tatsuro	038		Miwa Shirow	092
Kaneda Eiji	176		Morii Shizuki	172
Kato Hiromi	058		Morikawa Satoko	138
Kazama Raita	160		Morita Kazuaki	054
Kishida Mel	130		Nagahama Megumi	118
Kishida Takahiro	166		Nakamura Yusuke	174

HIJKLMN...

Nakazawa Kazuto — 168

Nekoshogun — 186

Nishimura Kinu — 056

OPQRSTU...

Oda Hiroyuki — 034

pako — 072

redjuice — 058

Sasaki Keigo — 094

Sasaki Masakatsu — 026

Sekiguchi Kanami — 130

Shimada Humikane — 148

Shimazaki Mari — 156

Shinkawa Yoji — 170

Soejima Shigenori — 044

Sudo Tomonori — 146

Suzuhira Hiro — 144

Takeyasu Sawaki — 028

Tameshige Eiko — 064

Tanaka Masayoshi — 020

tanu	018
toi8	122
Tsuchibayashi Makoto	100
Tsuji Santa	104
Tsunako	110
Umino Chika	138
Ushi	070

VWXYZ...

wagi	162
Watanabe Akio	136
Watanabe Mayumi	164
Yamai	070
Yamakawa Koji	098
Yamamura Hiroki	106
Yasuda Suzuhito	112
Yoshizaki Mine	032
Yuuya	134

【デザイナーインタビュー1】
『キャサリン』『ペルソナ3 ポータブル』『ペルソナ4』シリーズ キャラクターデザイナー 副島成記

大人気タイトル『ペルソナ』シリーズや、『キャサリン』等、見る者を魅了する
キャラクターを生み出す副島成記に『キャサリン』制作のお話を伺った。(※作品は本書p44〜53に掲載)

『ペルソナ』チームで挑んだ『ペルソナ』シリーズとは違うテイストの『キャサリン』。

——『キャサリン』制作までの経緯をお教えいただけますか。

副島 『ペルソナ3』と『ペルソナ4』を同じチームで作ったんですが、そのときにチーム内で「何か違うものも作りたいね」という話が出ていて、『キャサリン』を作りました。ハードの話をすれば、『ペルソナ3』『ペルソナ4』はPlayStation 2で、弊社としては、PlayStation 3のソフトをまだ作っていなかったんです。RPGは相当なボリュームで、いきなり次世代のハードに対して大きなソフトを作るのはリスキーなので、実験作でしかできない、『ペルソナ』ではできないような、やってみたいことをやろうという話がチーム内にありました。『キャサリン』はPlayStation 3というハードのきっかけにしつつ、やりたいことをやってみるという、内部的にはそういう意味合いのあるタイトルですね。

——キャラクターを描く上で苦労されたところは？

副島 ひとつは、3Dモデルのモデラーとのやりとりですね。それまでのゲームはバストショットがゲーム画面に出ていて、ゲーム中はポリゴンのキャラクターが立っていたりするんですけど、それにはちょっとデフォルメがかかっているんです。デザイン画そのままをモデリングすることは、実は今までなくて、それを作るときにどう表現するのが一番いいのかをやりとりするのが大変でした。自分の絵は漫画絵なので、立体図としては破綻してるんです。横顔と正面顔で顔のバランスが違っていたりするので、そのまま三面図というわけにはいかなくて。ゲーム中のモデルのどこをどうすれば、そのキャラクターらしく見えるか、そのやりとりをしているときに自分も発見があって、あとで役に立ちました。

女性スタッフからの声で、補強が入った「ヴィンセントいい人化計画」。

——描きやすかったキャラクターは？

副島 脇役ですね。脇役って表裏がなくて、キャラクターとしては一通りと言いますか、主人公は途中で改心したりとか複雑ですけど、脇役は「こういうキャラクターです」っ

Catherine, Persona3, Persona4 Series Interview with Soejima Shigenori, Character Designer

I'm talking with Soejima Shigenori, the creator of many captivating characters in the popular Persona Series, Catherine, and other titles, about the creation of Catherine. (*You can read about Catherine on pgs. 44 – 53.)

Catherine, a bit different than what the Persona team has ever worked on.

–Can you tell us what led to the creation of Catherine?

Soejima: Catherine was made by the same team that made Persona3 and Persona4. There was talk about making something different while we were making Persona, so we made Catherine. At the hardware level, Persona3 and 4 were for the PlayStation 2, but our company hadn't yet made any software for the PlayStation 3. RPGs are take a lot of memory, and suddenly creating huge software for a next-generation system is risky, so our team said let's do something we couldn't do with Persona, something we can only get away with an experiment. As a group, we decided that Catherine would be our chance to do everything we wanted to do using PlayStation 3 hardware.

–Were there any difficulties in drawing the characters?

Soejima: One was working with a 3D modeler. Until Catherine, games would have bust shots on the game screen, while within the game the characters were polygon characters. But we encountered some deformation. We had a tough time working out how best to express the modeling design as-is, which was something new for us. My drawings are manga drawings, so they would break down in single view drawings. The facial balance between profiles and head-on views are different, so they couldn't be used as orthographic views as-is. I made a discovery that came in handy later about when and how to do modeling in the game, how the characters should look, and how to go about it.

The women on the staff wanted Vincent to be more personable.

–What characters were easy to draw?

Soejima: The side characters. Side characters have no depth, and as characters are one-dimensional.

て言ったら最後までそうなので、キャラクターとして立てやすいと思うんですね。ジョニーとオーランドという主人公の悪友がいるんですが、彼らは描きやすかったです。脇役は最初に設定されたイメージが全面に出ますから、そのぶん魅力的にもなりますし、ブレのないキャラクターは描きやすい。自分の年齢が近いので、感情移入しちゃうっていうのもあります（笑）。

——主人公のヴィンセントも32歳ですね。

副島 ヴィンセントは基本かっこ悪い主人公なんです。最初から最後までヒーローではないんですよ。最初のプロットで、浮気はするわ、いつまでもウジウジしているわで、女性スタッフから「許しがたい」という意見が出ました（笑）。最後にこういう一言を言ってくれれば、まだ許せるという話があって、途中で「ヴィンセントいい人化計画」ということで、ヴィンセントにいろいろな補強が入ったんです。

——ヴィンセントに主人公補正が入ったんですね（笑）。

副島 顔も最初はそんなに崩れなかったんですが、ストーリーが進むにつれ、シリアスになってきて冗談じゃ済まなくなってくるんです。チャップリン演じる男のように、ひどい目に遭ってる男を見て笑って欲しいんですけど、あんまりシリアスだと苦しくて笑えないので「ここは笑いどころなんですよ」というように、一般の3Dモデルではあまりやらない漫画に近い顔の動きができるようにしました。デザインのほうも、最初は渋めに描いていたのを漫画っぽく描いてそれを再現できるようにしたり。補正する一番最初のきっかけは、ヴィンセントの立ちポーズが今はルパン三世みたいに猫背でガニ股なんですけど、その前はスッと背筋が伸びて斜に構えて立っていて、「それがムカつく」って話になったんです（笑）。何をかっこつけているんだと。最初はシリアスで真面目でかっこいい主人公というスタートだったんですけど、どうも何か噛み合わなくて喜劇役者のかっこ良さ、面白いかっこ良さを見てくれればいいなということで、全体のテイスト作りをするのと一緒にキャラクターも作られていきました。

——ふたりのキャサリンについてはいかがでしたか？

※ここではカバーイラストに使用されたキャサリン（CATHERINE）を浮気キャサリン、もうひとりのキャサリン（KATHERINE）を恋人キャサリンと書き分けています。

副島 ふたりのキャサリンはそんなに迷うことはなかったですね。浮気キャサリンは意外と早かったです。記号の集合体というか、色っぽくてありえないような衣装を着て主人公を誘惑するファンタジックなキャラクターなので、あまりブレがなかったんです。恋人キャサリンについては、最初のほうで若干の変遷がありましたね。基本的に主人公がどちらのキャサリンを選ぶかっていう話なんですが、恋人キャサリンはすごく厳しいんですね。恋人なんだけど、恐妻家みたいな、会う度にきついことばかり言ってくる。

Main characters can reform or become complex midway through the game, but side characters are set and stay that way until the end. I think they're easy to create as characters. Jonathan and Orlando are bad influences for our hero, but they were easy to draw. The initial image that the side characters give is their only image, so that becomes captivating. Simple characters are easy to draw. And they're close to my age so I empathize with them. (Laughs)

–Our hero Vincent is 32, right?

Soejima:Vincent is basically not a cool character. From beginning to end, he's not really a hero. In our first version, he would always have affairs and be passive. Our female staff said that he was "hard to forgive." (Laughs) They mentioned that in the end if he just said one thing then he could still be forgiven, so midway we added things on as part of a plan to make Vincent more personable.

–So Vincent got some heroic corrections. (Laughs)

Soejima:His face initially didn't change much, but as the story progressed it got more serious. We couldn't get away with jokes. Like the kind of guys Charlie Chaplin would play, we wanted him to laugh when he saw people in a terrible situation, but the tone was so serious we couldn't have him laugh. We thought "This isn't a funny situation," so we made facial movements more like manga, which isn't usually done on standard 3D modeling. With the design too, he was initially more mellow. We just drew it like manga and made sure that we could draw it again. Our very first chance for revisions was with Vincent's pose. Vincent's standing pose is more like Lupin the 3rd, with his hunched back and bowed legs. Before that he stood ram-rod straight and kind of askew. Some staff said that it looked gross. (Laughs) We asked ourselves what we were trying to show. At first we wanted him to be a serious, handsome hero, but somehow it just didn't fit. We thought it would be good if people saw him as "funny cute," as an interesting cute. So we created a character together with creating that overarching flavor.

–How did you feel about the two Catherines?

*This section talks about both the cheating Catherine, the illustration used on the cover, and the other girlfriend Katherine.

Soejima:There wasn't a lot of hesitation between

描きやすかったという悪友のひとりジョニー。主人公と違い脇役はプレイヤーとともに成長しないため、というのも理由のひとつ。

Jonathan, one of the bad influences, was easy to draw. One reason is that because like the players, and unlike the hero, the side characters don't grow.

そうすると、まず好かれない。好かれるためには、きつい
けど、母性があって包容力のあるキャラクターをと考えま
した。キャラクターを作るときに自分はキーワードを並べ
て、それに合ってるかどうか確かめながら描くんですが、
このふたりの場合は、片方は欲望、もう一方は理性、刺激
に対して安定とか、すべてにおいて対極に位置するように
対比表を並べていきました。ゲームの目的は迷わせること
なので、浮気キャサリンのキャラクターが固まっていると
いうこともあって、恋人キャサリンでバランスを取るとい
う感じですね。ムービーでも恋人キャサリンはヴィンセン
トがコーヒーを飲もうとすると、砂糖を２個入れるという
演出をあえて入れてみたりもしました。絵だけではなく、
設定も使うか使わないかわからないけど、プロファイリン
グ的なところまで掘り下げています。

街中で実際にいる人が
キャラクターデザインの素となる。

──キャラクターのコスチュームをデザインするときに参考に
しているものはありますか？

副島 ファッション誌をたくさん買ってきて並べて、いい
のがあるかな、という感じですね。一般の人の服はコスプレ
ではないので、「私、こういう人なんです」という自己主
張はないですよね。でも、キャラクターはある程度、その
キャラクターっぽい格好をしているべきだと思うんです。
一般の衣装を見ながら、街中にいてもおかしくないコー
ディネイトをされていても、何かしらの雰囲気があって、
そう見せている要因は何かというのを解釈します。余計な
ものを排除していって、その人がそれっぽく見える要素を
解読してそこだけを残す、覚えやすいデザインにしようと
心がけています。

──街中で人をよく観察したりしますか？

副島 しますね。メモが欲しくなります。忘れてしまうの
で（笑）。

──どういう人に目が留まりますか？

副島 普通のいろいろにヒントがあるときが多くて、一般
の人たちの中から「こういう普通の人いるよね」という人
を見つけると、嬉しくて覚えておこうと思います。ファッ
ションショーのテレビとかも見ますけど、あれがキャラク
ターデザインの参考になることはあまりないです。ああい
う人は知り合いにいないですからね。もちろん、デザイ
ン的にいろいろ趣向を凝らしているので、面白いんです
が、キャラクターというもののイメージ作りとしてはまた
ちょっと違うのかな。やっぱり実際にいる人にはかなわな
いですね。

──副島さんがキャラクターデザイナーを目指したきっかけは？

副島 昔から漫画が好きで、漫画のキャラクターが好き
でっていう、わかりやすいきっかけですね。自分は今、

the two Catherines. The cheating Catherine was actually quite quick. She's a fantastic character, the embodiment of signs, who wears sexy, almost impossible clothing to seduce our hero. So she was pretty direct. With the girlfriend Katherine, there were some changes at first. Basically it's a story of which Catherine our hero will choose, but the girlfriend Katherine is extremely strict. She's the girlfriend, but she's like a scary wife who criticizes people whenever we see her. So first, she's unlikable. But in order to make her likable, I thought she should be strict, but with a maternal instinct and tolerance. When I make a character, I make a list of all the key words for that character, and I check whether the character I'm drawing matches those key words. With these two Catherines, one was Desire, one was Reason, so I made a comparison list that positioned contrasted key words for each type, such as impulse and stability. The purpose of Catherine is to lead you astray, so the cheating Catherine had some concrete points to balance her out with the girlfriend Katherine. Even in the movie, when Vincent would drink coffee I tried a scene where the girlfriend Katherine puts in two packs of sugar. I don't know if I'll use the drawing or even as a character trait, but I delve into this kind of character profiling.

**Actual people on the street become
the essence of character designs.**

–Do you reference anything when you're designing character costumes?

Soejima:I buy a lot of fashion magazines and check them out to see if they have anything good. Most normal people don't wear cosplay clothing, so most people don't broadcast "I'm this kind of person." But I think characters should wear clothing that is like them. While looking people wearing normal clothing on the street, I try to figure out what image they're projecting, and what makes them want to project that image. I reject clothing that is too much, and what's left is what I figure are the elements that fit their look. Then I make sure to create a design that is easy to remember.

–Do you often observe people on the streets?

Soejima:Yes. I always want to take notes because I tend to forget things. (Laughs)

–What kind of people stand out?

プレイヤーの選択を迷わせるため、かわいそうな感じにならないように、厳しいだけの感じにもならないようにと絶妙のバランスで作り込まれてた「恋人キャサリン」

In order to confound players in their choice, the girlfriend Katherine was exquisitely balanced so that she was neither pitiful nor strict.

37歳ですけど、中学生くらいのときに『ロードス島戦記』とか、ファンタジーものにどっぷりハマり、『機動警察パトレイバー』や士郎正宗さんに影響されました。
——漫画家になろうとは思わなかったのですか？
副島 漫画をひとつも描いたことがないんです。子供の頃、『アニメージュ』とかに載ってるアニメの設定画を見て「かっこいいなあ、プロの仕事だなあ」と思うわけです。それで漫画を描こうと思ってキャラクター設定画を描くと満足して、漫画を描かずに次の設定画を描き始めるんです（笑）。かっこいいシーンだけは描くんですよ。ボードみたいに。でも漫画は描かない（笑）。絵が描きたいだけの人だったんですね。
——アニメの『ペルソナ4』の監修もされていますが、アニメ用のキャラクターデザインについていろいろと話し合ったりはしたのでしょうか？
副島 アニメの監督含め、スタッフさんも『ペルソナ4』をよく知っている方々なので、ゲームで描かれた絵もたくさんありますし、どういうキャラクターなのかはそんなにブレることはなかったですね。キャラクターが、そのキャラクターっぽく見えるポイントというのはお伝えしましたが、全体の雰囲気はお任せしました。逆に原作側が「ああして下さい、こうして下さい」と言うと窮屈な作品になってしまいますよね。アニメは「こんなふうだったんだ」とか「ペルソナ大きいなあ」とか楽しんで見ています。ペルソナはゲームだと画面に収まりきらないので、小さくしていますが、アニメだと実際のフル等身で描かれているので迫力ありますね。
——副島さんがキャラクターを描く上でこだわっているところは？
副島 わかりやすさですね。漫画でもアニメでもゲームでも何でもいいんですが、見ている側は初見でキャラクターが好きかどうかの判断をすると思うんです。その作品に触れるきっかけを作るのはキャラクターに頼っている部分があると思うので、そこは責任を感じています。我々が作っている作品をなるべく多くの人に見てもらうためには、独自性もありつつ、好かれるキャラクターでなくてはいけない。好き嫌いがはっきり分かれるキャラクターをあまり良しとしないというか、とがっててかっこいいけど、あまり人に見てもらえないものでは、我々も作った意味がない。特にゲームはお金を出して買って下さった方にしか内容を見ることができないものなので、中にはきっと面白い作品が詰まっているんだという期待を裏切らないものにしたい。それをイントロダクションでキャラクターが阻害するようではいけないと考えています。だから、キャラクターは見たまんまが好きですね。「見ればわかりますよ」というシンプルな記号をどれだけ飽きないように厚みを持たせるかというところを大事にしています。『キャサリン』の

Soejima: Often I see a lot that hints at normality. I love it when I find someone that stands out as normal in a sea of normal people, so I try to remember them. I sometimes watch fashion TV shows, but usually they aren't good as references for character design. I don't know anyone like those people. Design-wise there is a lot of variety, which is interesting, but as an inspiration for a character it's a little different. They're not on the same level as actual people.

-What made you decide to become a character designer?

Soejima: I've always liked manga, and I've always liked manga characters. Pretty simple, right? I'm 37 now, but when I was a junior high school student I was totally hooked on Record of Lodoss War and other fantasy series. I was influenced by Mobile Police PATLABOR and Shirow Masamune.

-Did you think about becoming a manga artist?

Soejima: I've never drawn a single manga. When I was a kid I would look at the set-up screen on Animage or whatever and think, "Wow, that looks so cool. That's the work of a pro!" So I thought I would draw manga, but I was actually satisfied with drawing characters for set-up screens, so I forgot about the manga and started drawing more and more set-up screens. (Laughs) I just draw cool screens, like boards. But I don't draw manga. (Laughs) I was someone who just wanted to draw pictures.

-You were supervisor on the Persona4 anime. Did you talk a lot about character designs for anime?

Soejima: The staff and even the anime director knew a lot about Persona4, so there were a lot of drawings from the game. There weren't a lot of discussion as to what kind of characters there would be. I told them that the main point was that the characters looked like the characters from the game, but I left the overall feel to them. Saying "do this" or "do that" on the story side would make it feel too restricted. I watch the anime and am excited to see what it's like and how big Persona is. As a game, there's only so much that can fit on the screen, so Persona is small, but as anime you can draw Persona to full size. It makes quite an impact.

-Is there anything you get hung up on when drawing characters?

Soejima: Their simplicity. Manga, anime, games, or whatever, when you first look at a character you decide whether you like that character or not. I think part of the reason why you will go for a game is driven by the character, so I have a lot of responsibility. I need characters that are unique and that people will like in order to get as many people as possible to check out our game. While it's not really good to have characters that you decide you like or dislike easily, there's no point in us making

ような、内容としてはとがっているものでも、キャラクターはどこか安心感がある窓口の広さは必要だと思います。こだわっているのはその点です。

――副島さんから、キャラクターデザイナーを目指す方へアドバイスをいただけますか?

副島 アドバイスというと「好きこそ物の上手なれ」じゃないですけど、描きたいときにたくさん描いて下さいということになるでしょうか。面白いと思うことを一生懸命やるのが一番いいかなと思います。自分は好きだから描いているのももちろんですが、まず第一に人に喜んでもらいたくて一生懸命描いています。最近気がついたことですが、自分が絵を描く仕事をずっと続けていられるのは、「好きで楽しい」ことの他に、自分が若い頃に好きで、楽しませてもらった作品がたくさんあり、そういう作品を作ってくれた先輩たちがいるからなんですね。そのせいか、自分が若い頃に夢中になっていたのと同じ楽しみを今度は自分の年代とは違う人たちとも共有したいという感覚が生まれたんです。児童書を書く人たちと同じ気持ちでしょうか。読むのは今の自分じゃないんです。子供たちに読んでもらいたいんですというものです。キャラクターデザイナーを目指している学生さんは20歳前後でしょうか。ゲームやアニメを一番楽しめる年頃ですが、そのときに一番好きだから仕事にしたいというだけではなく、自分以外の人たちに楽しみを提供したいとか、「どうやったら人に楽しんでもらえるかな」と、過去自分の好きだった作品や、今の時流を加味して喜んでもらえるものを作ろうとする感覚も必要かもしれません。そういう気持ちの整理をすると、若いうちからでも、勉強の仕方や作品の見方がちょっと変わってくるのかなと思います。

stand-out cool looking characters if people aren't going to look at them. Especially, games have content only viewable to people who actually shell out money and buy the game, we don't want to betray their expectations that the game will be filled with interesting content. It's important at the beginning not to undermine the character. That's why I like characters that are as they look. It's important that characters are rounded enough that even though you know all about them when you see them, you don't get tired of them. Even with a game like Catherine, an exciting game, the characters need to be easily accessible. This is what I get hung up on.

-Do you have any advice for aspiring character designers?

Soejima: I'm not going to say "get good at what you like," but I'd like to say that if you want to draw, you should draw a lot. I think it's best if you put all of your effort into what you enjoy. You should draw what you like, of course, but first you should draw your best to make people happy. Recently, I've realized that the reason I've continued to draw as a job isn't just because I like it and it's fun, but there were a lot of things There were things that I liked as a kid, and the people that made those things are still around. I don't know if that's the reason, but it instilled in me a desire to share that same joy with other people of my generation. People who write children's books probably feel the same way. You don't read them now – you want your children to read them. Students maybe 20 years old want to become character designers. It's an age when they love video games and anime the most, but it's not just when they want to become a character designer because it's when they love these things the most. It's when they want to give this joy to others, "They need to not only think" How can I share this with others," as well as feel the need to make something that appeals to modern sensibilities. If you can manage those feelings, then I think it will change the way you study and look at things when you're young.

副島は『ペルソナ3』の途中から、下描きからすべてデジタルで描く。使用ソフトは『ペイントツールSAI』。

Midway into Persona3, Soejima started drawing everything by computer, including rough sketches. He uses Easy Paint Tool Sai.

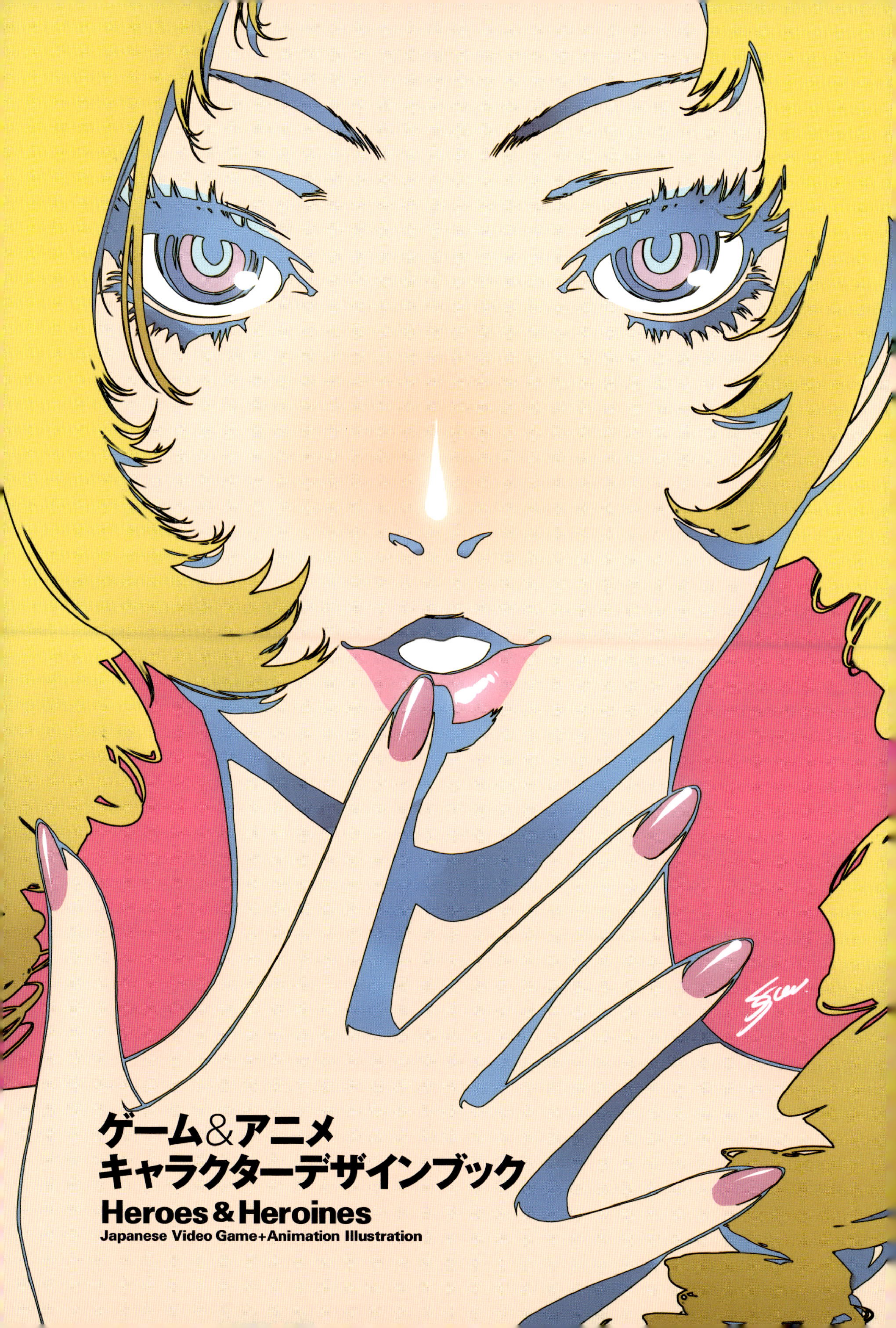

ゲーム&アニメ キャラクターデザインブック
Heroes & Heroines
Japanese Video Game+Animation Illustration

Game

『AKIBA'S TRIP』
● AKIBA'S TRIP

キャラクターデザイン
tanu
tanu

[代表作]『AKIBA'S TRIP』

リアルな秋葉原の街を舞台に、"カゲヤシ"と呼ばれる吸血鬼と戦うアクションアドベンチャーゲーム。メイド、アイドル、オタクやジャンクパーツ屋のオヤジなど、秋葉原を象徴する様々な人物を活写した新進気鋭のイラストレーター・ｔａｎｕ。今後の活躍にも期待大だ。

Set on a real Akihabara street, players in this action adventure game fight against the vampire "Kageyashi". Illustrated by tanu, it realistically depicts cosplay maids, pop idols, otaku, old junk store owners, and other real-life denizens of Akihabara. More exciting work is expected of this up-and-coming illustrator!

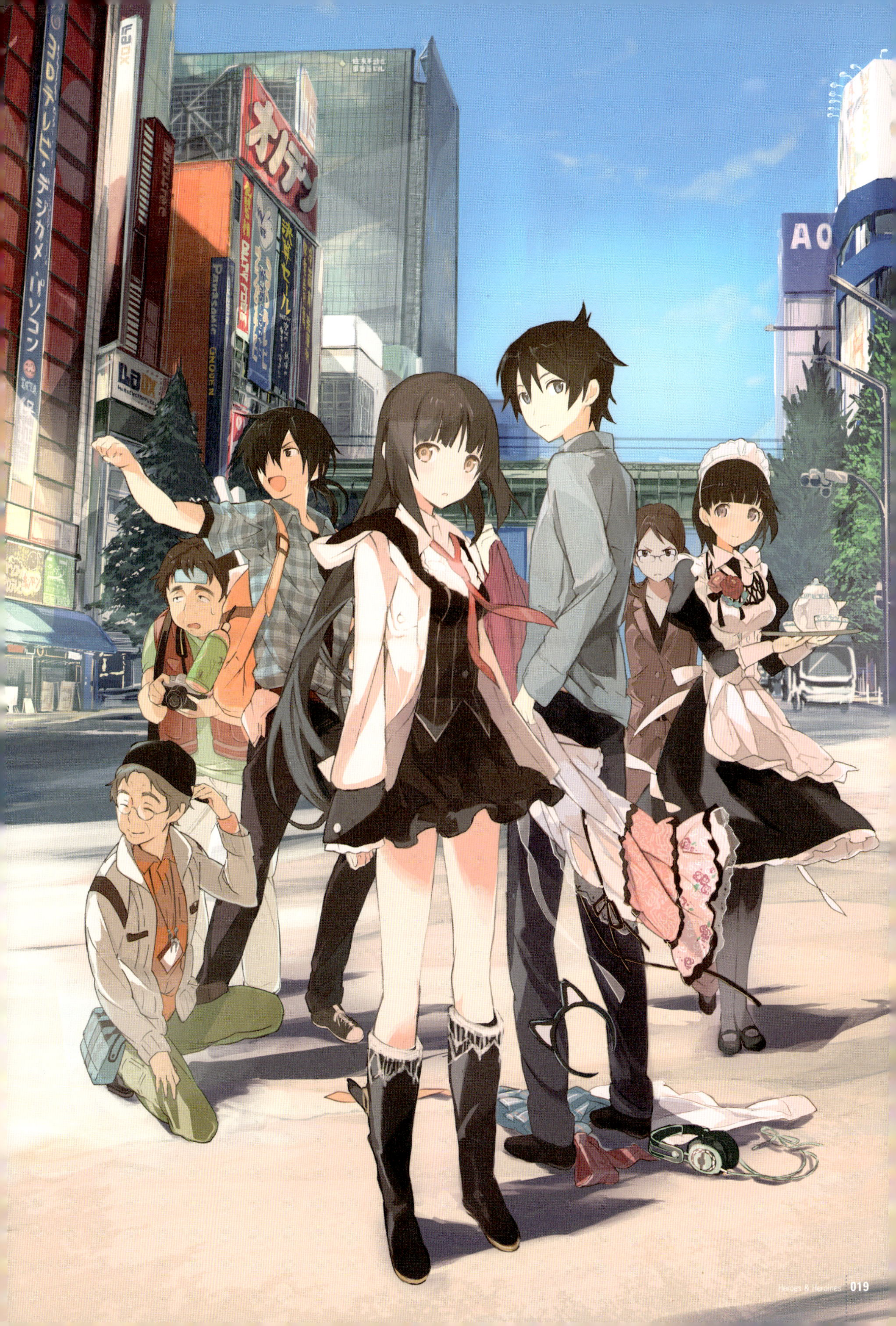
オノデン
AO

Animation 『あの日見た花の名前を僕達はまだ知らない。』
● Anohi mita hanano namaewo bokutachiha mada shiranai

キャラクターデザイン
田中将賀
Tanaka Masayoshi

[代表作]『学園黙示録 HIGHSCHOOL OF THE DEAD』
『家庭教師ヒットマン REBORN!』

誰もが通り過ぎる少年少女時代の淡い恋、嫉妬や羨望、罪の意識を丁寧に描いたドラマ性の高いストーリーで視聴者の胸を打ち、テレビ放映終了後も、物語のモデルとなった土地へファンが訪れるなど、話題を呼んだ。田中将賀は第1話、最終話の作画監督も担当した。

This striking dramatic story beautifully captures the passionate love, jealousies, and feelings of guilt that all young women have. Even after its run on TV it is a model story that fans return to again and again. Tanaka Masayoshi was executive supervisor on the first and last parts.

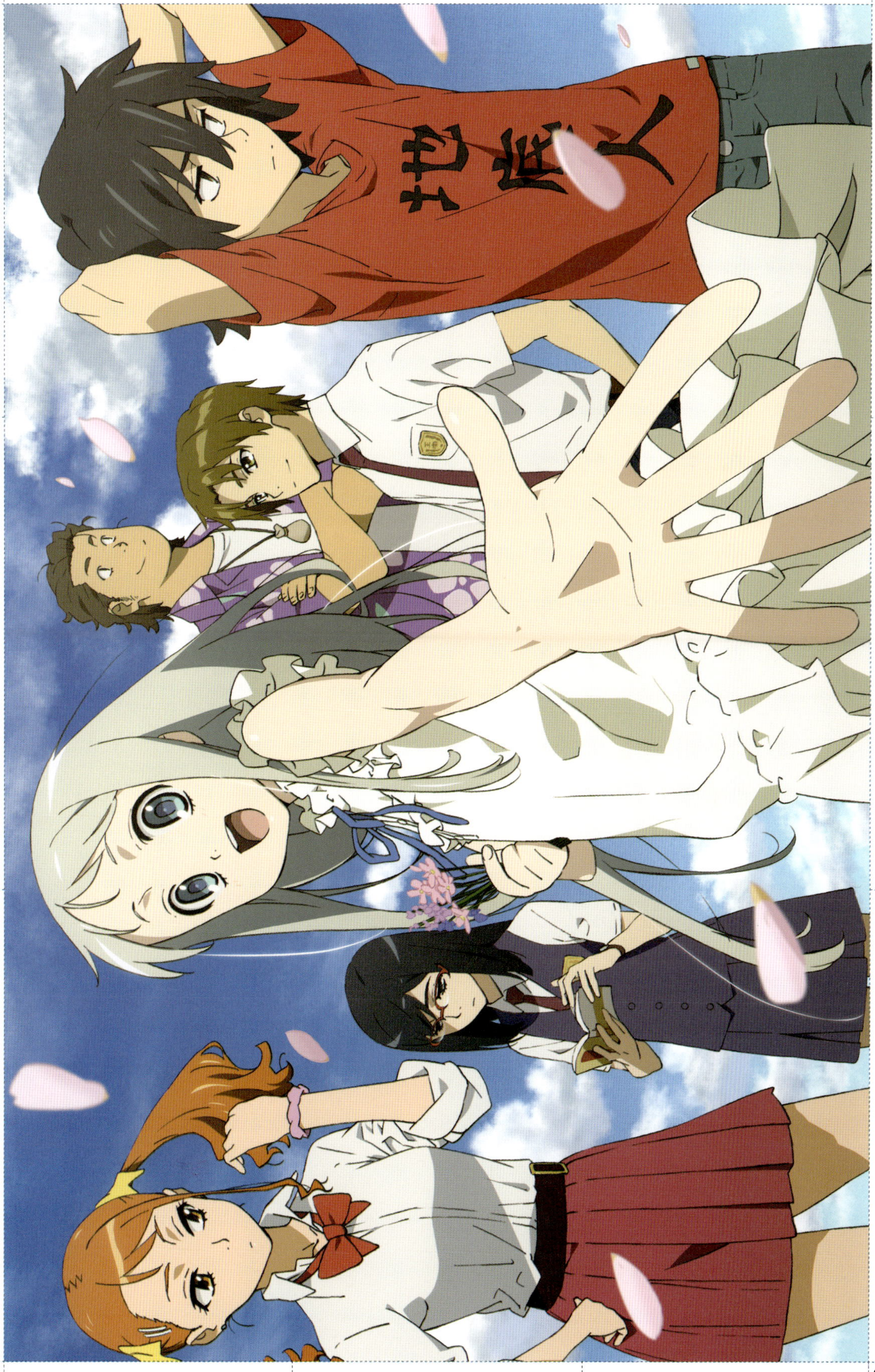

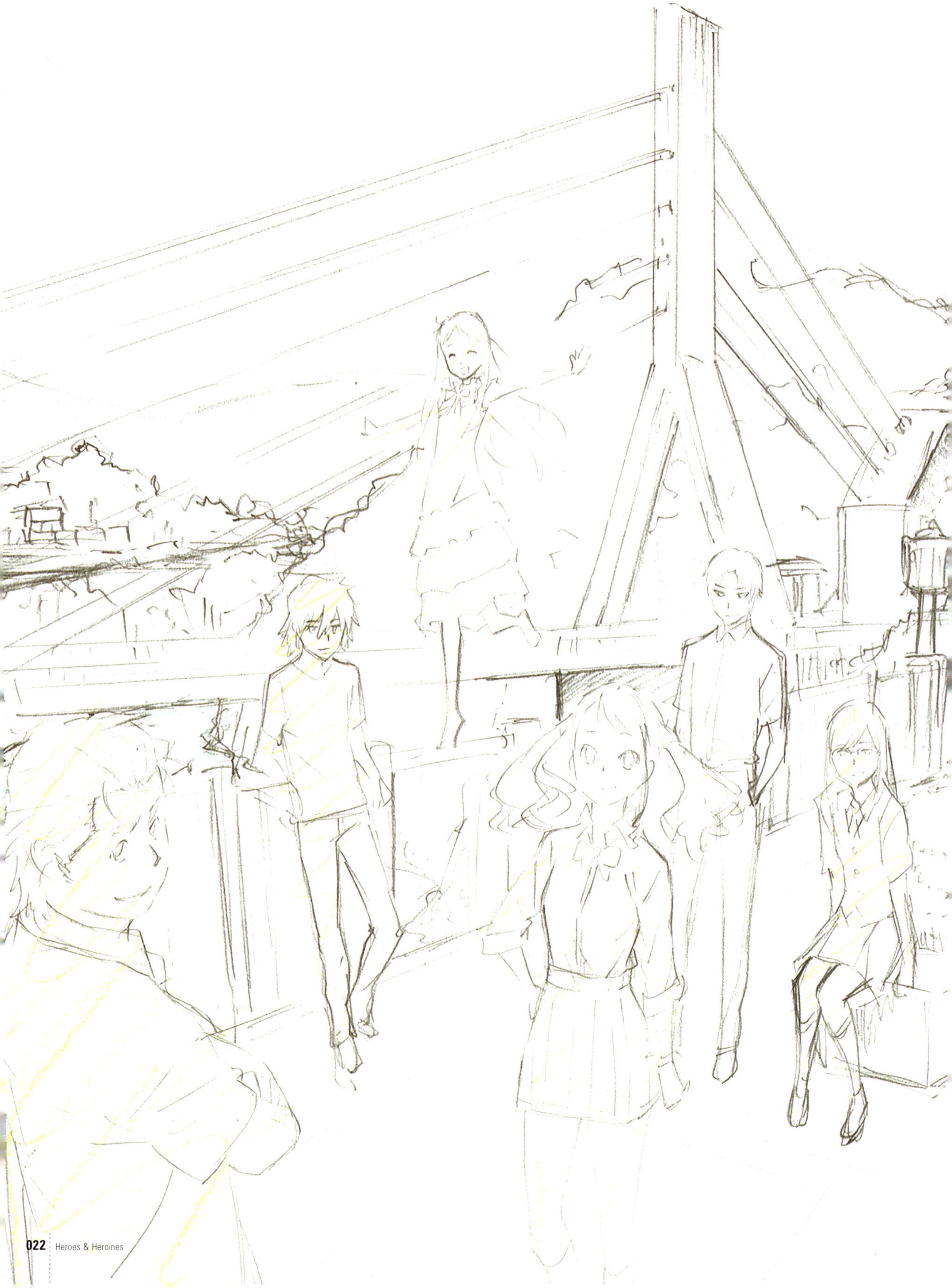

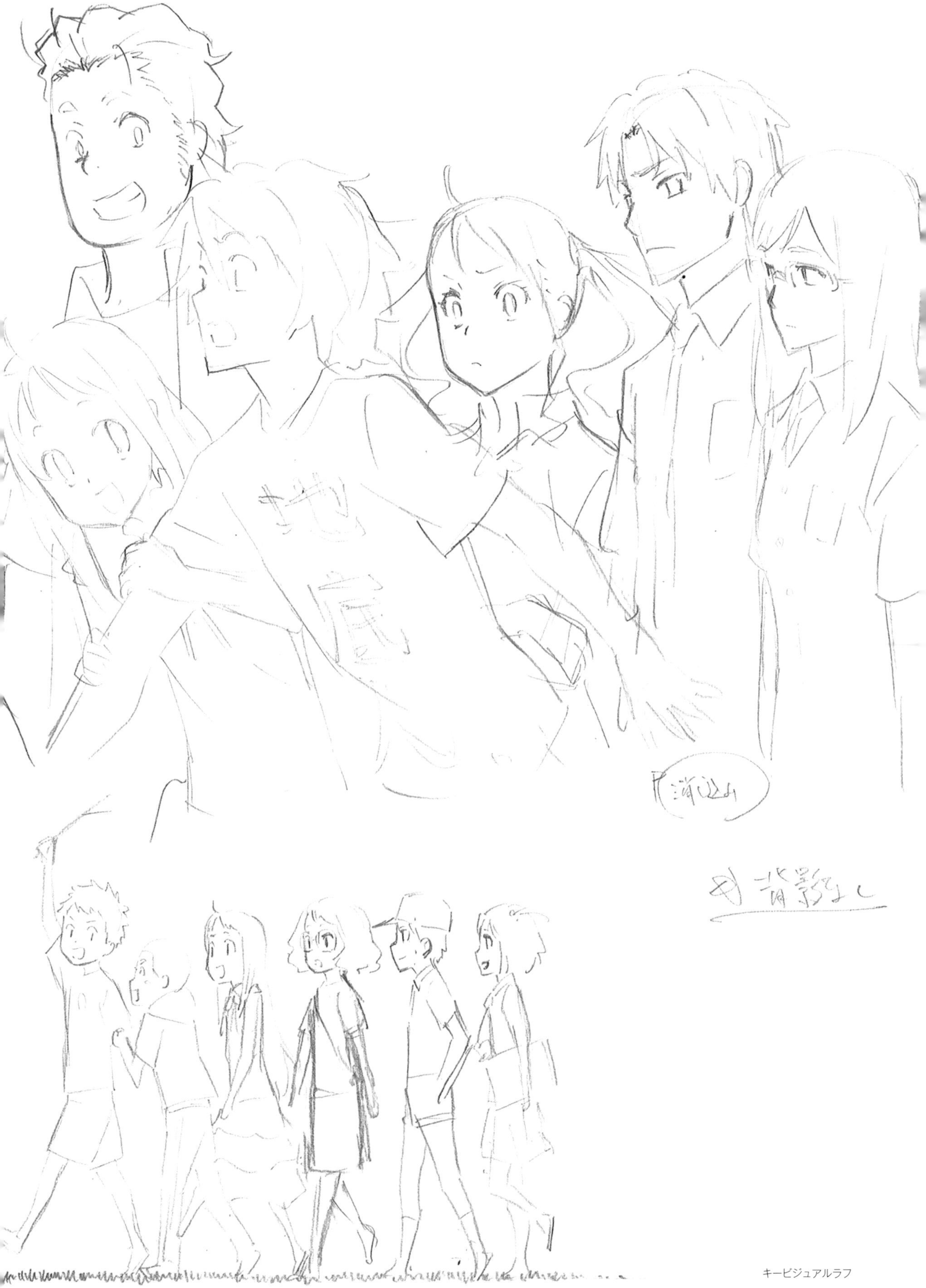
消込み
背影なし

キービジュアルラフ

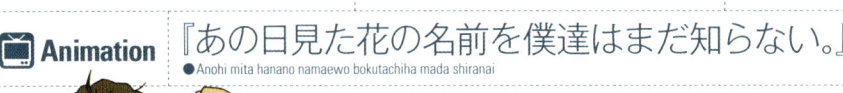

『あの日見た花の名前を僕達はまだ知らない。』

● Anohi mita hanano namaewo bokutachiha mada shiranai

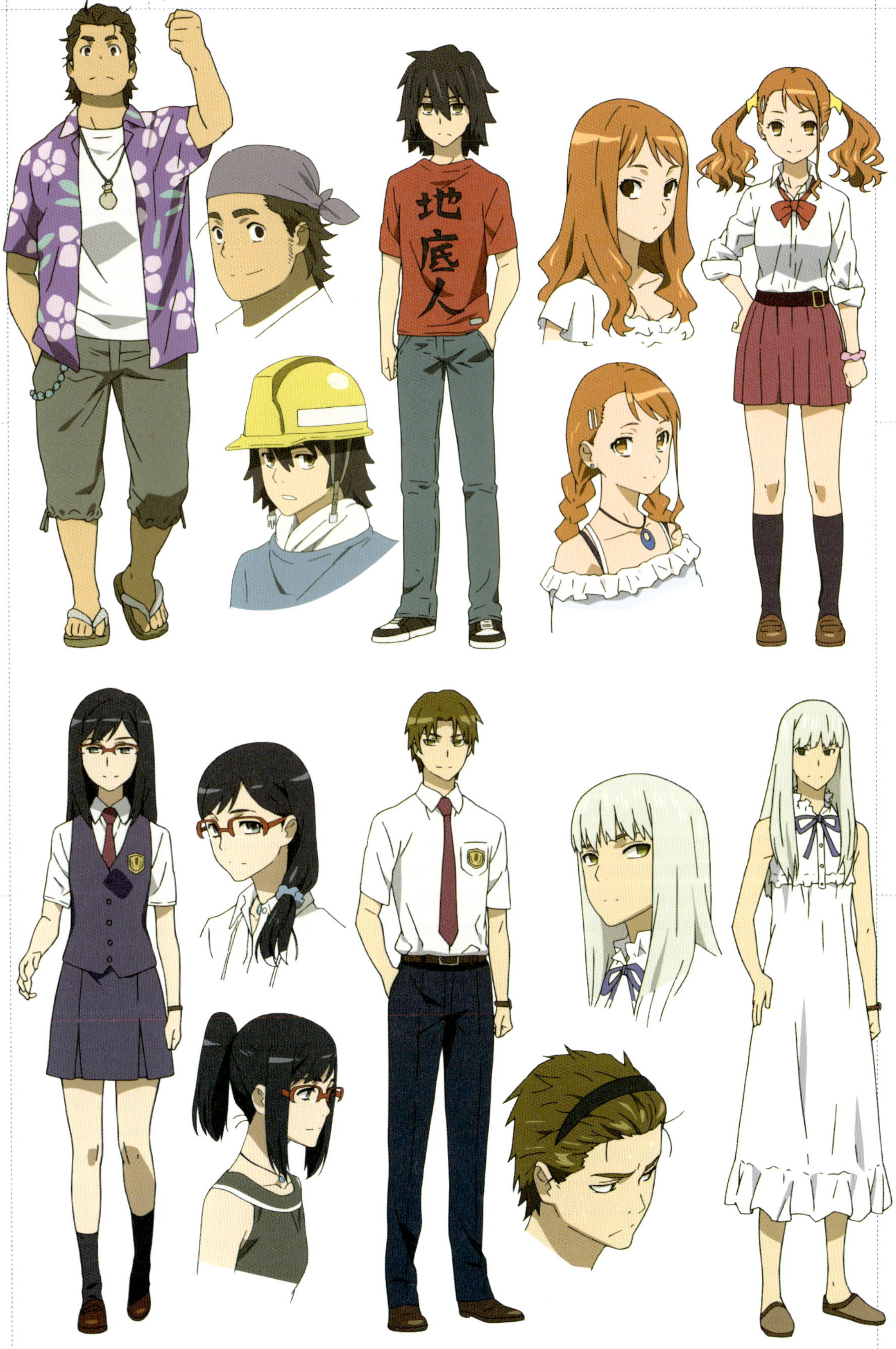
地底人

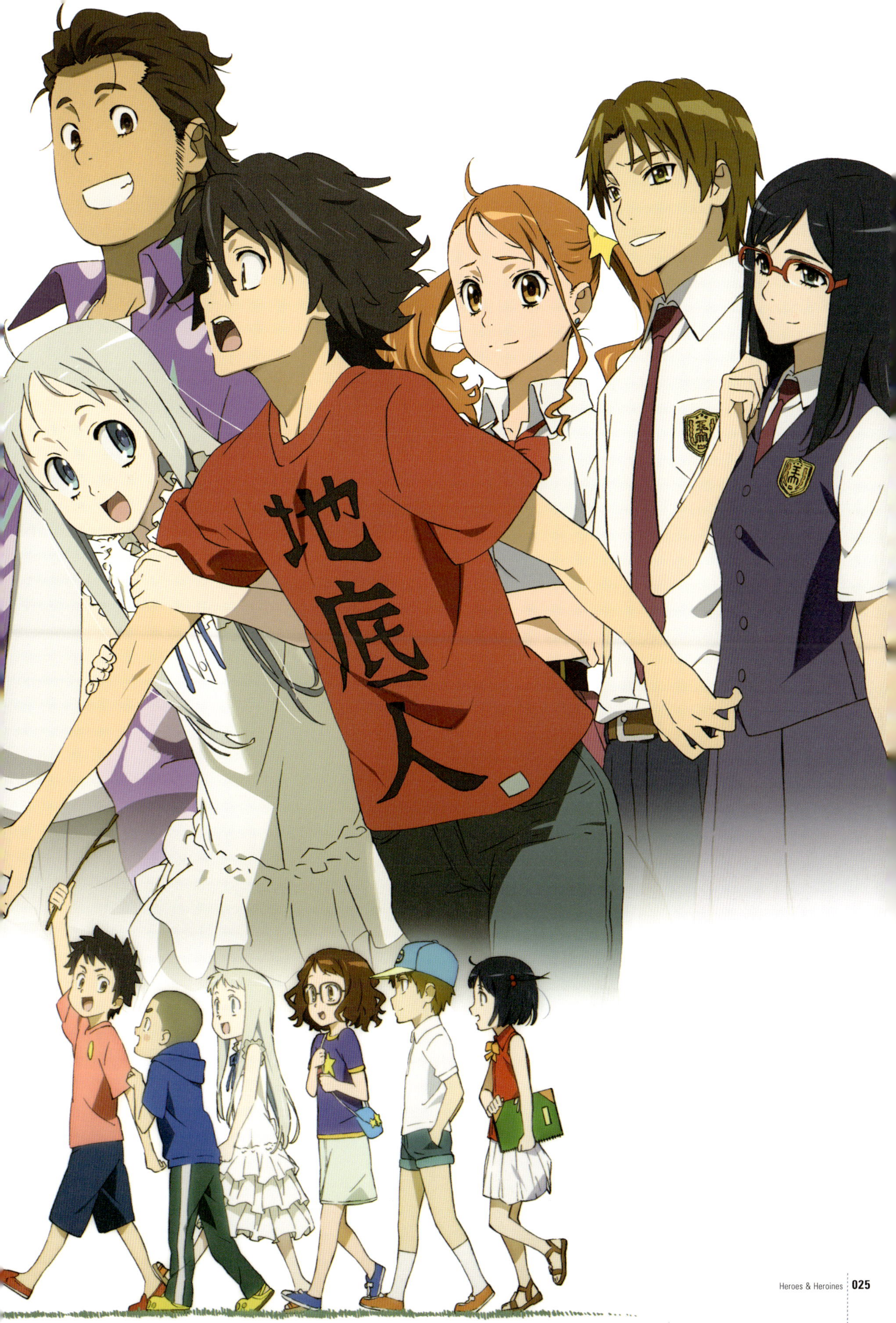
地底人

キャラクターデザイン

佐々木政勝

Sasaki Masakatsu

[代表作]『咲 -Saki-』

黒田bb原作の4コマギャグ漫画のテレビアニメーション。るん、トオル、ナギ、ユー子の女子高生4人の日常を描いている。キャラクターデザインを務める佐々木政勝は、1980年代からアニメーターとして、テレビ、映画、ゲーム等数々の作品を手がけている。

A TV anime of the original 4-panel manga by Kuroda bb telling the story of the daily life of four high school girls: Run, Toru, Nagi, and Yuko. Sasaki Masakatsu, who worked on the character design, has been drawing anime since the 80s, and has also been involved in TV, movies, and video games.

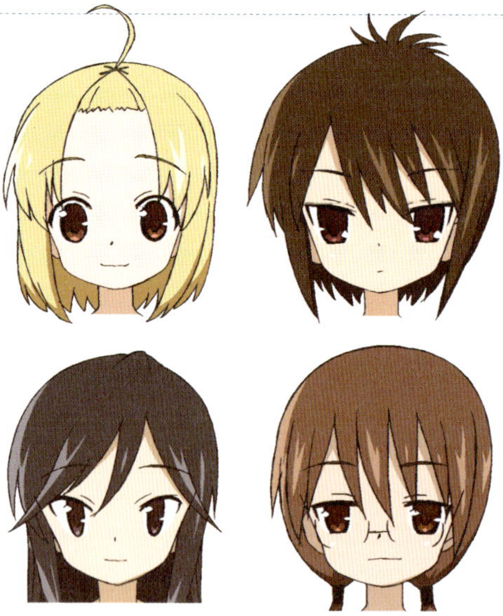

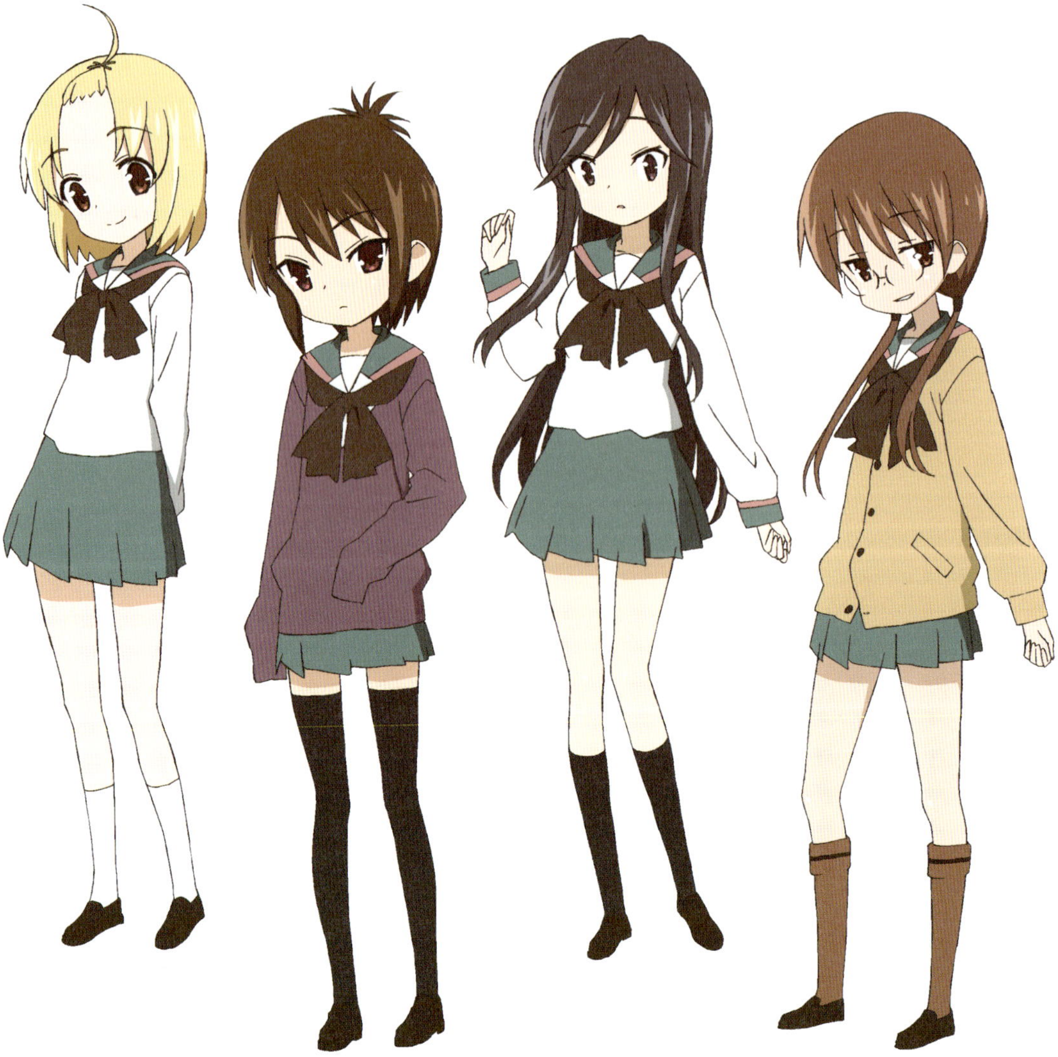

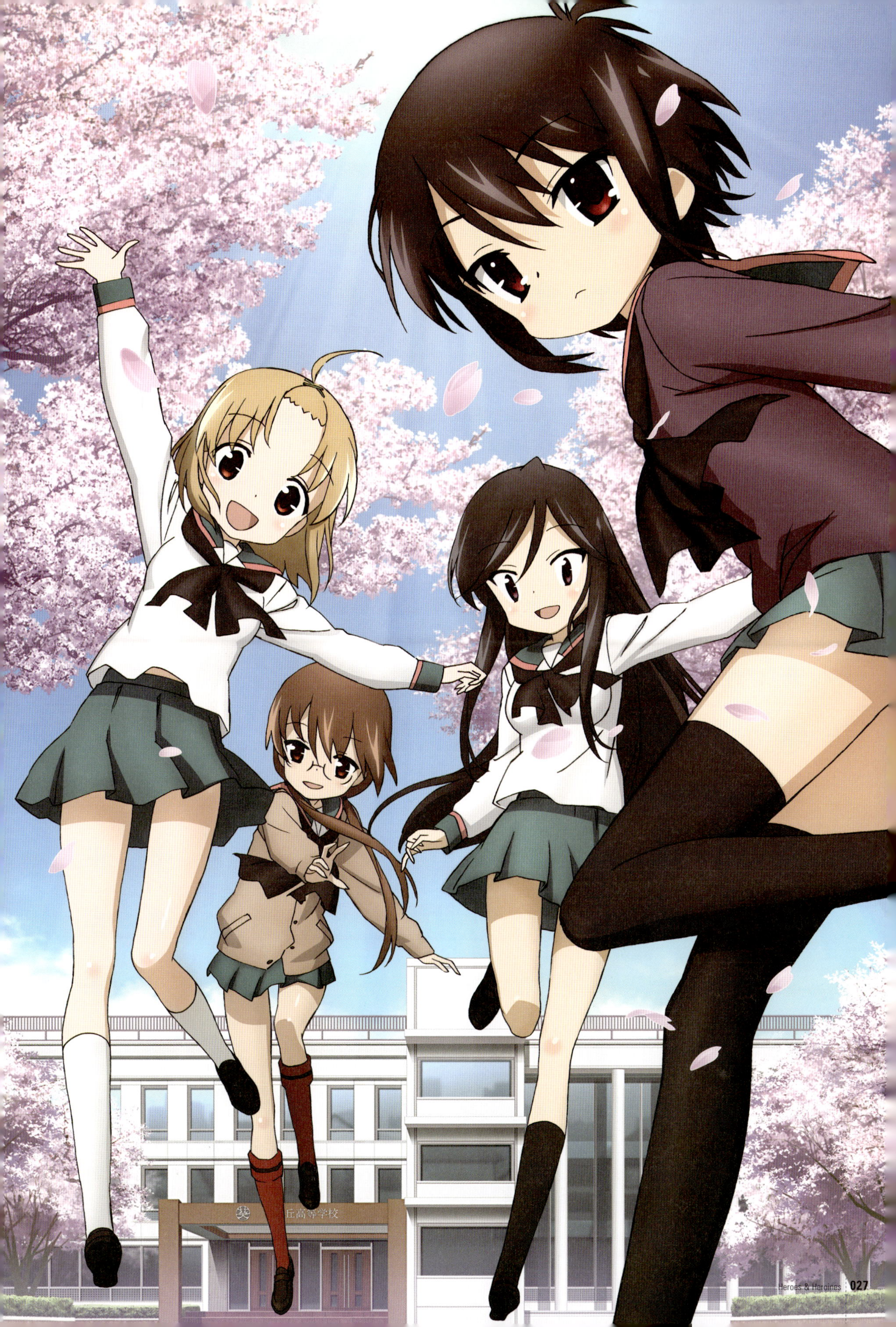
丘高等学校

🎮 Game 『エルシャダイ』
● El Shaddai

ディレクター・キャラクターデザイン
竹安佐和記
Takeyasu Sawaki

[代表作]　『Devil May Cry』（モンスターデザイン）
　　　　　『大神』（妖怪デザイン、イベントイラスト）

発売前に発表された本作品のトレーラーを見た者はみな、その世界観と強いキャラクター性に夢中になり、期待と話題を呼んだ。大天使ルシフェルの天使のイメージを覆す、黒シャツ、ブラックジーンズ、手にはビニール傘という出で立ちは、竹安佐和記独特の感性が爆発している。

Everyone that saw the pre-release trailer for this game was mesmerized by the worldview and by the strength of the characterizations, eliciting anticipation and discussion. The black shirt, black jeans, and plastic umbrella used by the "great angel" Lucifer destroys his image as an angel and erupts with Takayasu's unique sensibilities.

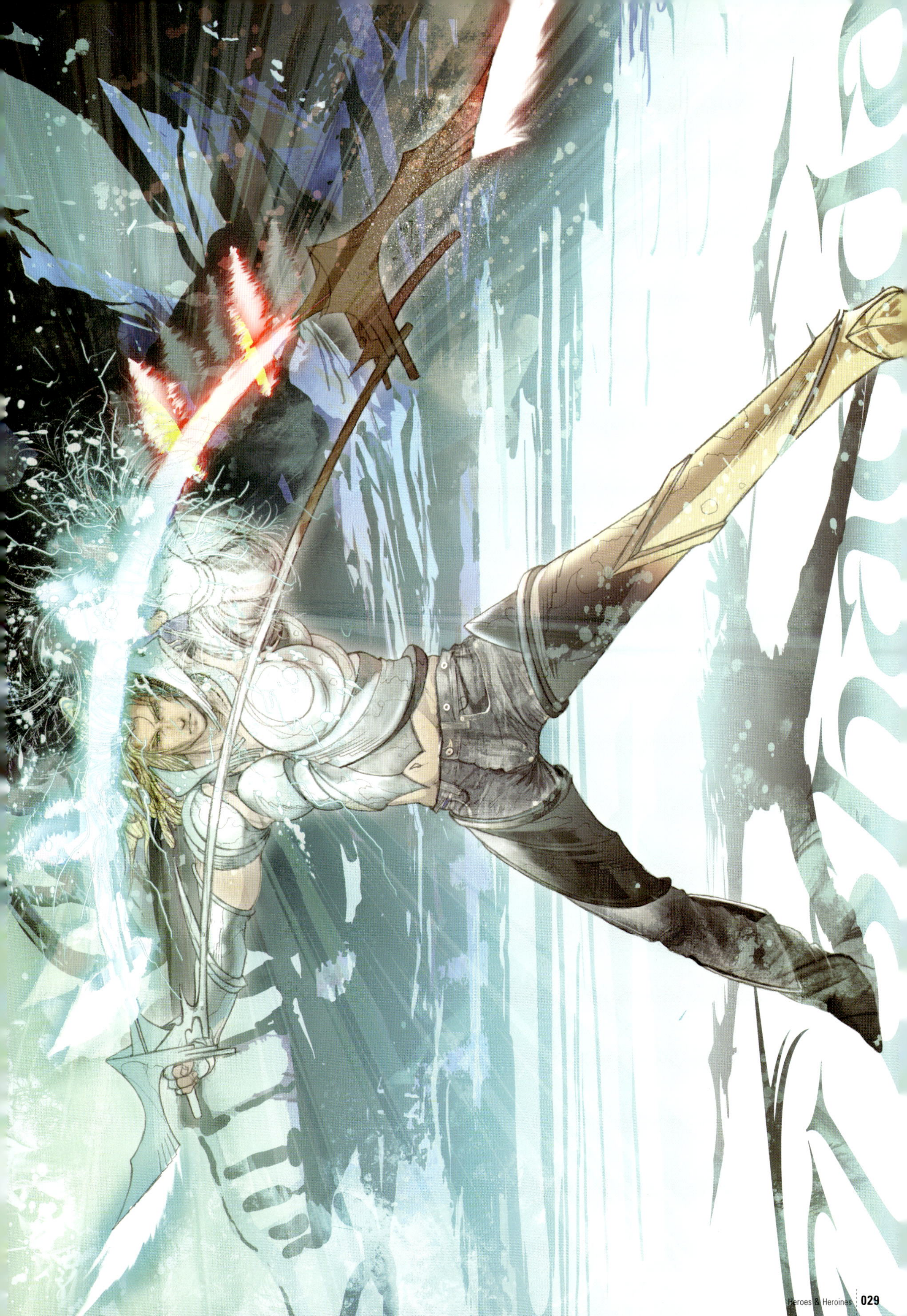

『エルシャダイ』

● El Shaddai

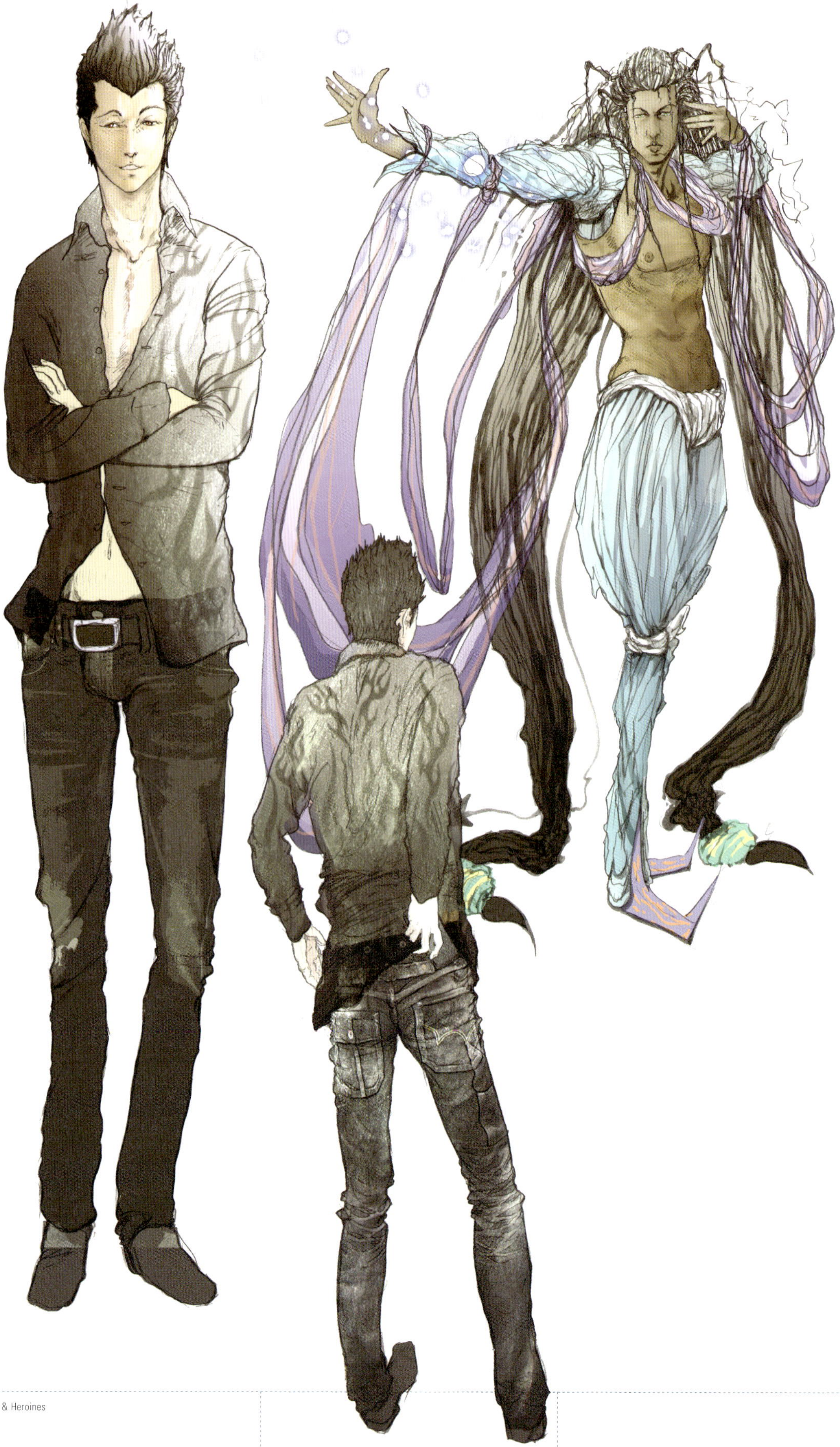

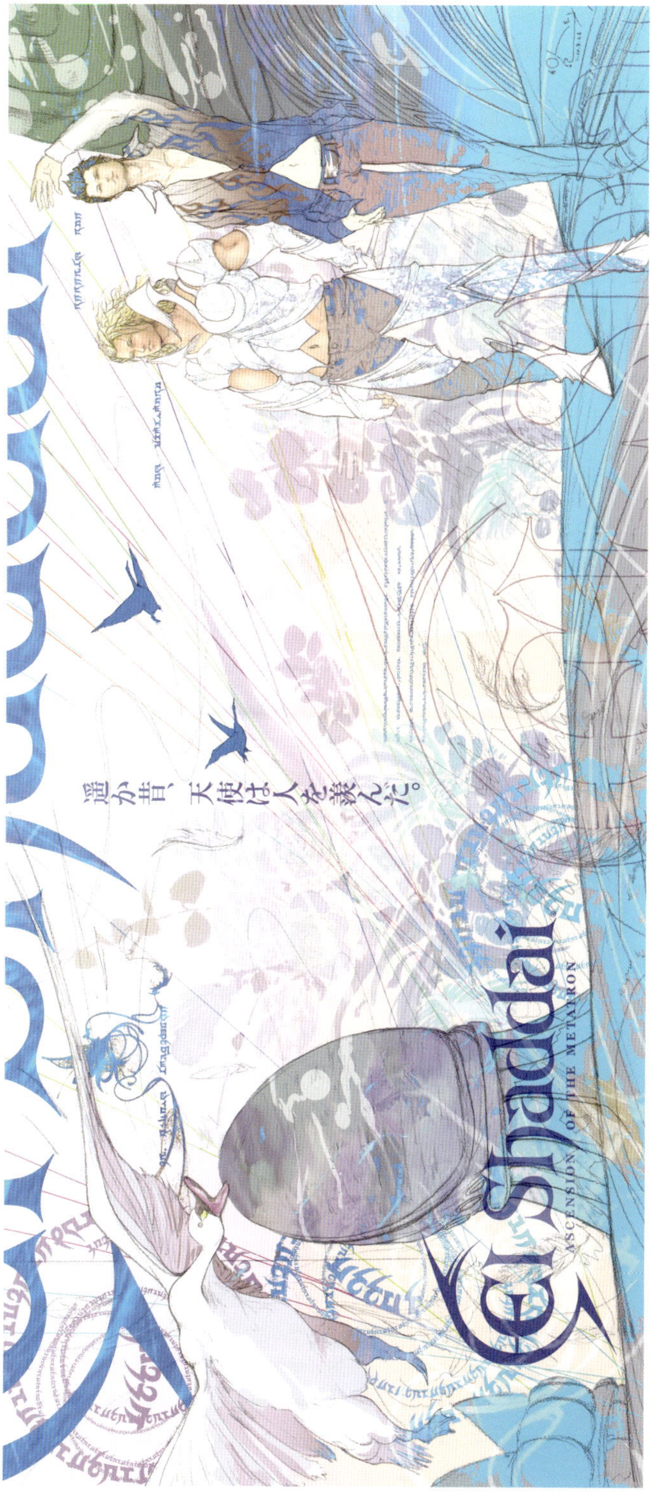
遥か昔、天使は人を羨んだ。
El Shaddai
ASCENSION OF THE METATRON

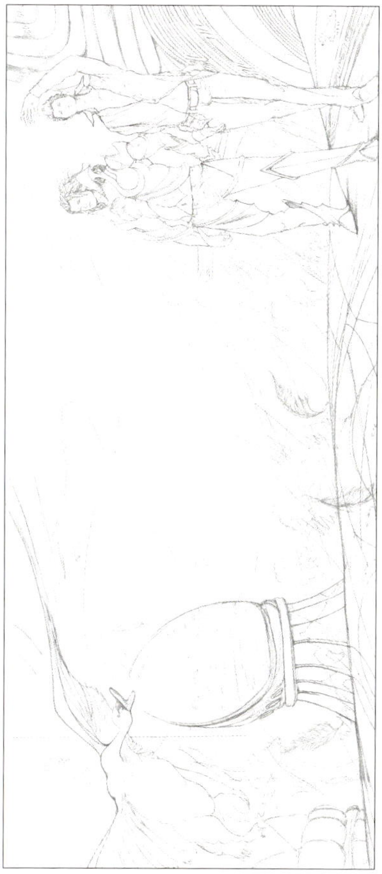

Game
『オトメディウスX(エクセレント!)』
● OTOMEDIUS EXCELLENT

キャラクターデザイン

吉崎観音
Yoshizaki Mine

[代表作]『ケロロ軍曹』(漫画)『七人のナナ』(キャラクター原案)

宇宙の彼方から地球に襲いかかる巨大な闇の力と戦う「天使」たちが活躍するシューティングゲーム。タイトルどおり、戦うのは「天使」と呼ばれるうら若き乙女たちである。可憐な天使たちを描くのは、人気漫画『ケロロ軍曹』の作者でもある吉崎観音。

In this shooting game, Angels from beyond time and space fight against dark powers on earth. These beautiful young angels are drawn by Yoshizaki Mine, the popular manga artist behind Sergeant Frog.

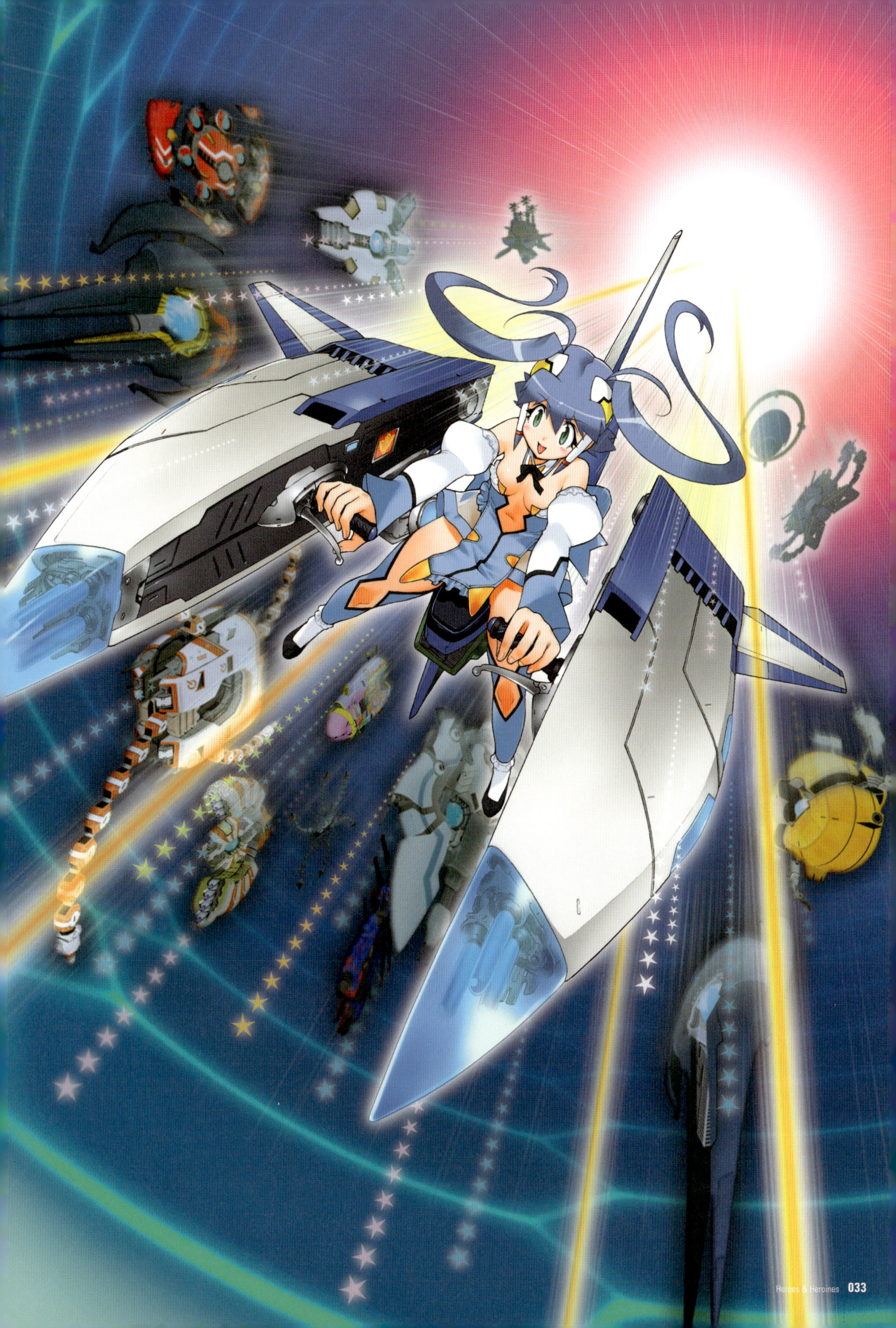

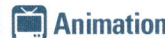

キャラクターデザイン

織田広之

Oda Hiroyuki

[代表作]『GOSICK』(ED原画)『みなみけ おかわり』(OP原画)

ごく普通の男子高校生・高坂京介は、数年前から口もきかなくなった人生勝ち組でリア充な妹・桐乃から突如人生相談を持ちかけられる。かんざきひろ名義で同タイトル原作小説の挿絵を担当。アニメ化にあたり、キャラクターデザインも手がけた。

Kosaka Kyosuke is a completely regular boy attending high school, when one day his "winning at life" little sister Kirino, whom he had not spoken with for years, suddenly asks him for life advice. Oda Hiroyuki managed the illustrations for the novel of the same name under the name Kanzaki Hiro. Mr. Oda also worked on character design for the animation version.

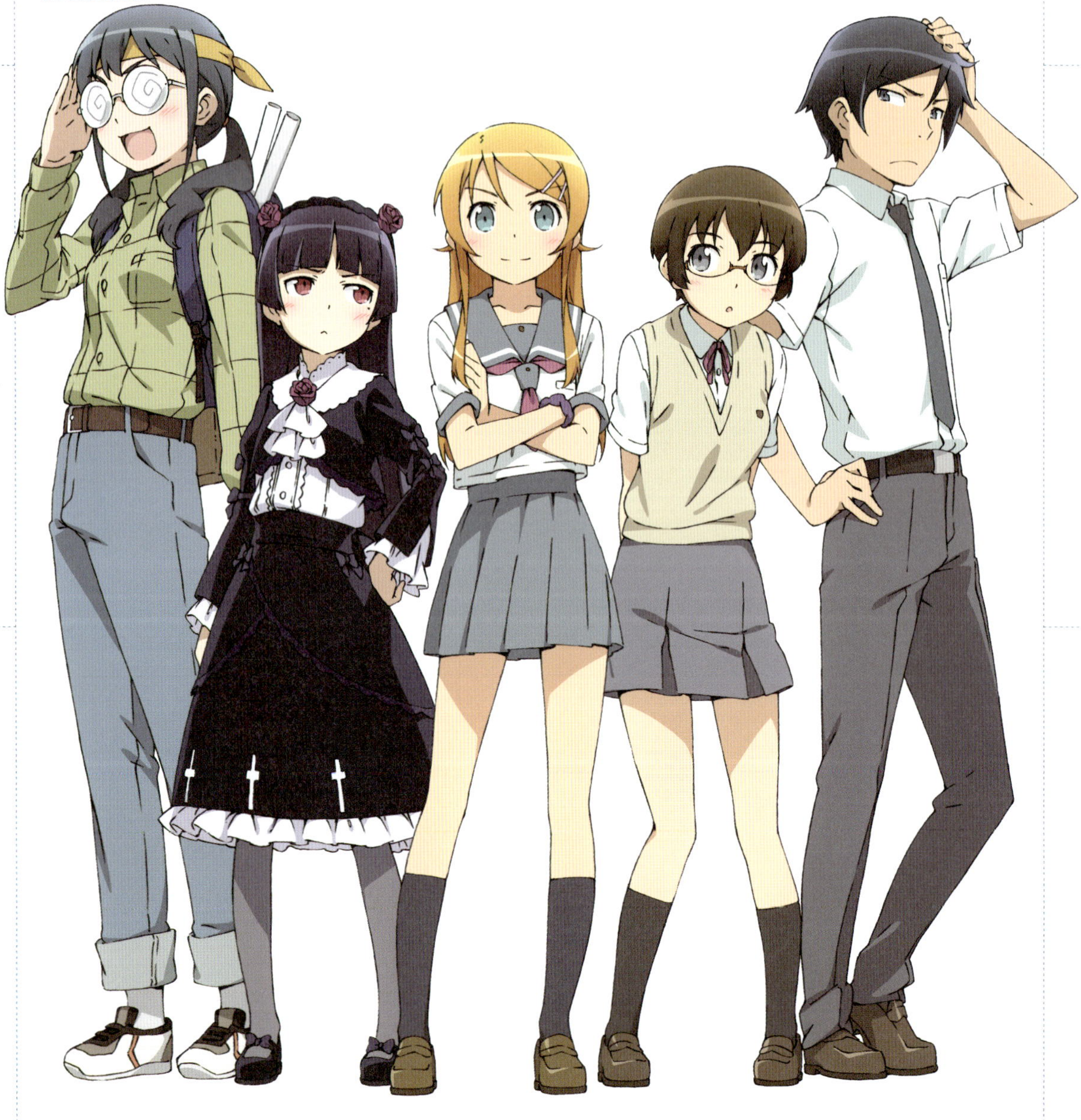

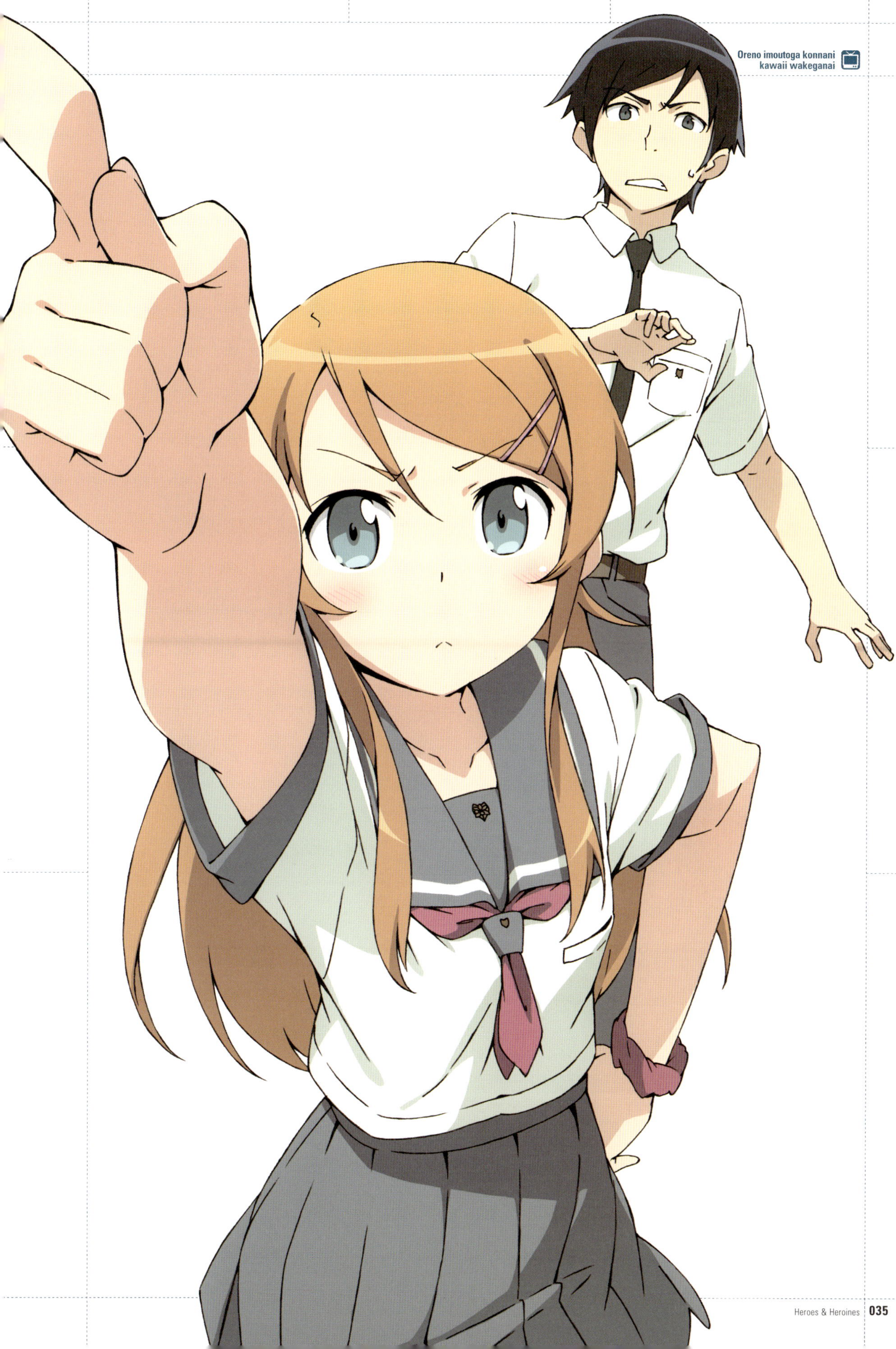

Game

『ガチトラ！ ～暴れん坊教師 in High School ～』
● Gachitora:The Roughneck High School Teacher

キャラクターデザイン
円居雄一郎
Enkyo Yuichiro

［代表作］『くるくる◇プリンセス ～ときめきフィギュア☆めざせ！バンクーバー～』（メインキャラクターデザイン）

任侠集団の若頭・梶虎男がとある理由から高校教師となり、問題児ばかりのクラスの生徒それぞれの悩みを型破りな方法で解決していく学園アクションアドベンチャー。生徒たちひとりひとりがどこにでもいそうな高校生でいながら、実に個性的に丁寧に描き分けられている。

This is a school action-adventure game in which Kaji Torao, a yakuza leader, has for certain reasons become a high school teacher and must use an unconventional method to resolve the issues of his classroom full of problem youths. While each student is like a high school student one might encounter anywhere, the individuality of the students is in fact carefully illustrated.

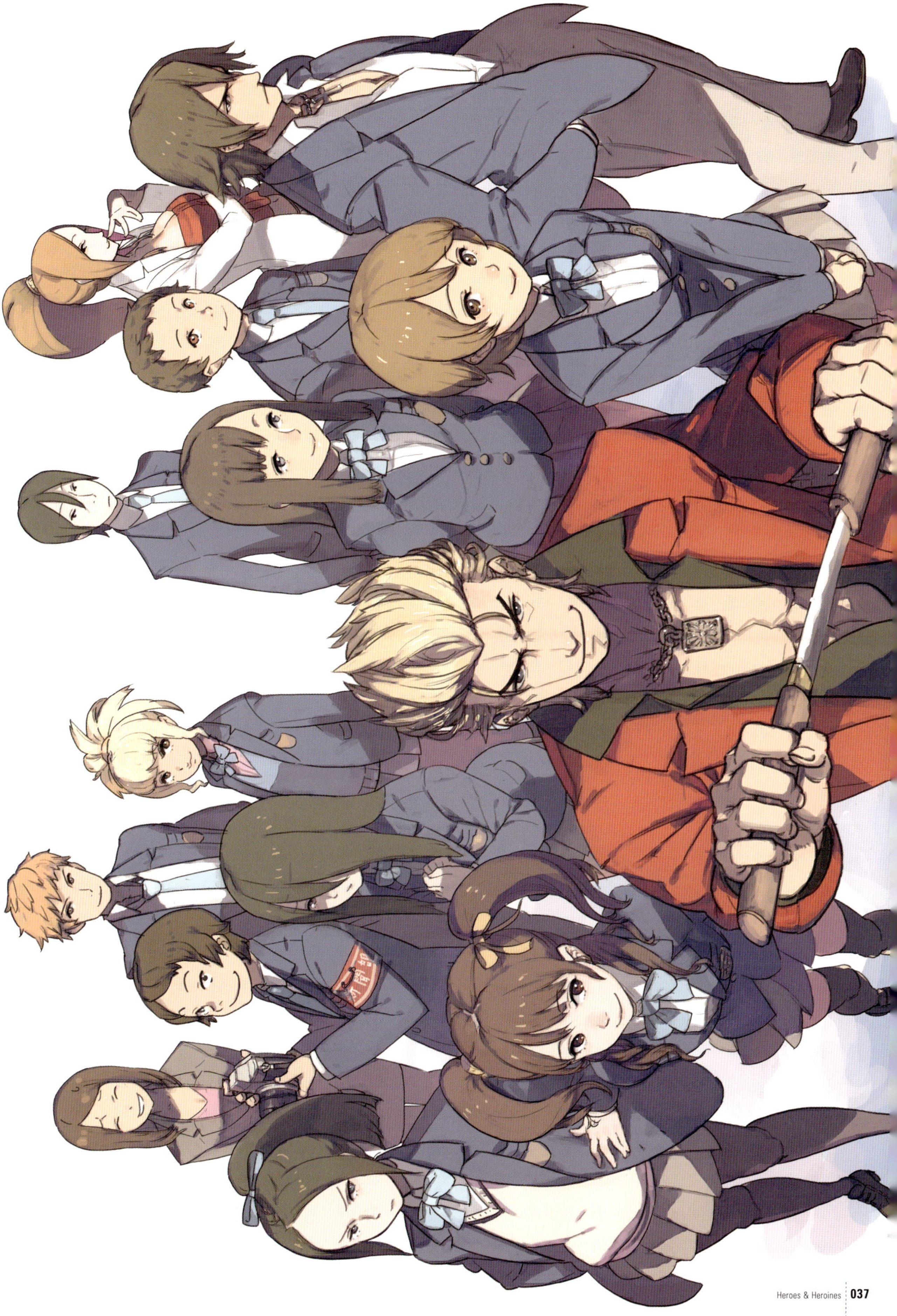

Game

『逆転検事』シリーズ
● 『Ace Attorney INVESTIGATIONS: Miles Edgeworth』SERIES

キャラクターデザイン
岩元辰郎
Iwamoto Tatsuro

[代表作]『逆転裁判』『逆転裁判2』『逆転裁判3』『逆転検事』『逆転検事2』

2001年に発売された『逆転裁判』は「法廷バトル」という今までのゲームになかったジャンルを確立し、大人気シリーズとなった。『逆転検事』でキャラクターデザインを務める岩元辰郎は、この逆転シリーズの最初のタイトルからのスタッフである。

The first game in the popular "Ace Attorney" series was released in 2001, and it established the previously non-existent "court battle" genre. Iwamoto Tatsuro works on character design for "Ace Attorney Investigations" and has been a staff member since the first title in the Ace Attorney series.

キャラクターデザインラフ

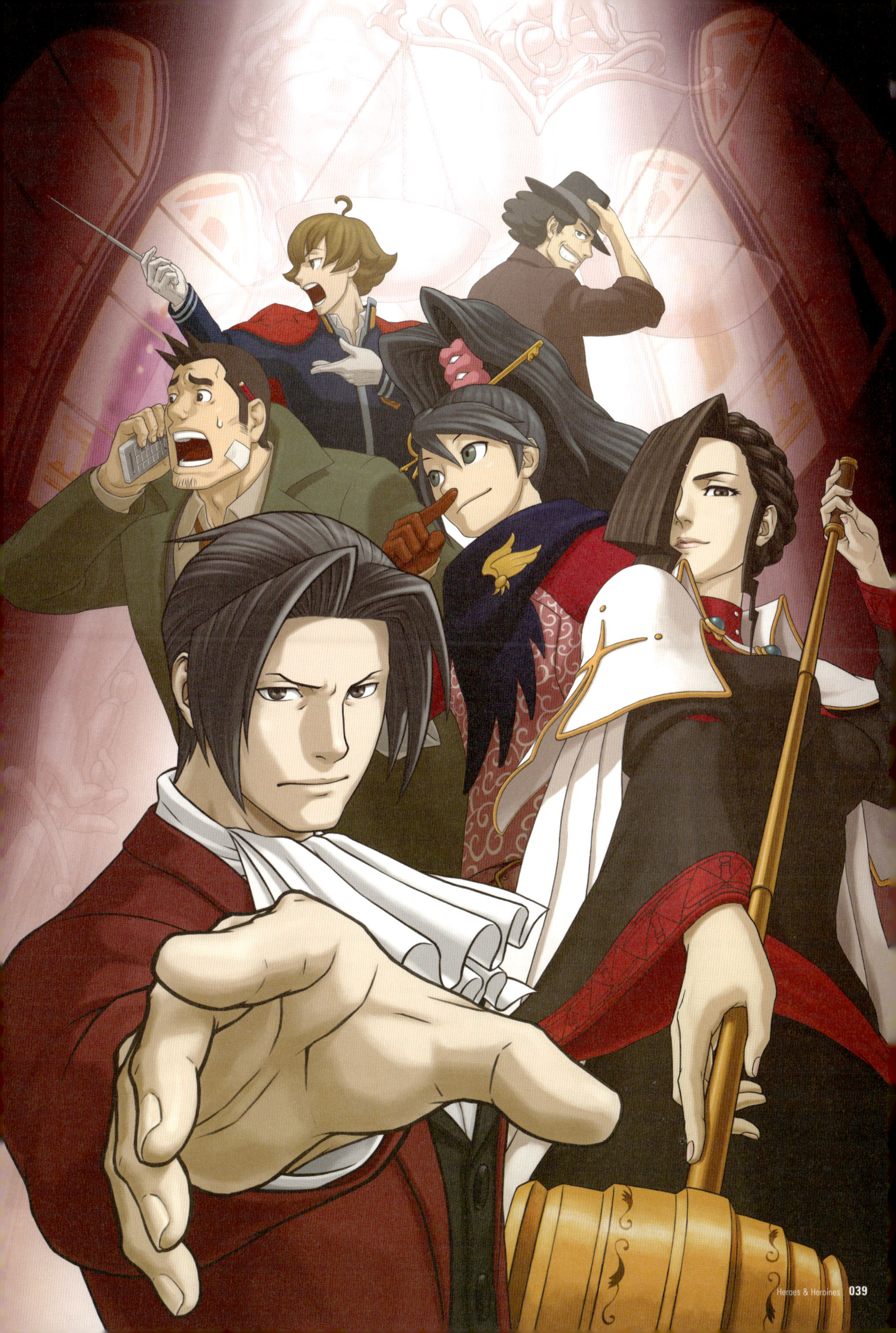

Game

『逆転検事』シリーズ
●「Ace Attorney INVESTIGATIONS: Miles Edgeworth」SERIES

『Ace Attorney INVESTIGATIONS: Miles Edgeworth』 SERIES

Heroes & Heroines | 041

Game
『逆転検事』シリーズ
●「Ace Attorney INVESTIGATIONS: Miles Edgeworth」SERIES

042　Heroes & Heroines

「Ace Attorney INVESTIGATIONS: Miles Edgeworth」SERIES

Heroes & Heroines | 043

Game

『キャサリン』『ペルソナ3 ポータブル』『ペルソナ4』シリーズ
● CATHERINE / Shin Megami Tensei: Persona3 Portable / Persona 4 / Persona4 The ULTIMATE in MAYONAKA ARENA / Persona4 The GOLDEN

アートディレクション・キャラクターデザイン
副島成記
Soejima Shigenori

[代表作]『キャサリン』『ペルソナ4』

謎の美女キャサリンと一夜を共にしたことからヴィンセントは毎夜悪夢にうなされ始め、現実と悪夢の境界は曖昧になっていく。サスペンスフルな展開でユーザーたちを驚かせたゲーム。副島成記は『キャサリン』『ペルソナ4』ではアートディレクションも担当している。

Vincent has been tormented by nightmares every night since spending an evening with the mysterious beauty Catherine, and now the boundary between reality and nightmares is becoming indistinct. This is a game that surprised players with the suspenseful way it unfolded. Soejima Shigenori is also in charge of art direction for "Catherine" and "Persona 4."

『キャサリン』

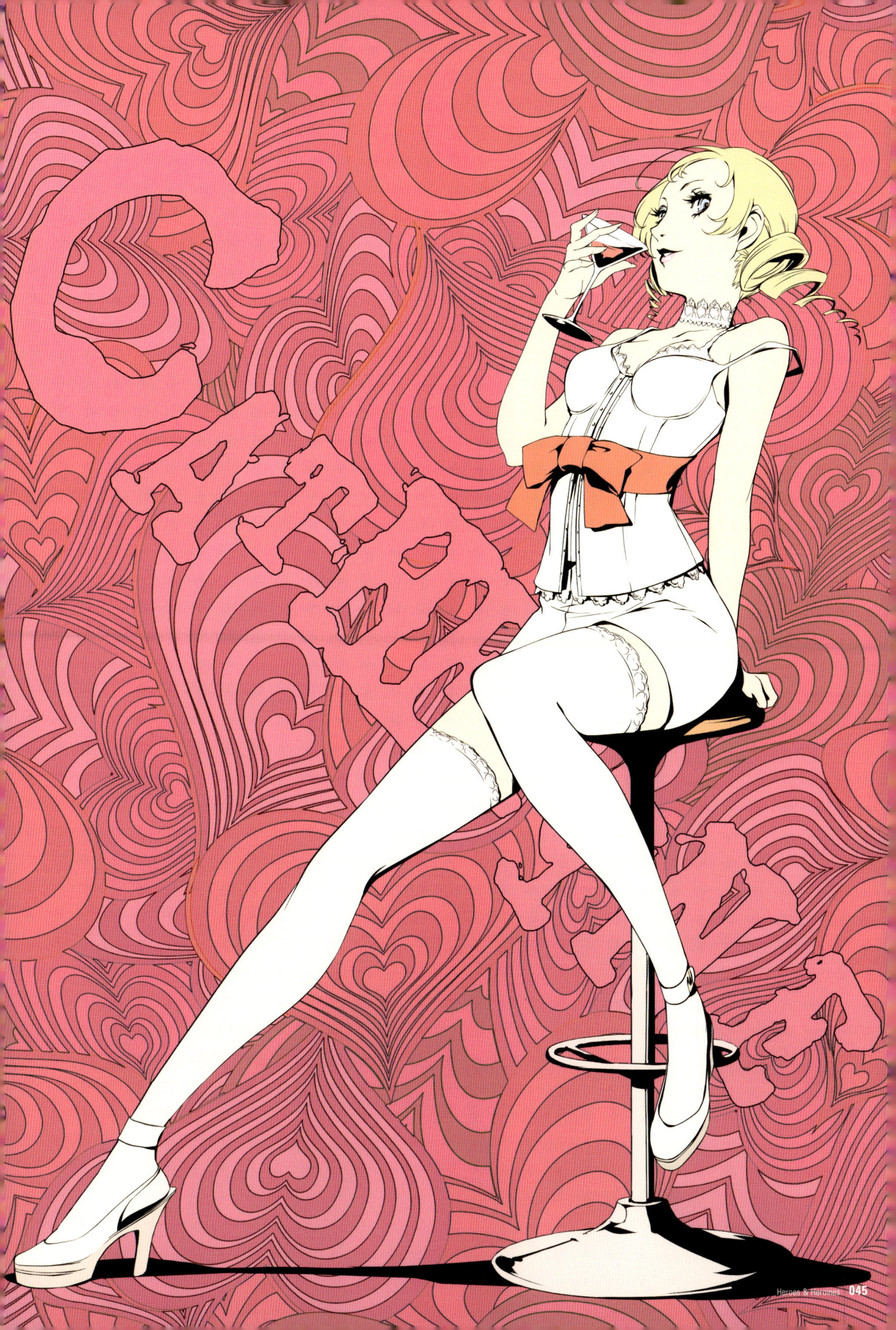

Game
『ペルソナ３ ポータブル』
● Shin Megami Tensei: Persona3 Portable

『Persona3 Portable』

Heroes & Heroines 047

『Persona3 Portable』

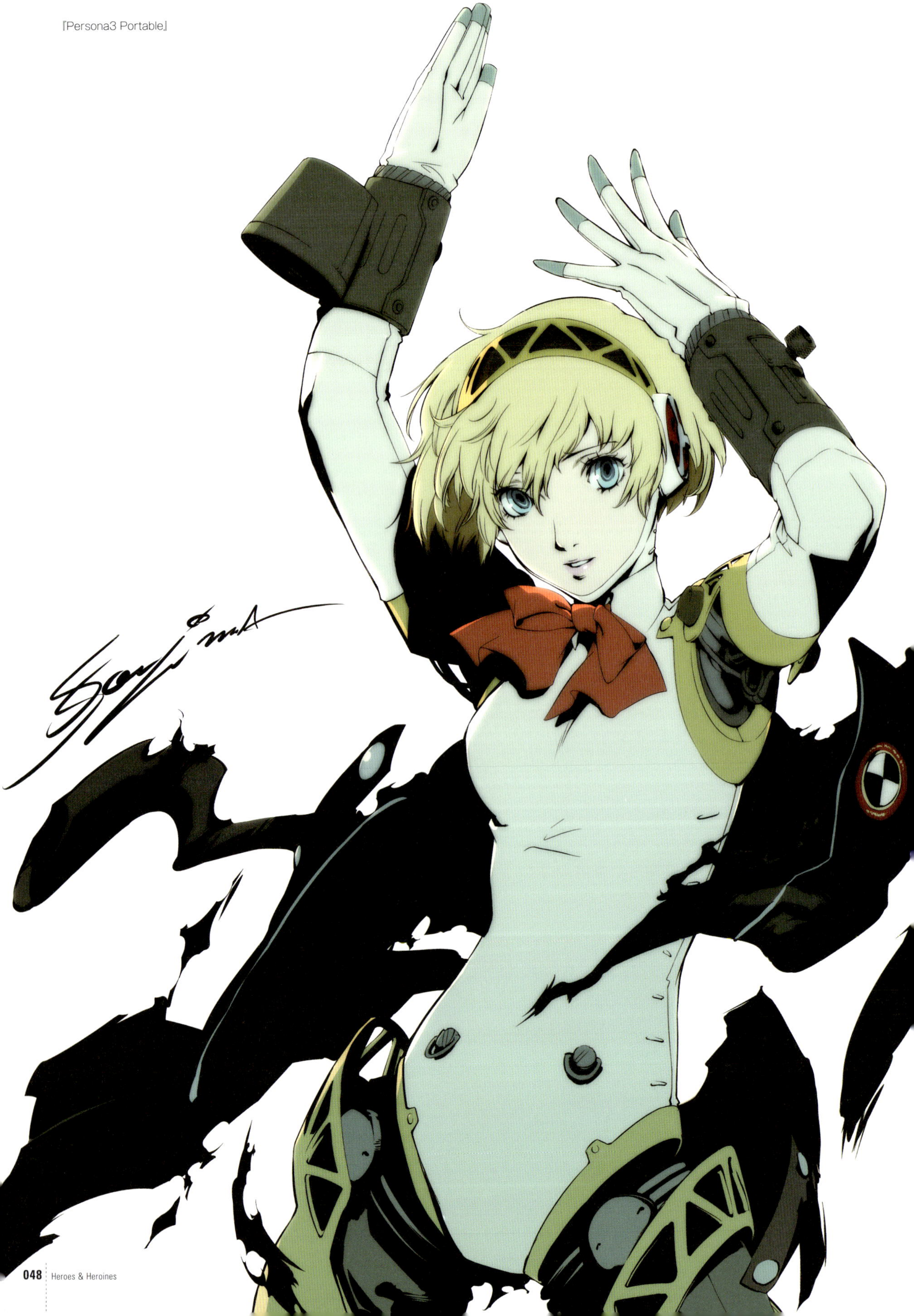

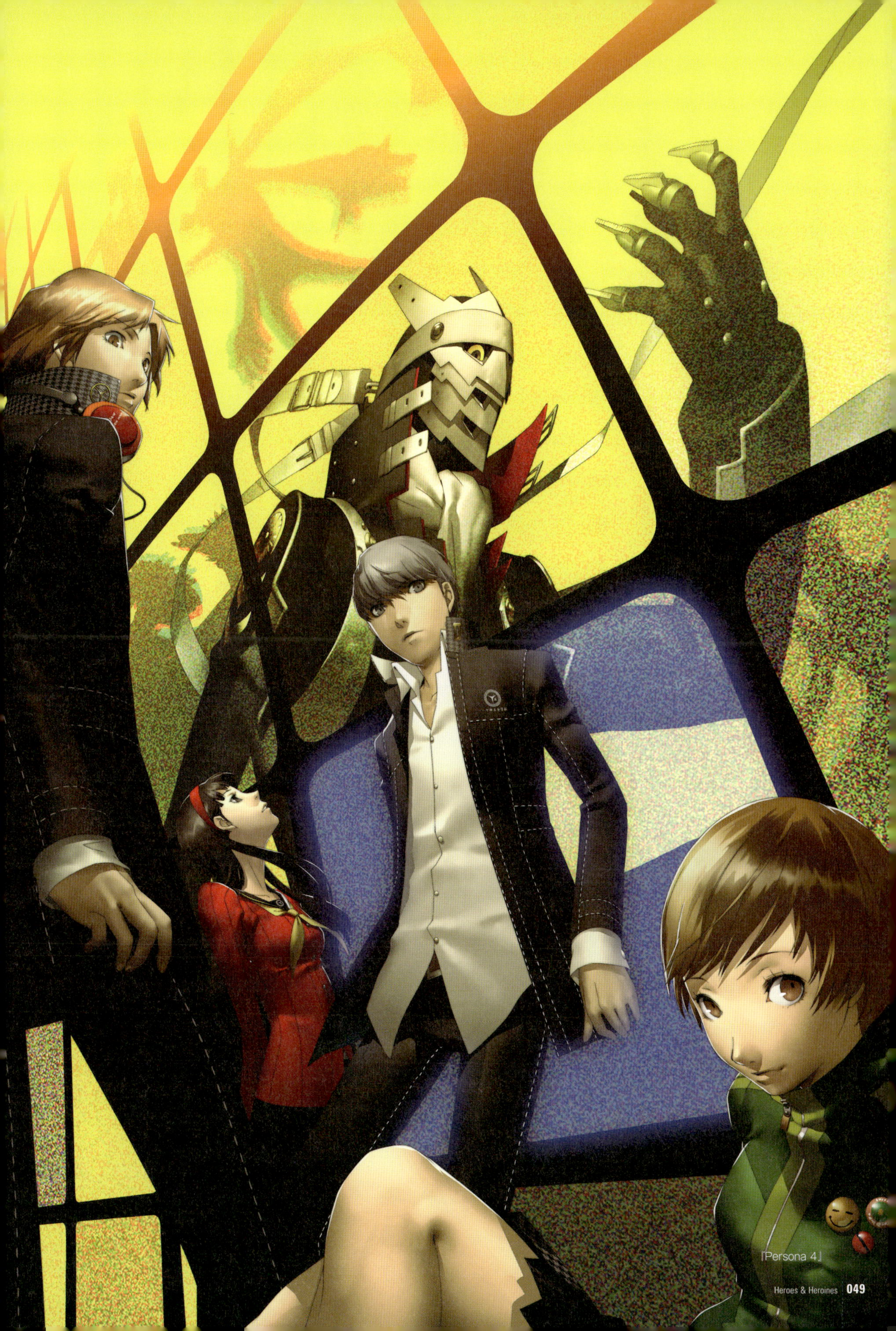

[Persona 4]

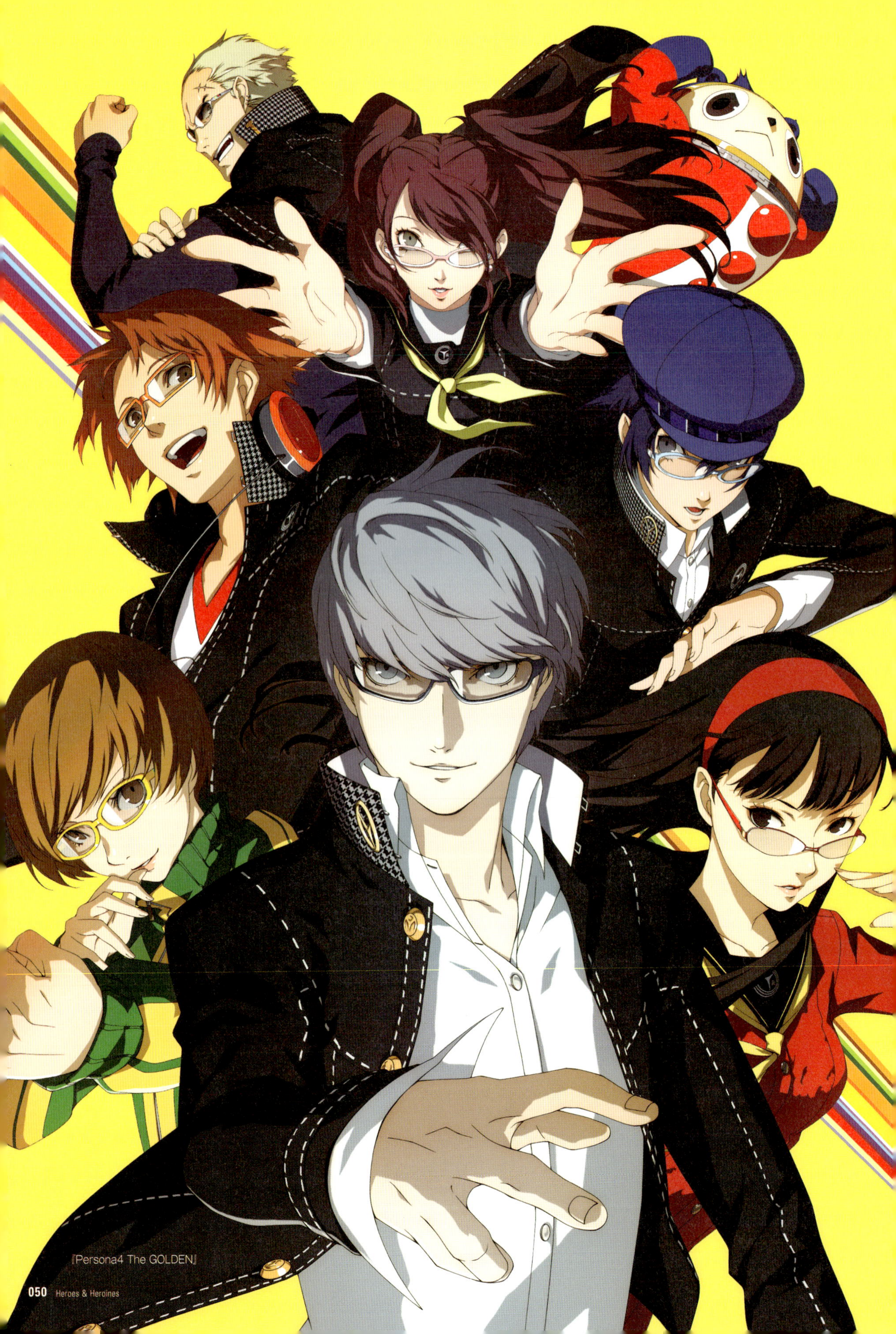

『Persona4 The GOLDEN』

『Persona4 The ULTIMATE in MAYONAKA ARENA』

Game 『Persona4 The ULTIMATE in MAYONAKA ARENA』
● Persona4 The ULTIMATE in MAYONAKA ARENA

Persona4 The ULTIMATE in MAYONAKA ARENA

Animation
TVアニメ『ペルソナ4』
● TV animation『Persona4』

キャラクターデザイン

森田和明
Morita Kazuaki

[代表作]『神様ドォルズ』『瀬戸の花嫁』

大ヒットRPG『ペルソナ4』をテレビアニメーション化。『ペルソナ』シリーズに通底している独特の色味、湿った空気とスタイリッシュな雰囲気そのままに物語を楽しめる。森田和明はこれまでにも数多くのアニメーション作品のキャラクターデザインを手がけている。

The massively popular RPG Persona4 is now an anime program. All of stand-out scenes and involving, stylish atmosphere of the Persona Series is still here. Morita Kazuaki has also had a hand in the character design for numerous other anime works as well.

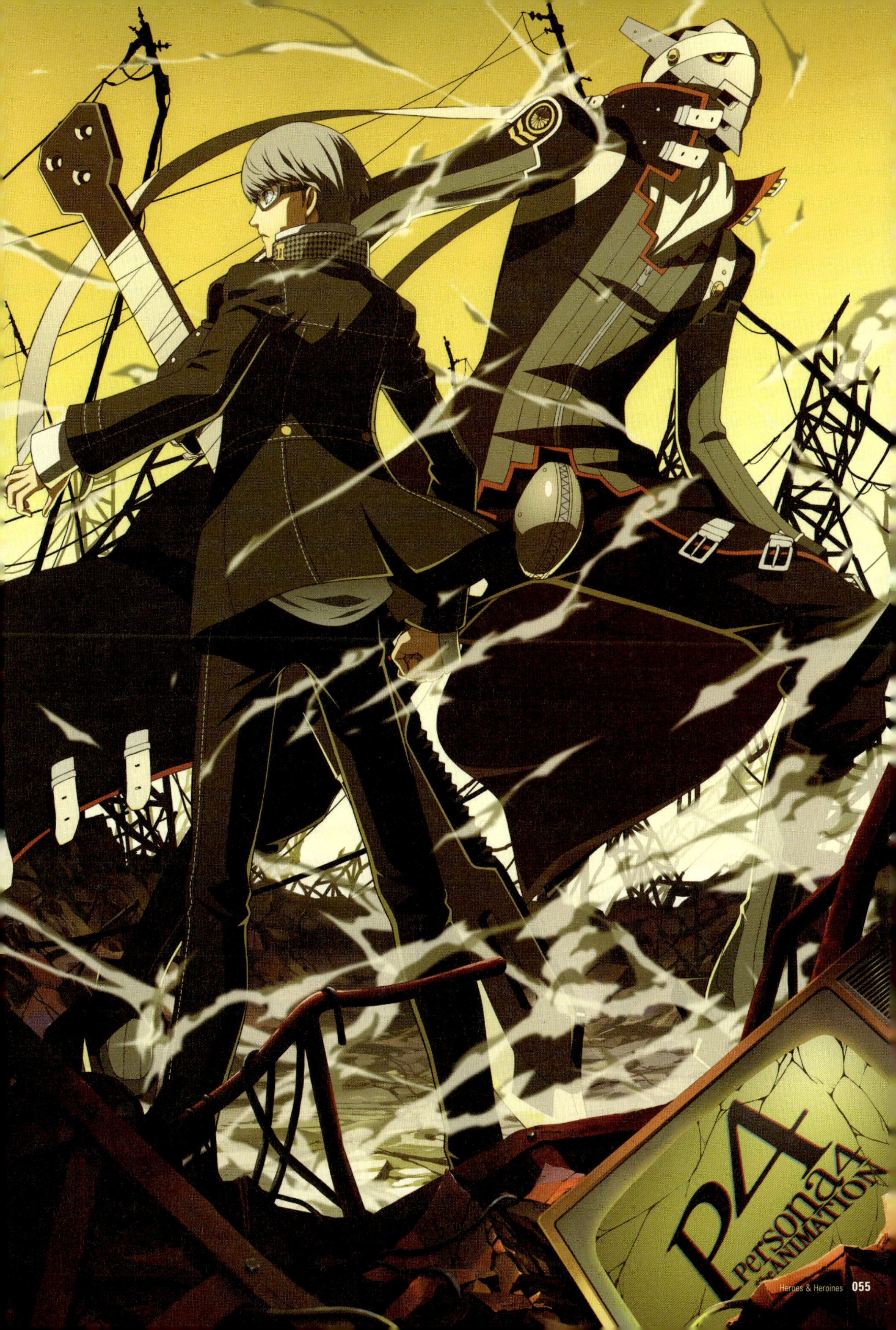
P4
persona4
the ANIMATION

🎮 Game 『極限脱出 9時間9人9の扉』
NINE HOURS NINE PERSONS NINE DOORS

キャラクターデザイン
西村キヌ
Nishimura Kinu

[代表作]『ストリートファイター』シリーズ（イラスト）

見知らぬ古い客船の密室に閉じこめられた大学生・淳平たちの生死をかけた脱出ゲームが始まった。西村キヌはゲームクリエイターのみならず、近年では小説のキャラクターデザインやイラストレーターとしても活躍の場を広げている。

University student Junpei and others have been shut away in the secret room of an old unknown passenger ship, and their life-and-death game to escape has begun. Nishimura Kinu is not only a game creator; recently she has also become expanded her activities into novel character design and illustrations.

NINE HOURS NINE
PERSONS NINE DOORS

Animation 『ギルティクラウン』
● GUILTY CROWN

キャラクター原案
redjuice / 加藤裕美
redjuice　　　　キャラクターデザイン　Kato Hiromi

[redjuice 代表作] supercell『さよならメモリーズ』CD（ジャケットイラスト）
『ワールドイズマイン』（イラスト）
[加藤裕美代表作]『こばと。』（キャラクターデザイン）
『とある魔術の禁書目録Ⅱ』（総作画監督）

2039年の日本。高校2年生の桜満集の平和な日常は、ひとりの少女に出会ったことから一変する。「罪の王冠」を背負うことによって……。supercellとして、今や押しも押されもせぬ人気イラストレーターとなったredjuiceが初めてテレビアニメーションのキャラクターデザインを務めた。

Japan, 2039. The peaceful life of high school second year student Oma Shu is changed when he meets a young girl. When the "Crown of Sins" is donned... This is the first time that the extremely popular illustrator "redjuice" has worked on character design for an animated television program as a "supercell."

加藤裕美

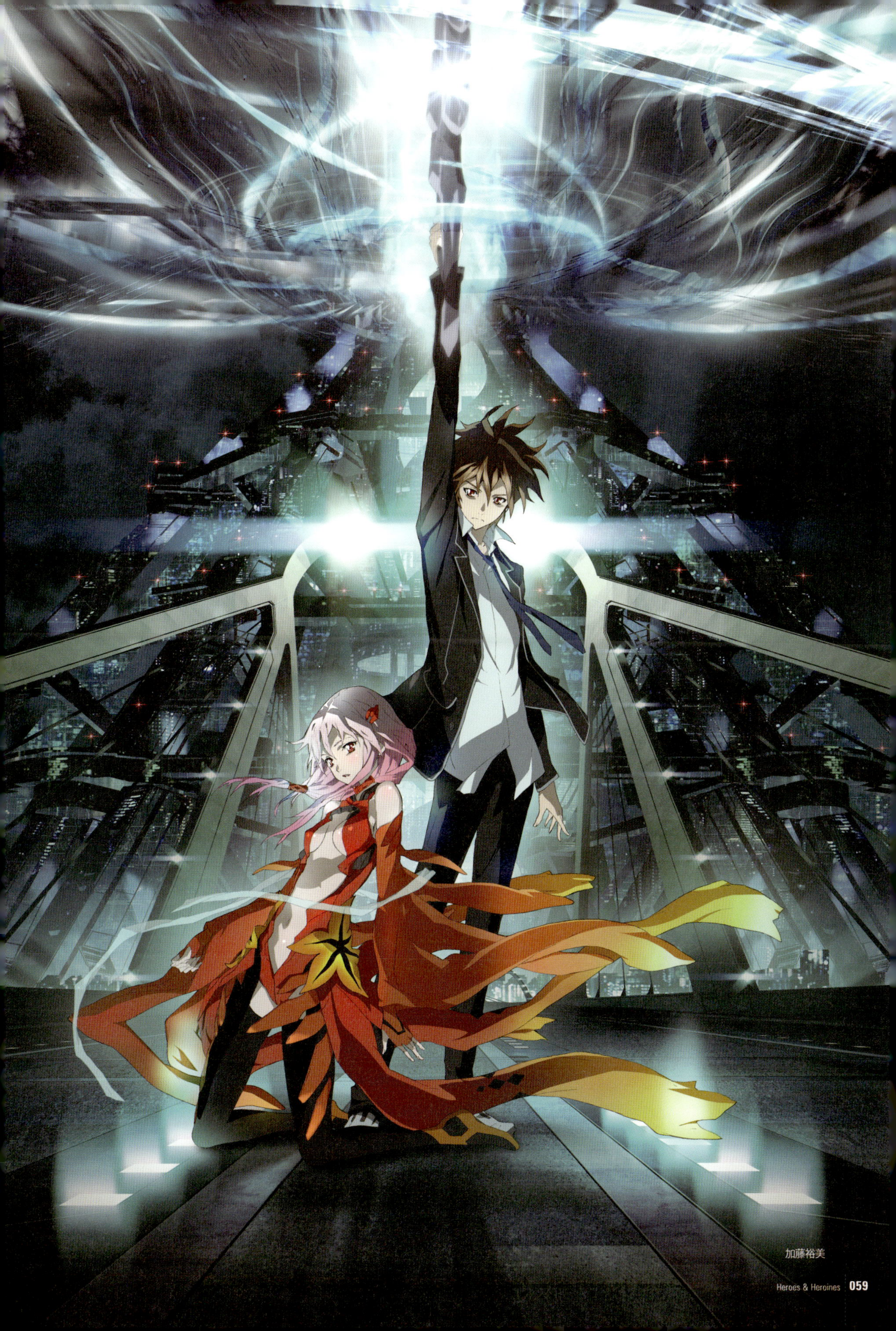

加藤裕美

Animation 『ギルティクラウン』
● GUILTY CROWN

redjuice

redjuice

Heroes & Heroines 061

Animation 『ギルティクラウン』
●GUILTY CROWN

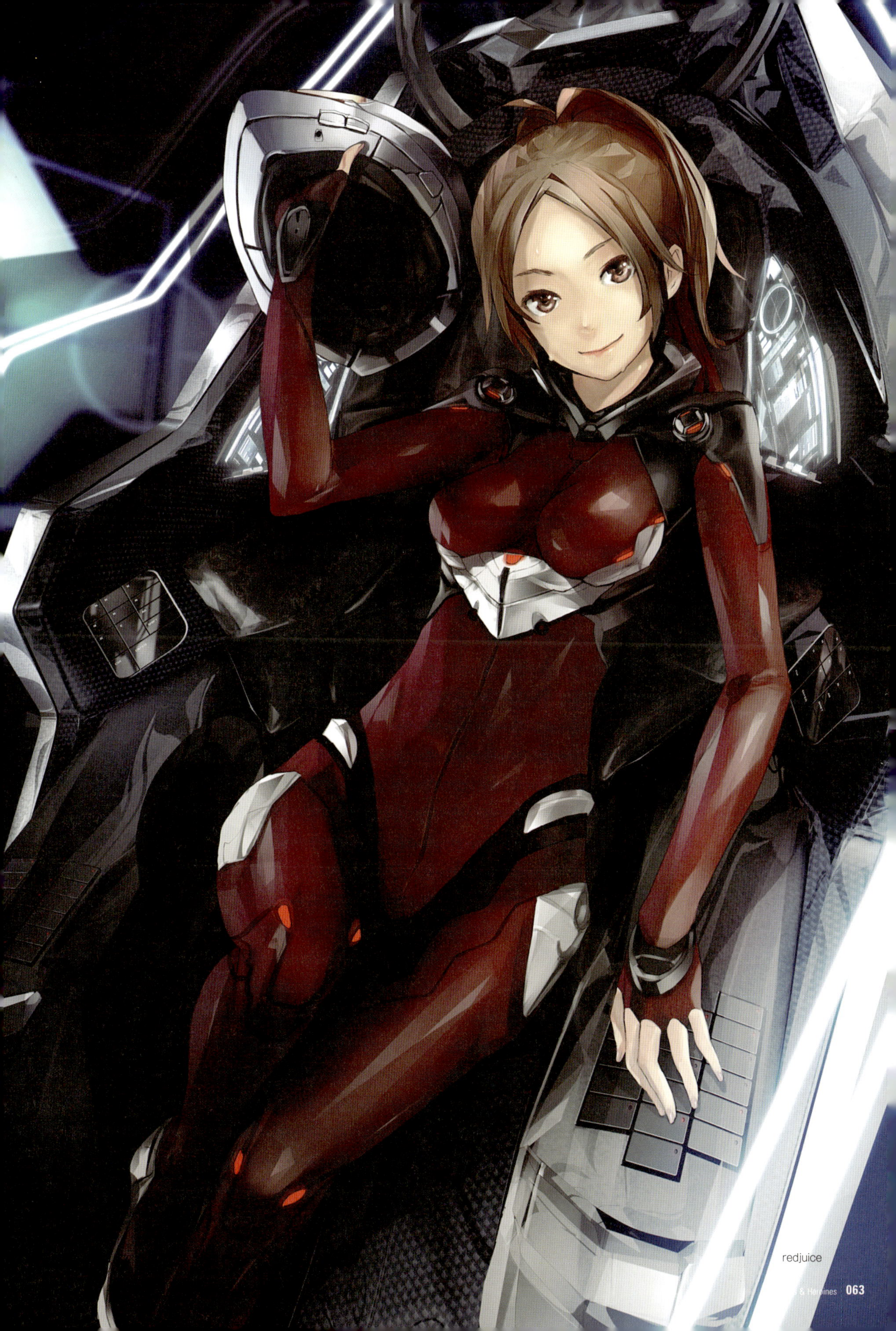

redjuice

Game

『グロリア・ユニオン—Twin fates in blue ocean—』
● Gloria Union Twin fates in blue ocean

キャラクターデザイン
こにしひろし／為重英子
Konishi Hiroshi　　　　　　Tameshige Eiko

[こにしひろし代表作]『ラジアントヒストリア』
[為重英子代表作]『ドカポンキングダム』

シミュレーションRPG『ユニオン』シリーズの第3弾は、爽快系海賊たちのド派手軍勢バトル。ふたりのキャラクターデザイナーにより人間、獣人、人魚等、数多くのキャラクターが描かれた。個性的なキャラクターがかっこよく、可愛らしく、冒険とバトルを盛り上げる。

The third installment in the simulation RPG "Union" series features flamboyant military battles between carefree pirates. The humans, monsters, fish, as well as many other characters were drawn by a pair of character designers. The individualistic characters are both cool and cute, and add excitement to the adventures and battles.

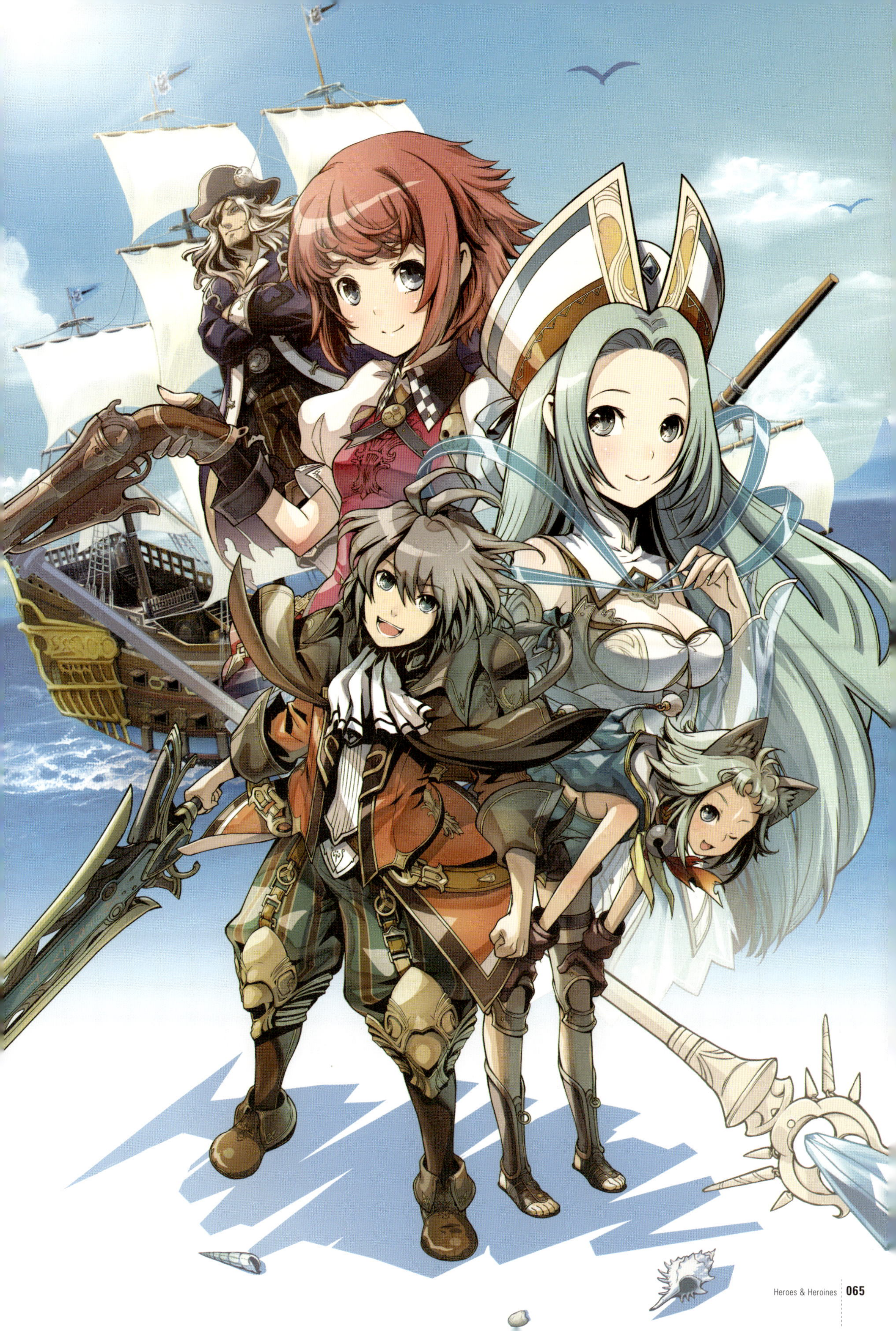

『グングニル ―魔槍の軍神と英雄戦争―』

● Gungnir: Inferno of the Demon Lance and the War of Heroes

キャラクターデザイン

きゆづきさとこ

Kiyuduki Satoko

[代表作]『ユグドラ・ユニオン』
『GA 芸術科アートデザインクラス』(漫画)

少年と魔槍グングニルが歴史に革命を刻むタクティクス系シミュレーションRPG。魔槍や軍神といったファンタジー的世界観に差別、血統、共生などの現実的テーマが交錯する戦乱の物語。重厚な世界観に、きゆづきさとこの愛らしいキャラクターが華を添える。

This is a tactical simulation RPG in which a youth and the demon lance Gungnir carve out a revolution in history. This is a story about the disturbances of war, and it blends a fantasy world of demon lances and war gods with realistic themes including discrimination, bloodlines and coexistence. Kiyuduki Satoko's cute characters give beauty to the profound worldview of this game.

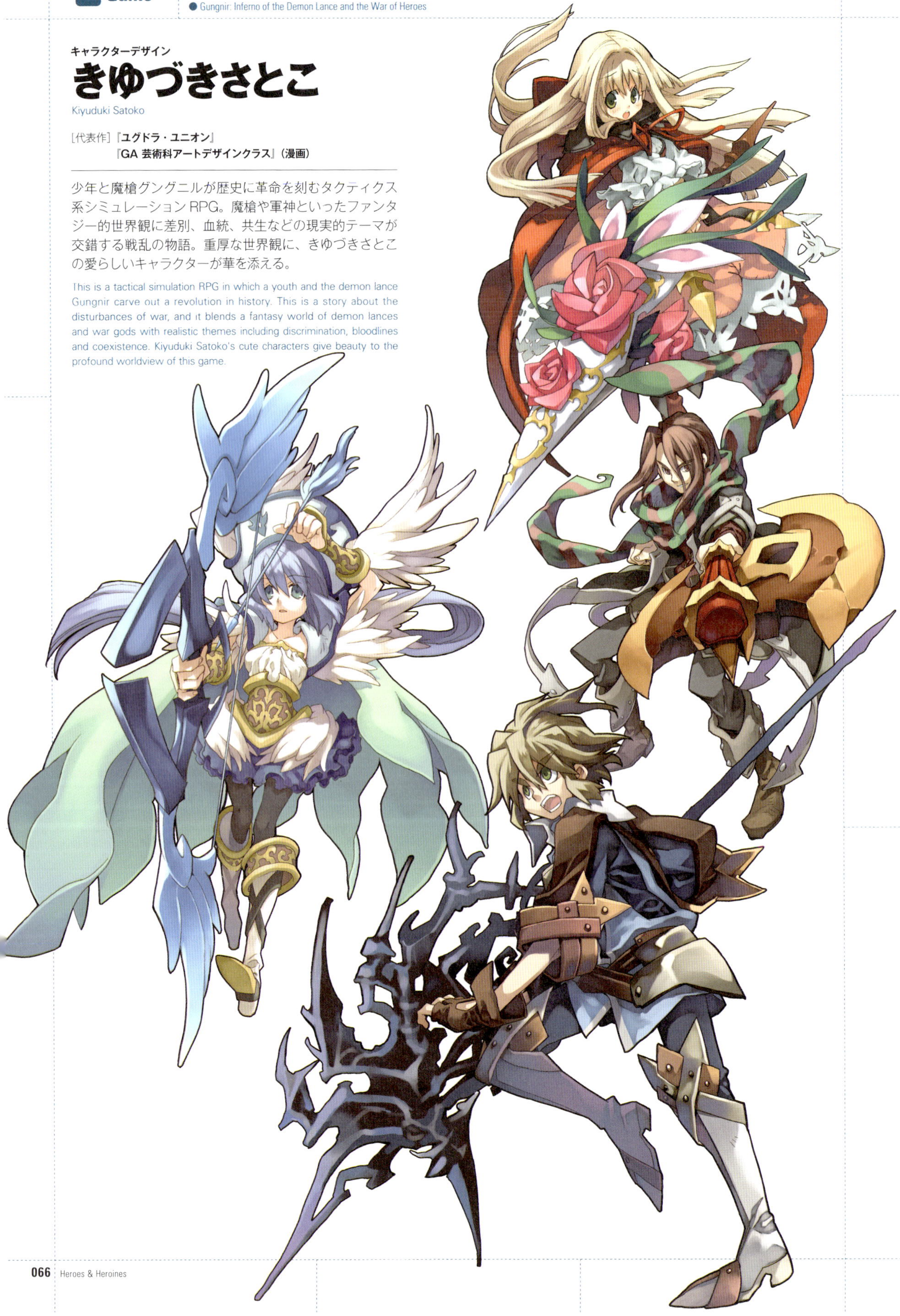

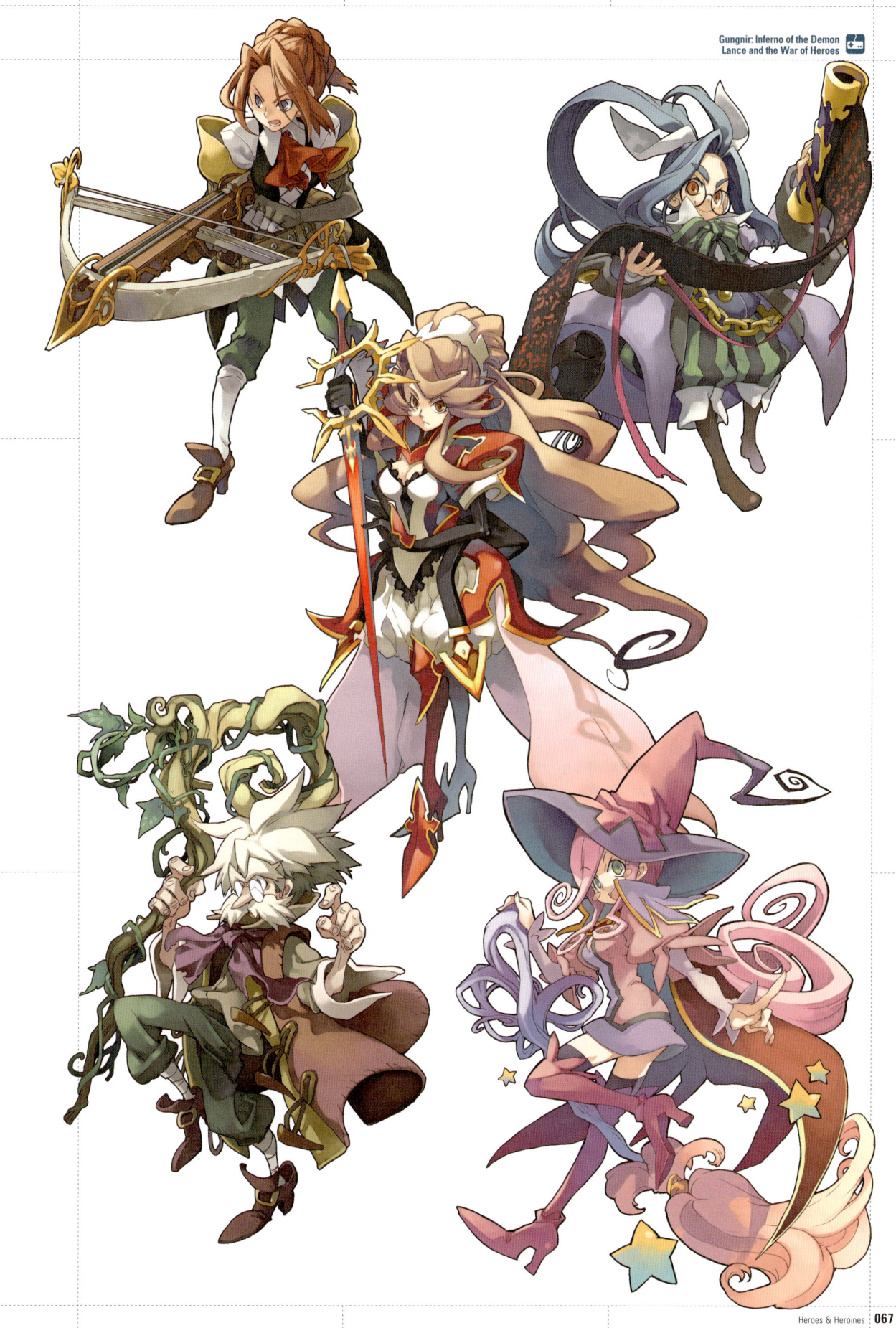

Gungnir: Inferno of the Demon Lance and the War of Heroes

Heroes & Heroines

Game

『月華繚乱ROMANCE』
● Gextukaryouran ROMANCE

キャラクターデザイン

黒裄
Kuroyuki

[代表作]『月華繚乱ROMANCE』

全寮制セレブ学園である白桜学園に転入することになった主人公・なずなは容姿端麗な子息たちが繰り広げる恋愛遊戯に巻き込まれてしまう！ 繊細な描線と淡い色味で表現された美しい男の子たちは夢の中の王子様のよう。彼らの個性的な制服の着こなしにも視線は釘付けだ！！

When the heroine Nazuna transfers to the celebrity Hakuoh Boarding School, she gets mixed up in a love game unleashed by a group of handsome boys! The delicate lines and light colorations of the beautiful boys are like princes from a dream. The way the boys wear their individualistic uniforms is also a point of attention!!

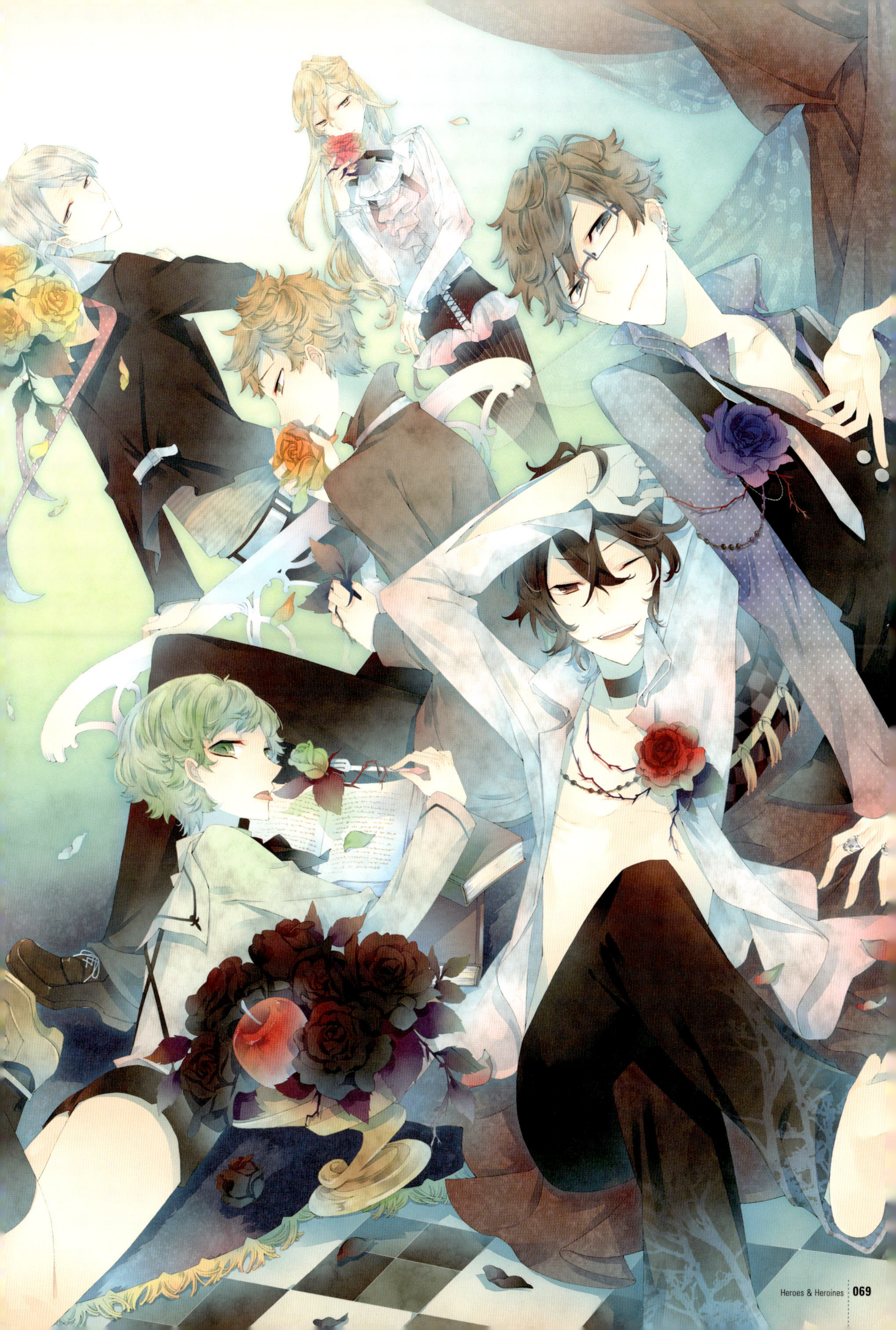

Game

『剣と魔法と学園モノ。Final ～新入生はお姫様！～』
● Class of Heroes Final: Her Royal Highness, the Freshman

キャラクターデザイン
病／うし
Yamai　　Ushi

[病代表作]『剣と魔法と学園モノ。』シリーズ
[うし代表作]『剣と魔法と学園モノ。』シリーズ

『剣と魔法と学園モノ。』、愛称『ととモノ。』シリーズ第4弾。冒険者を育てる学園の生徒たちが世界中に出現した迷宮を探索するダンジョンRPG。ヒューマンからエルフ、ディアボロスほか、キャラクターは多種多様。本シリーズのキャラクターデザインを務めている病とうしは実の兄弟でもある。

The 4th in Class of Heroes, or Totomono, Series. In this dungeon RPG, the students at the school study to become adventurers and seek out the world's labyrinths. Choose from humans, elves, diabolos, or one of many other characters. Yamai and Ushi, who worked on the character design for the series, are brothers.

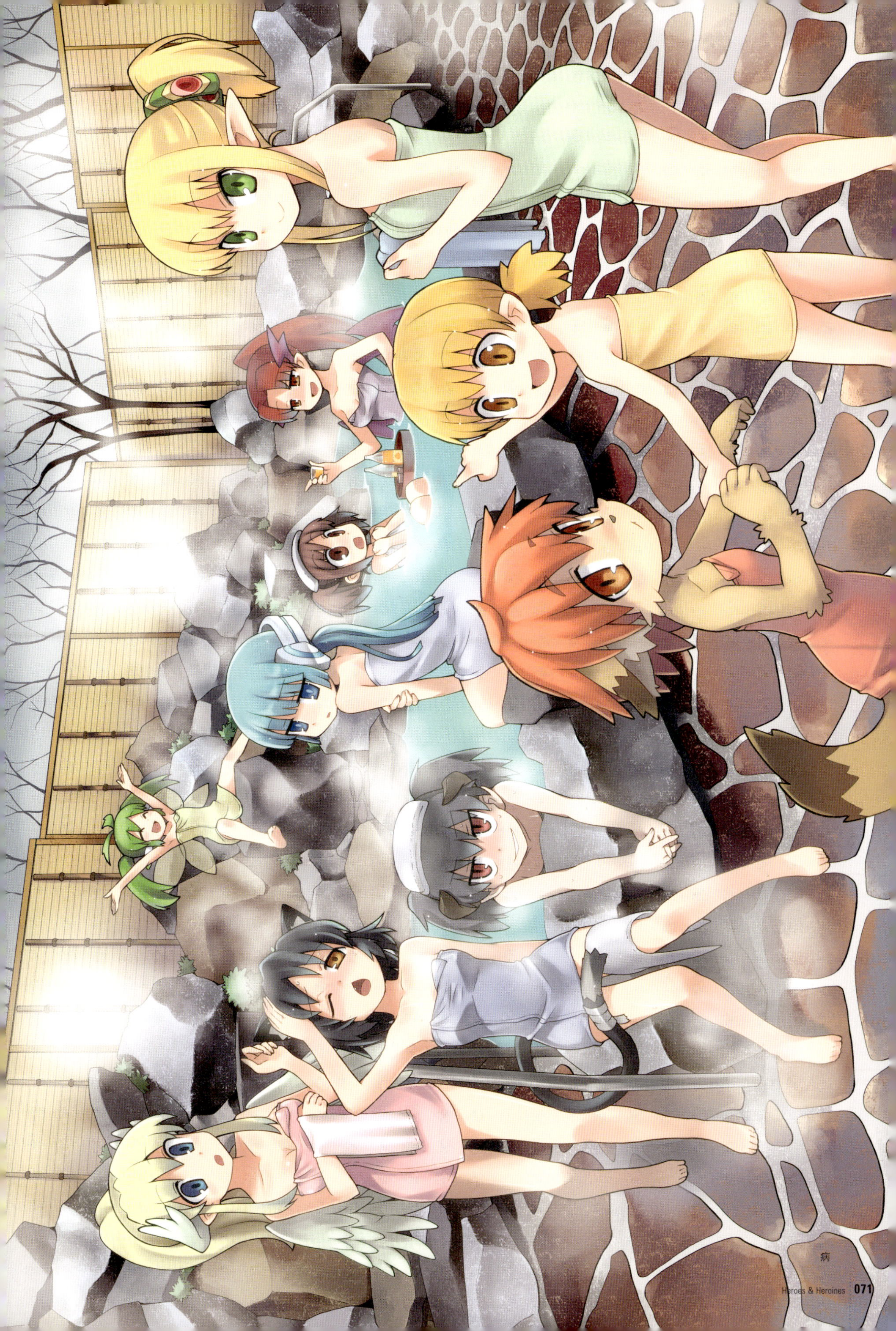

病

Game

『シャイニング・フォース』シリーズ
● Shining Force Feather / Shining Force EXA

キャラクターデザイン
pako／いとうのいぢ
pako　　　　　　　　　　　Ito Noizi

[pako 代表作]『シャイニング・フォース イクサ』
[いとうのいぢ代表作]『涼宮ハルヒ』シリーズ小説（挿絵）

人気のシミュレーションRPG『シャイニング』シリーズに、『レンタルマギカ』の挿絵を担当するpako、『涼宮ハルヒ』『灼眼のシャナ』の挿絵で知られる、いとうのいぢと、ふたりの人気イラストレーターがキャラクターデザインを務めることでも話題を呼んだ。

Shining Force series created waves when it was heard that the popular illustrators pako, in charge of art for the popular simulation RPG Shining Series and Rental Magica, and Ito Noizi, known for her work on Haruhi Suzumiya and Shakugan no Shana, would be involved.

いとうのいぢ

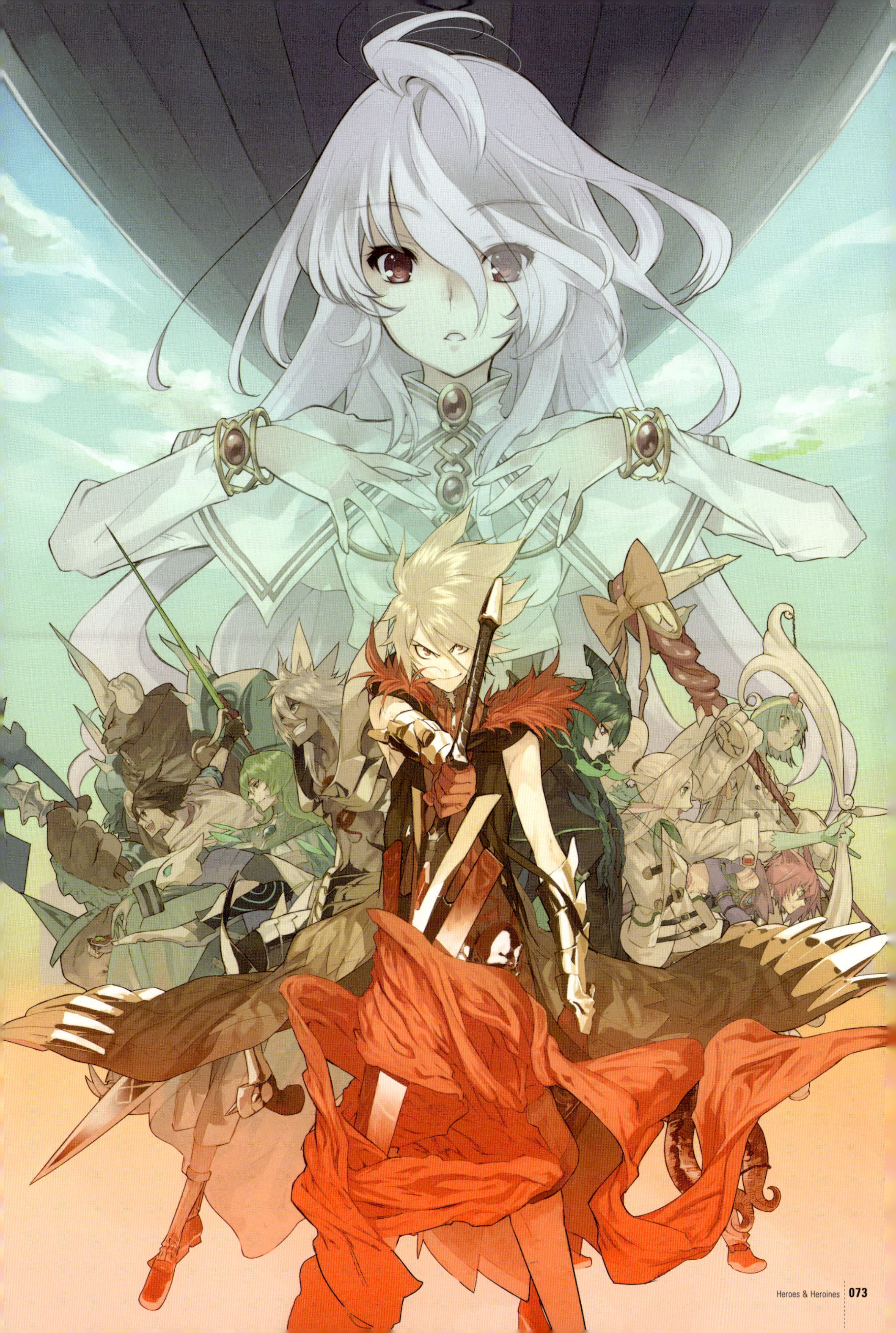

Game

『シャイニング・フォース フェザー』
● Shining Force Feather

Shining Force Feather

いとうのいぢ

Heroes & Heroines | 075

Game
● Shining Force Feather
『シャイニング・フォース フェザー』

pako

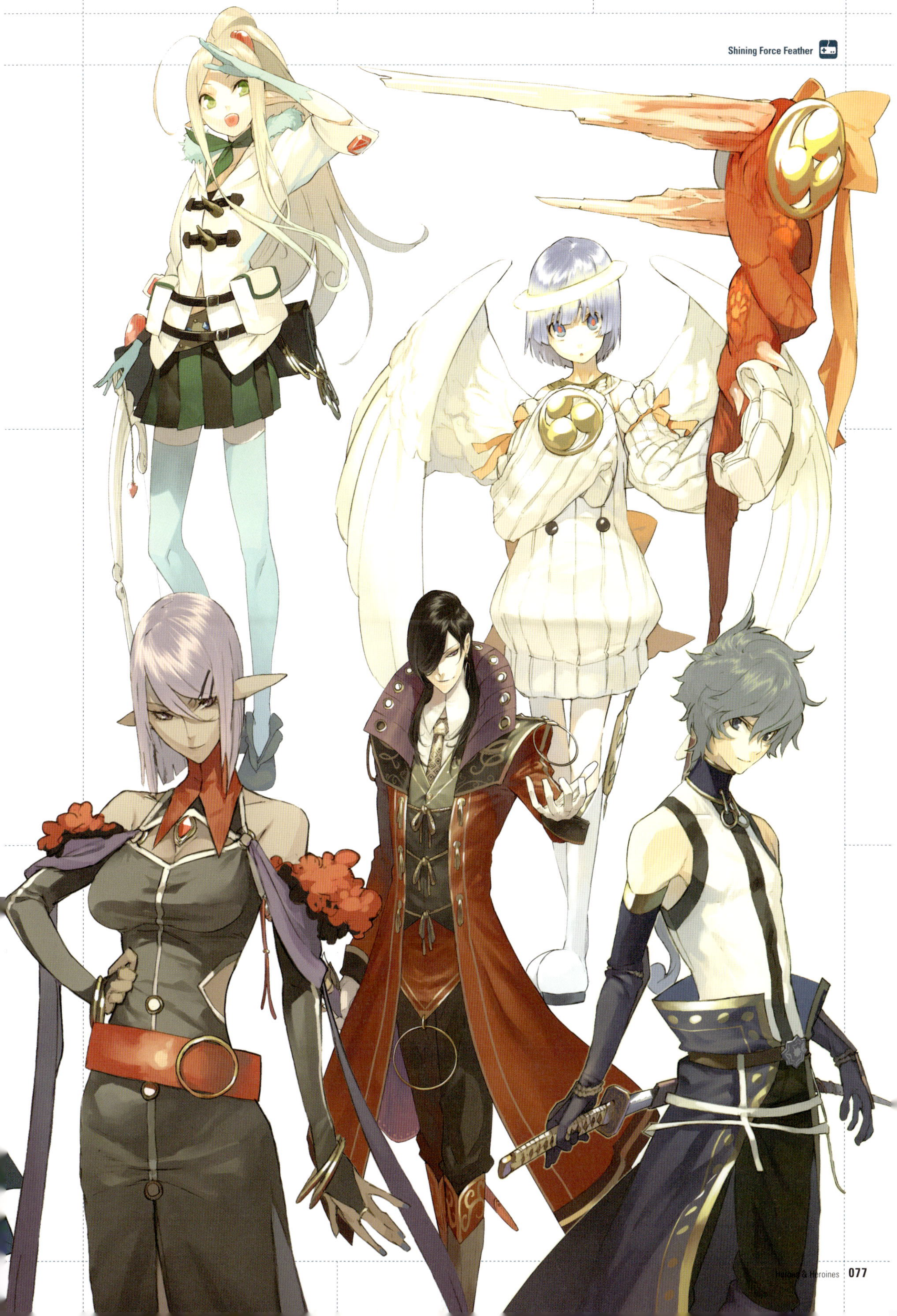

Game

『シャイニング・フォース イクサ』
● Shining Force EXA

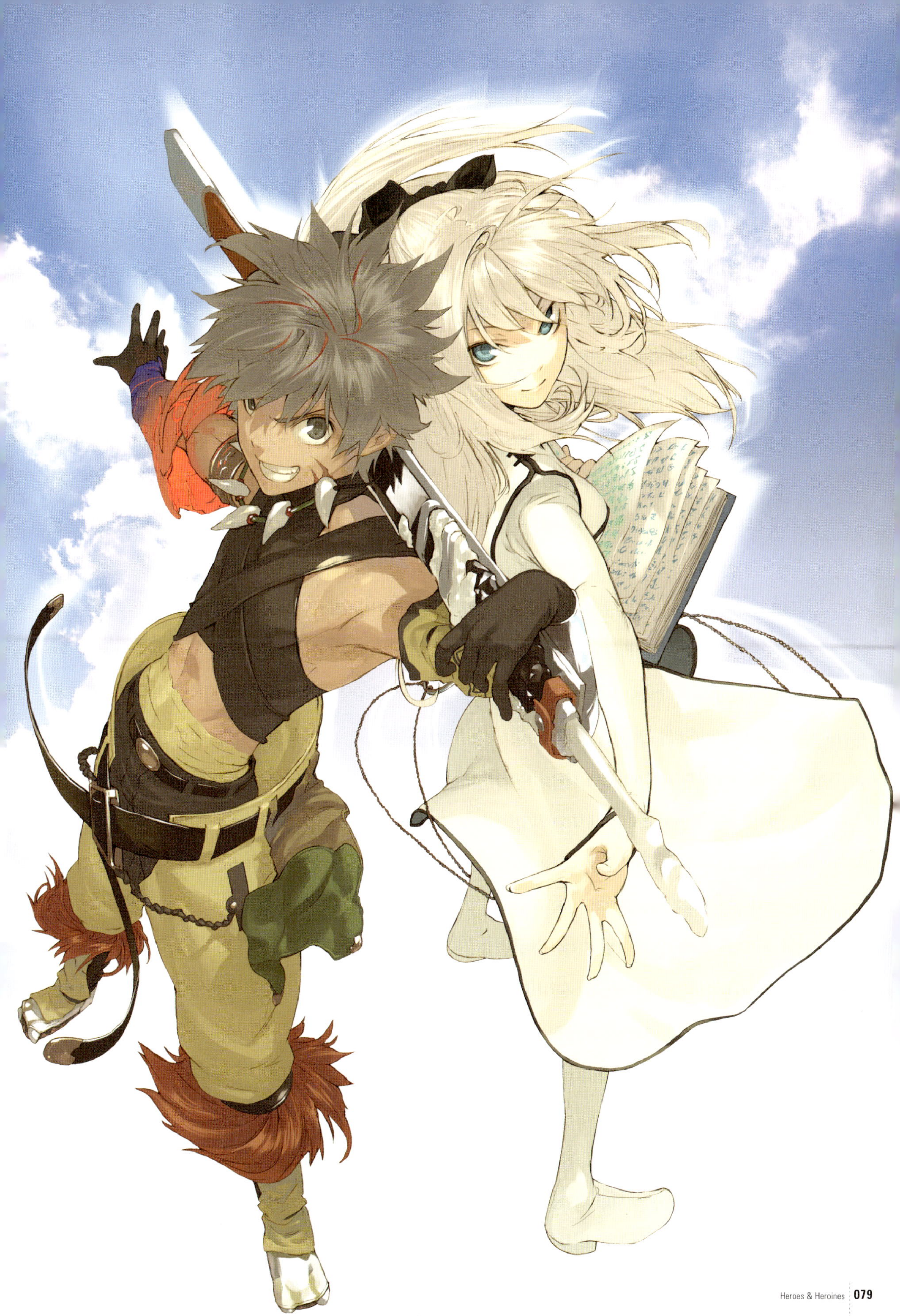

Game

『シャイニング・フォース イクサ』
● Shining Force EXA

pako

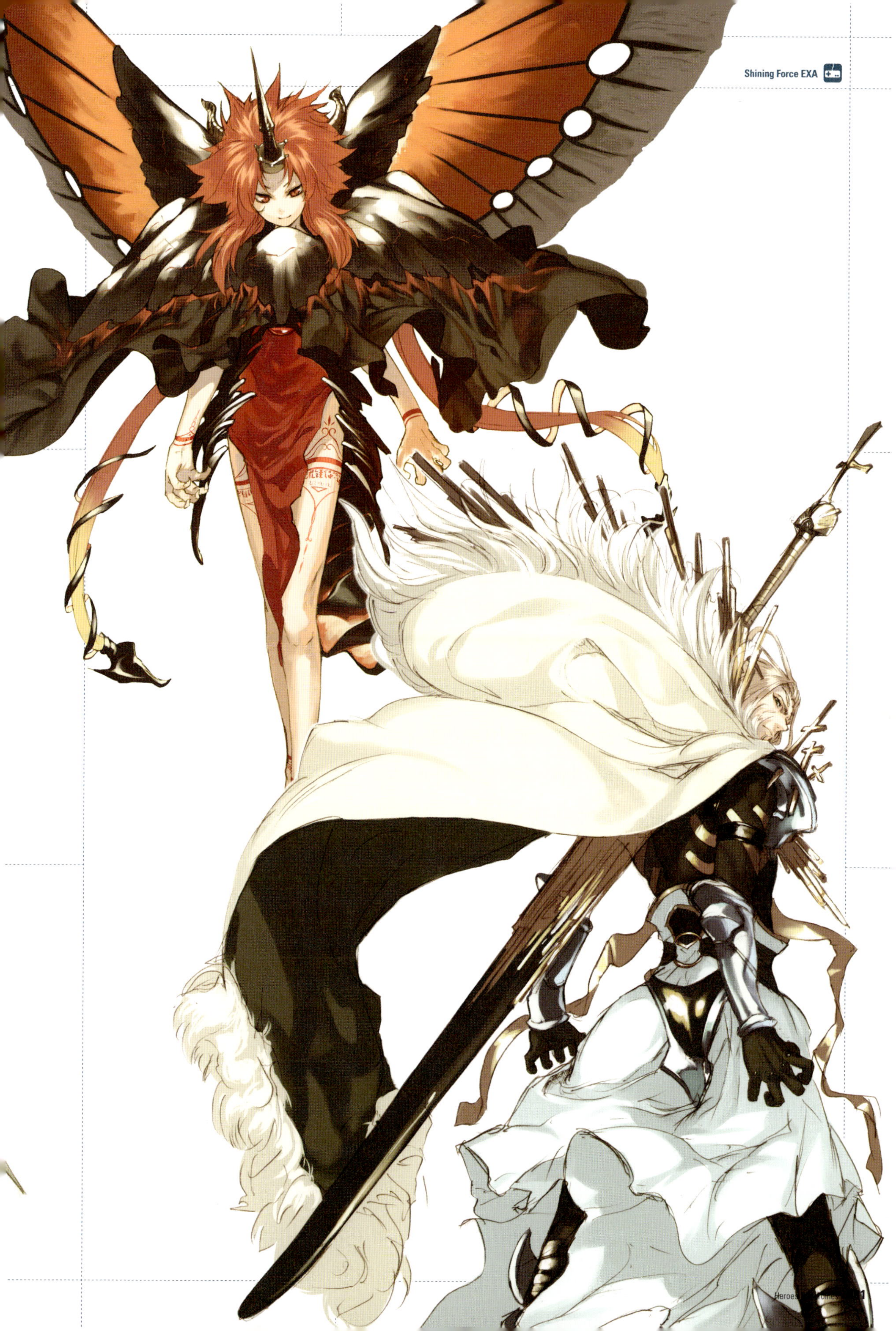

Game

『STEINS;GATE』シリーズ
● STEINS;GATE / STEINS;GATE hiyokurenri no darling

キャラクターデザイン

huke
huke

[代表作]『ブラック★ロックシューター』
『METAL GEAR SOLID PORTABLE OPS』

秋葉原を舞台とした想定科学アドベンチャーゲーム。スピンオフ作品、テレビアニメ、劇場版アニメと、幅広いエンターテインメント作品として広がりを見せている。hukeの描く無機質にも見えるスタイリッシュな美少女が多くのゲームユーザー、視聴者の心を捕らえた。

An envisioned science adventure game set in Akihabara. The series has spread widely as a wide-ranging entertainment work with spin-offs, TV animations, and a theatrical animated feature. The stylish, beautiful girl that almost looks cold and inorganic has captured the hearts of many game users and viewers.

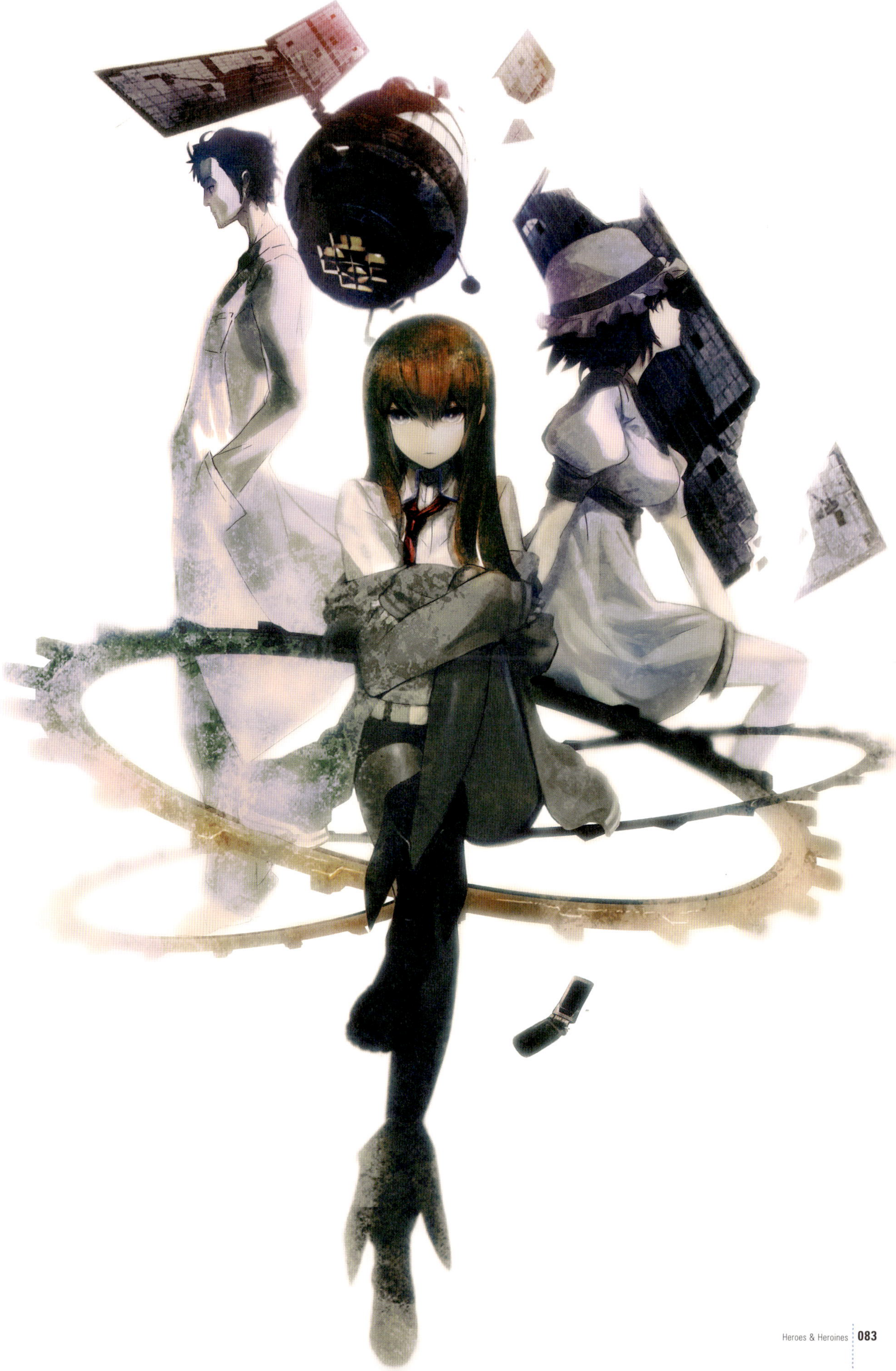

Game

『STEINS;GATE』シリーズ
● STEINS;GATE / STEINS;GATE hiyokurenri no darling

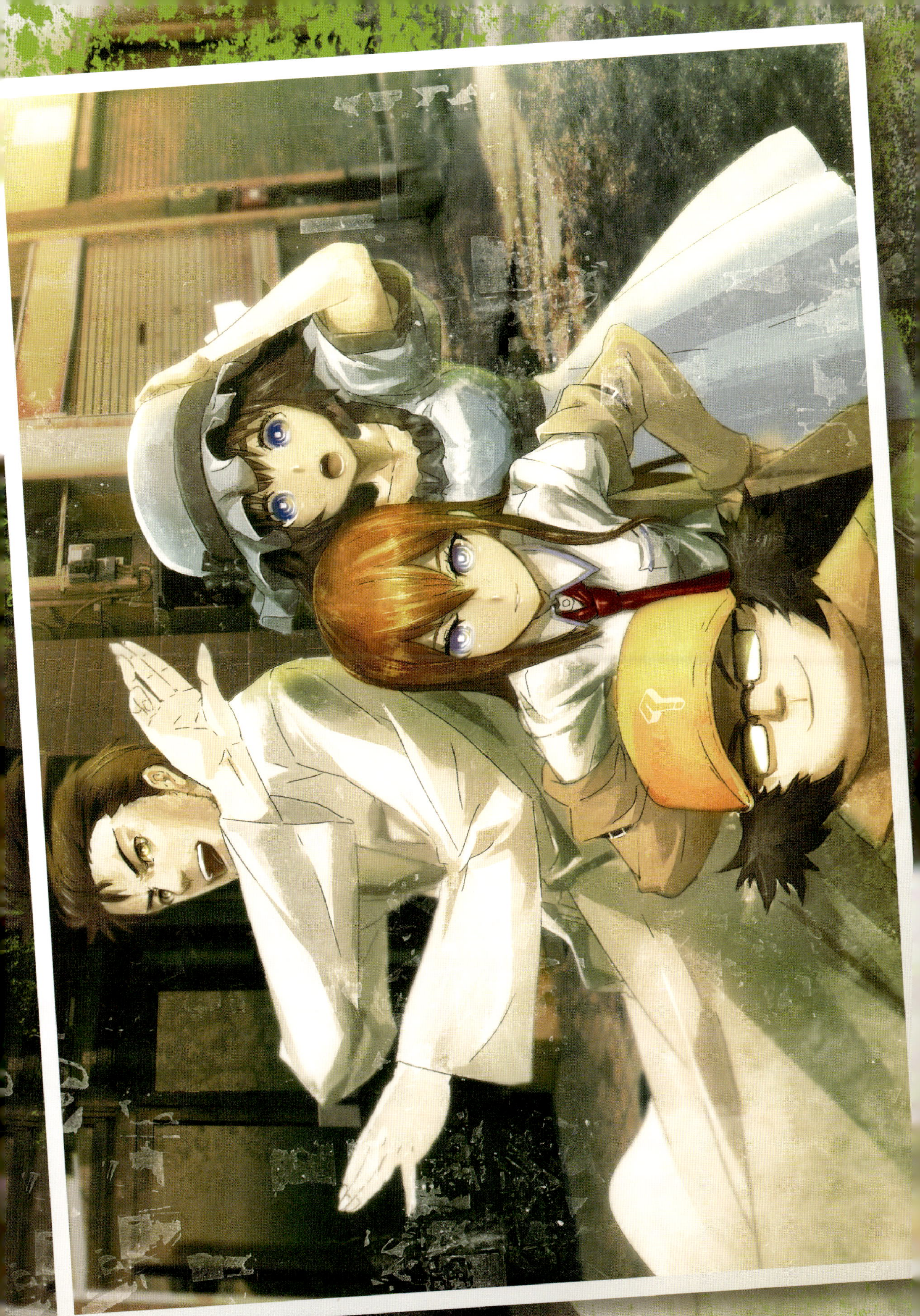

Animation 『世紀末オカルト学院』
● OCCULT ACADEMY

キャラクターデザイン
千葉崇洋
Chiba Takahiro

[代表作]『かみちゅ!』『青の祓魔師』（メインアニメーター）

オカルトを題材にしつつも、主人公である女子高校生・マヤの女王様ぶりと、その尻にしかれるヘタレ男・文明の作り込まれたキャラクターが作品を明るく照らす。長野県を舞台にした田舎の美しい風景描写も見どころ。千葉崇洋は本作品の総作画監督も務めている。

Occult themed, it's the characters that really bring this world to life- the heroine, a high school girl and princess Maya, and the cowardly men who yell at her from behind. The countryside of Nagano makes for a breathtaking backdrop. Chiba Takahiro is the executive animation director as well.

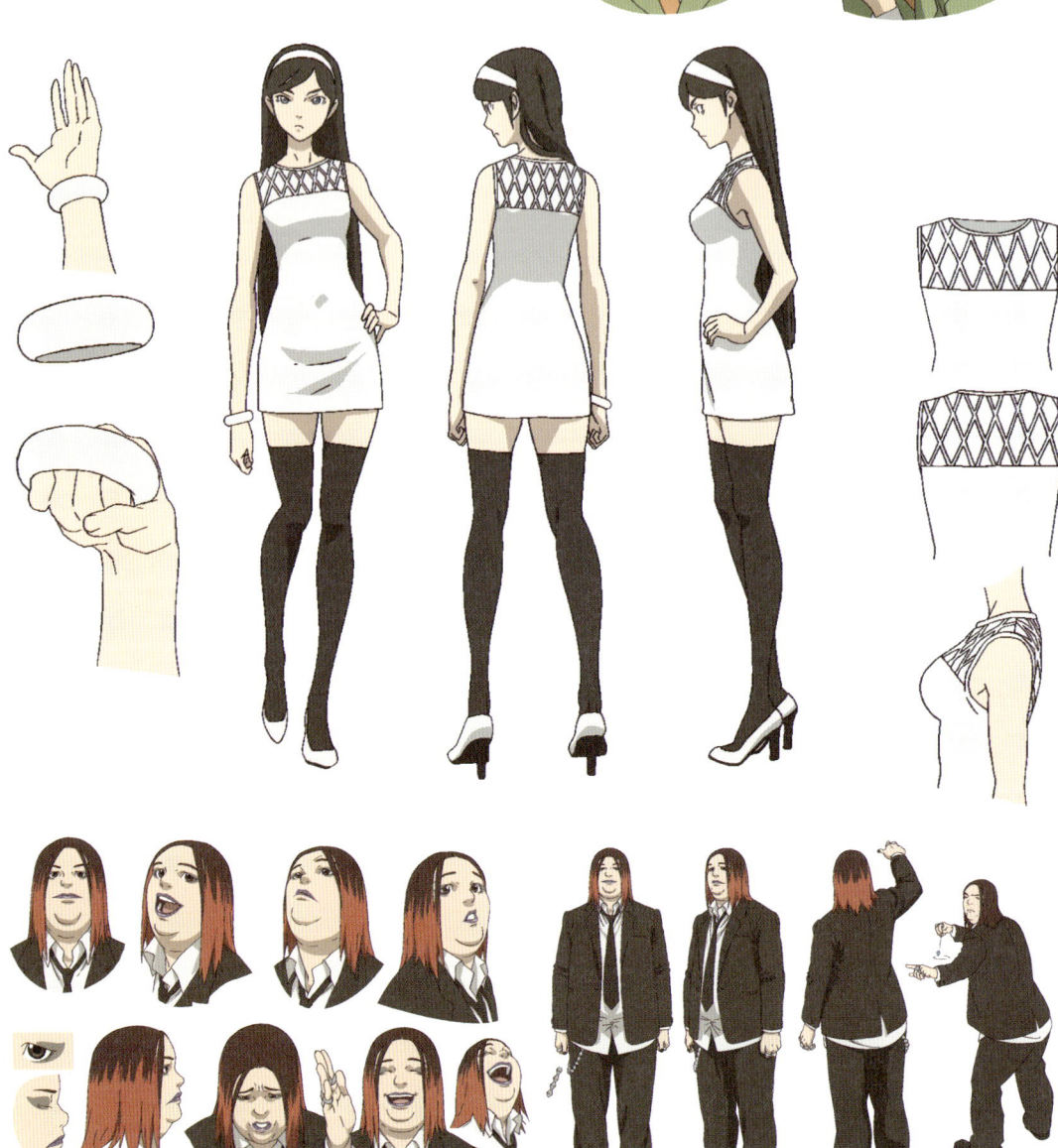

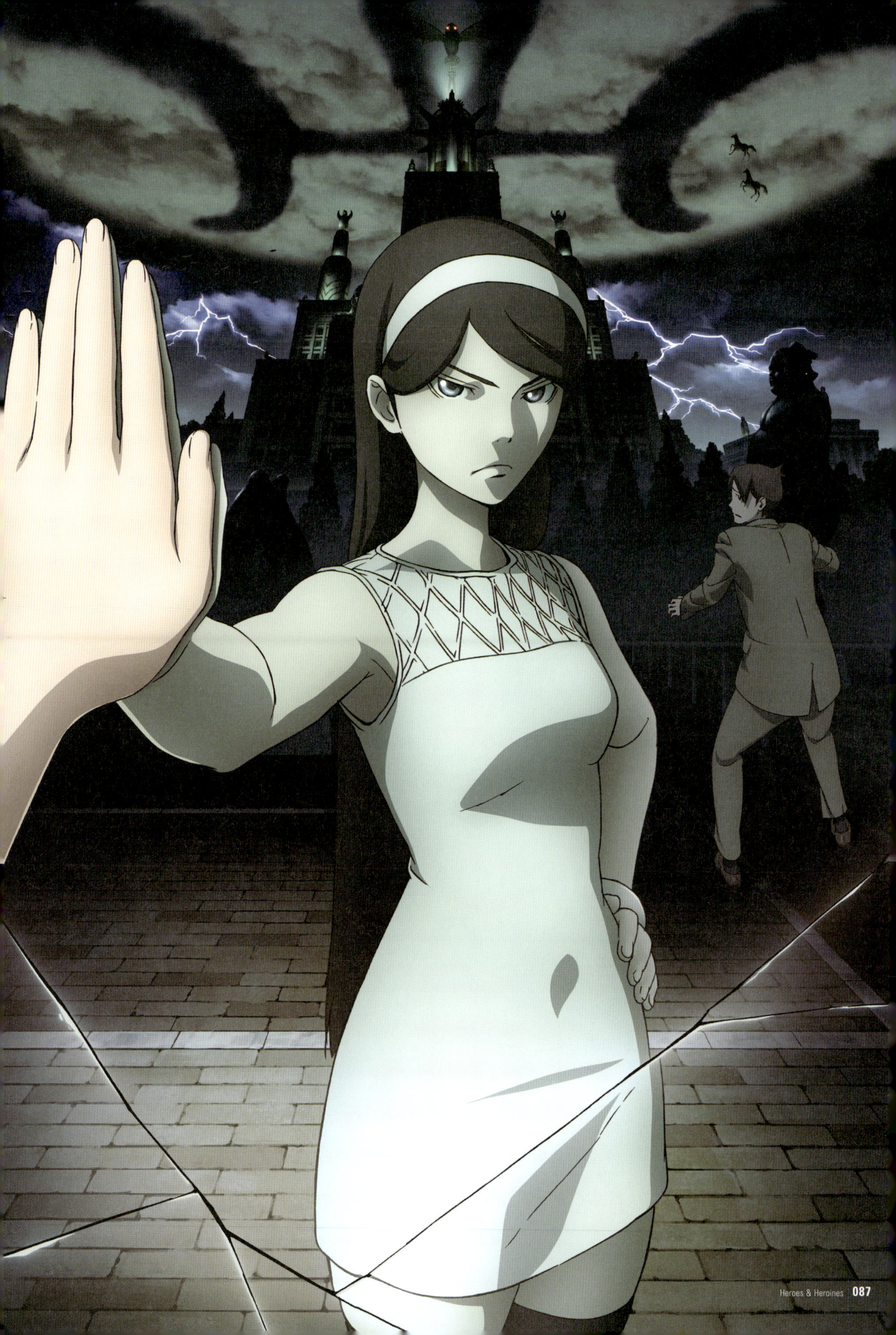

Game

『世界樹の迷宮』シリーズ／『ノーラと刻の工房 霧の森の魔女』
● Etrian Odyssey / Etrian Odyssey II: Heroes of Lagaard / Etrian Odyssey III: The Drowned City / Noora to Toki no Koubou: Kiri no Mori no Majo

キャラクターデザイン
日向悠二
Himukai Yuji

[代表作]『世界樹の迷宮』シリーズ
『吉永さん家のガーゴイル』小説（挿絵）

2007年にダンジョンRPG『世界樹の迷宮』が発売されると、そのクラシカルなシステムや冒険への好奇心をかきたてる世界観でたちまち大人気タイトルとなった。愛らしいイラストで人気の日向悠二がこの『世界樹の迷宮』シリーズと『ノーラと刻の工房 霧の森の魔女』のキャラクターデザインを務めた。

When the dungeon RPG "Etrian Odyssey" was released in 2007, it quickly became a hit title due to its classic system and world view that elicits a sense of curiosity toward the adventure. Himukai Yuji, popular for his cute illustrations, worked on character design for the "Etrian Odyssey" Series and for "Noora to Toki no Koubou: Kiri no Mori no Majo."

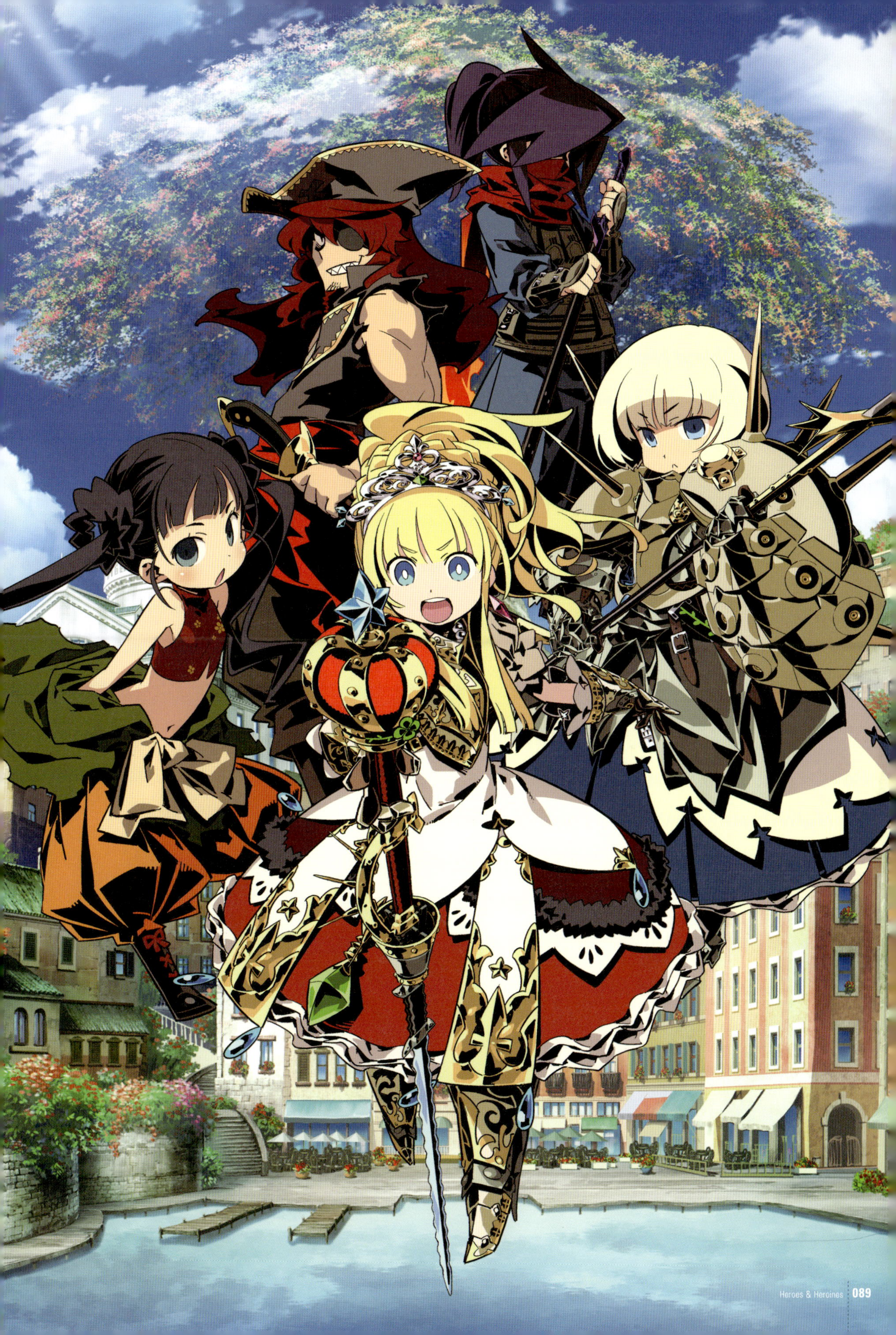

Game

『世界樹の迷宮』シリーズ／『ノーラと刻の工房 霧の森の魔女』
● Etrian Odyssey / Etrian Odyssey II: Heroes of Lagaard / Etrian Odyssey III: The Drowned City / Noora to Toki no Koubou: Kiri no Mori no Majo

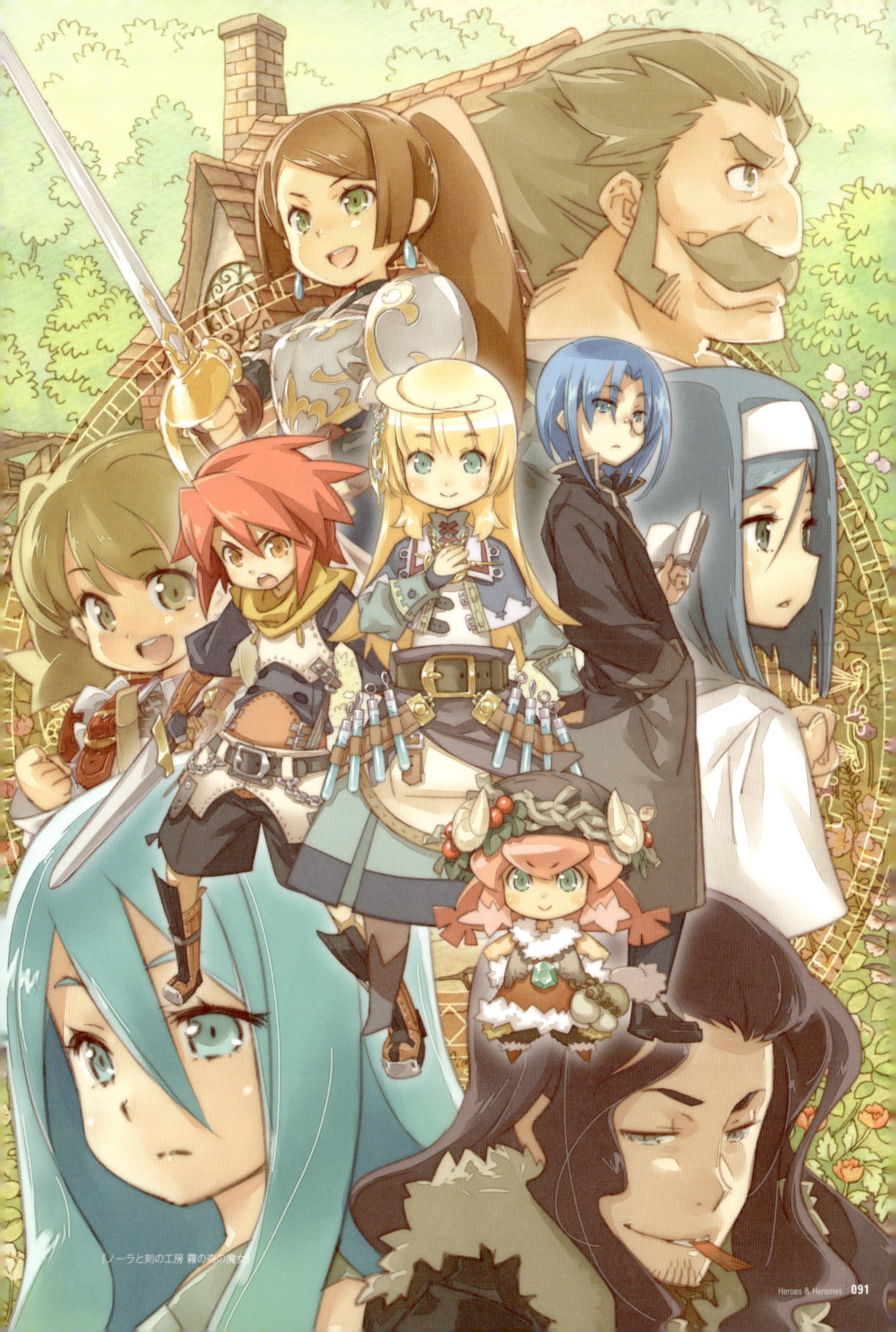

『ノーラと刻の工房 霧の森の魔女』

Game 『セブンスドラゴン2020』
● 7TH DRAGON 2020

キャラクターデザイン
三輪士郎
Miwa shirow

[代表作]『狗 -DOGS-』
『DOGS/BULLETS&CARNAGE』(漫画)

西暦2020年の東京を舞台に人類とドラゴンが戦うRPG。外見、職業、ボイスを自由に組み合わせることができるキャラクターメイキングが魅力。キャラクターデザインを務めるのは、漫画家、イラストレーターとして活躍中の三輪士郎。

An RPG where humans and dragons fight in Tokyo in 2020. A key feature is character creation, where you can freely combine your character's look, profession, and voice. Miwa Shirow, a manga artist and illustrator, worked on the character design.

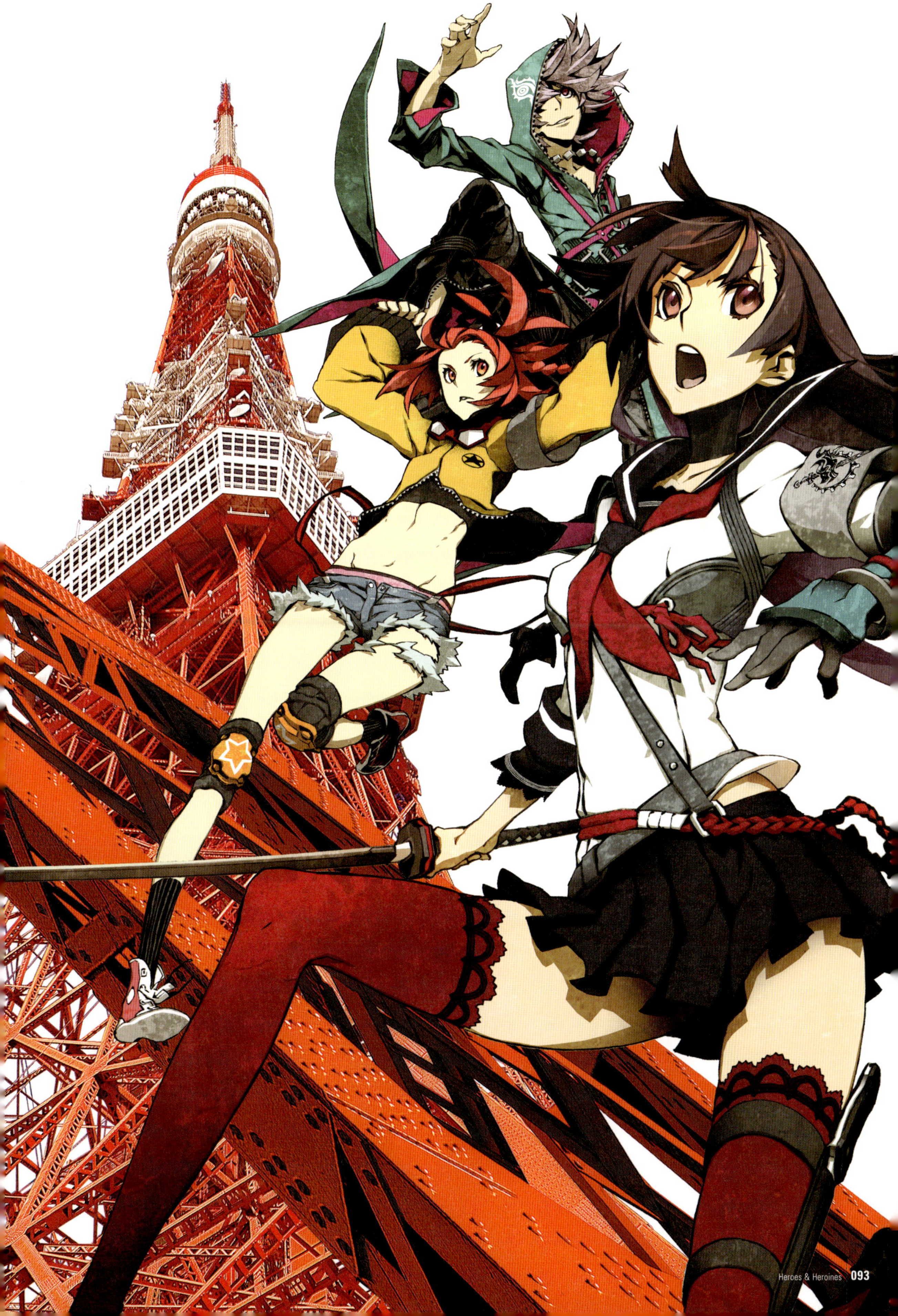

Animation

『閃光のナイトレイド』
● Senko no NIGHT RAID

キャラクターデザイン

佐々木啓悟
Sasaki Keigo

[代表作]『青の祓魔師』『戦国BASARA 弐』(デザインワークス)

1931年の国際都市・上海を舞台に、日本陸軍中のスパイ組織「桜井機関」に属すメンバーたちが暗躍するオリジナルアニメーション。漫画家上条明峰をキャラクター原案に迎え、佐々木啓悟がアニメ用に仕上げている。佐々木啓悟は他人気作品でも原画や作画監督を務めるなど、要注目のアニメーターである。

Set in cosmopolitan Shanghai in 1931, this original anime tells the tale of behind the scenes of the Sakurai Syndicate, a spy organization of the Japanese Army, and its members. Original character design was by the manga artist Kamijo Akimine, and made into anime by Sasaki Keigo. Sasaki Keigo is an up-and-coming animator and animation director behind other popular stories.

Heroes & Heroines

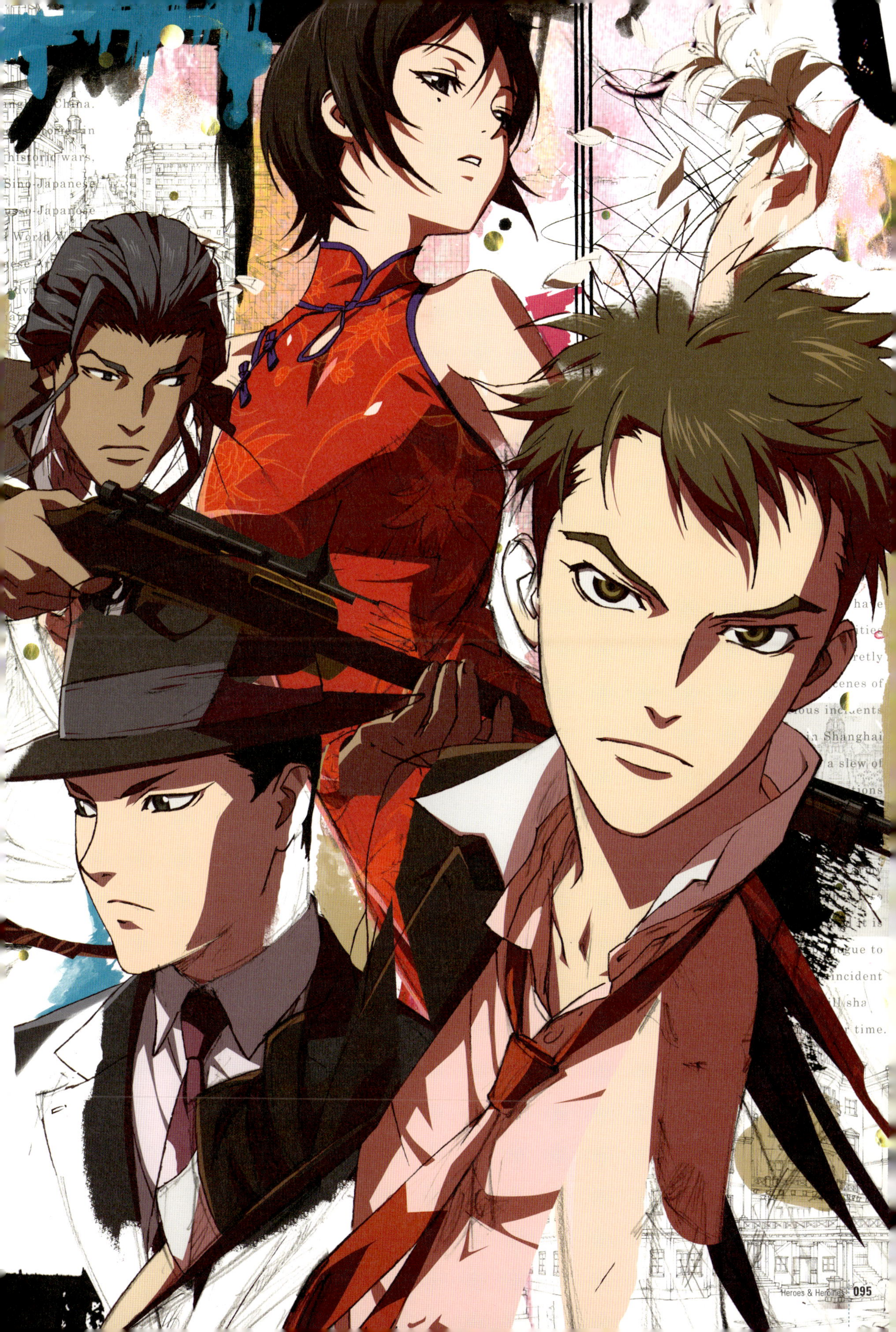

Animation 『青の祓魔師』
● Blue Exorcist

キャラクターデザイン

佐々木啓悟
Sasaki Keigo

[代表作]『閃光のナイトレイド』『戦国BASARA 弐』(デザインワークス)

加藤和恵のダークファンタジーコミックをアニメーション化。青年誌に連載中の原作だが、アニメ化により、親しみやすい絵柄やポップな配色が女性や子供の支持も得、人気が浸透した。

The animated version of Kato Kazue's dark fantasy comic. The original work was often featured in young adult comics, but once animated it grew in popularity by gaining the support of women and children for its easy to understand story and eye catching colors.

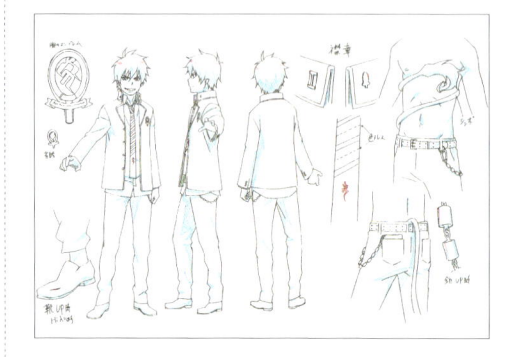

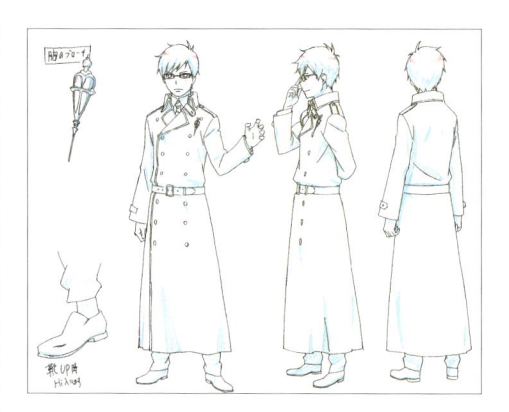

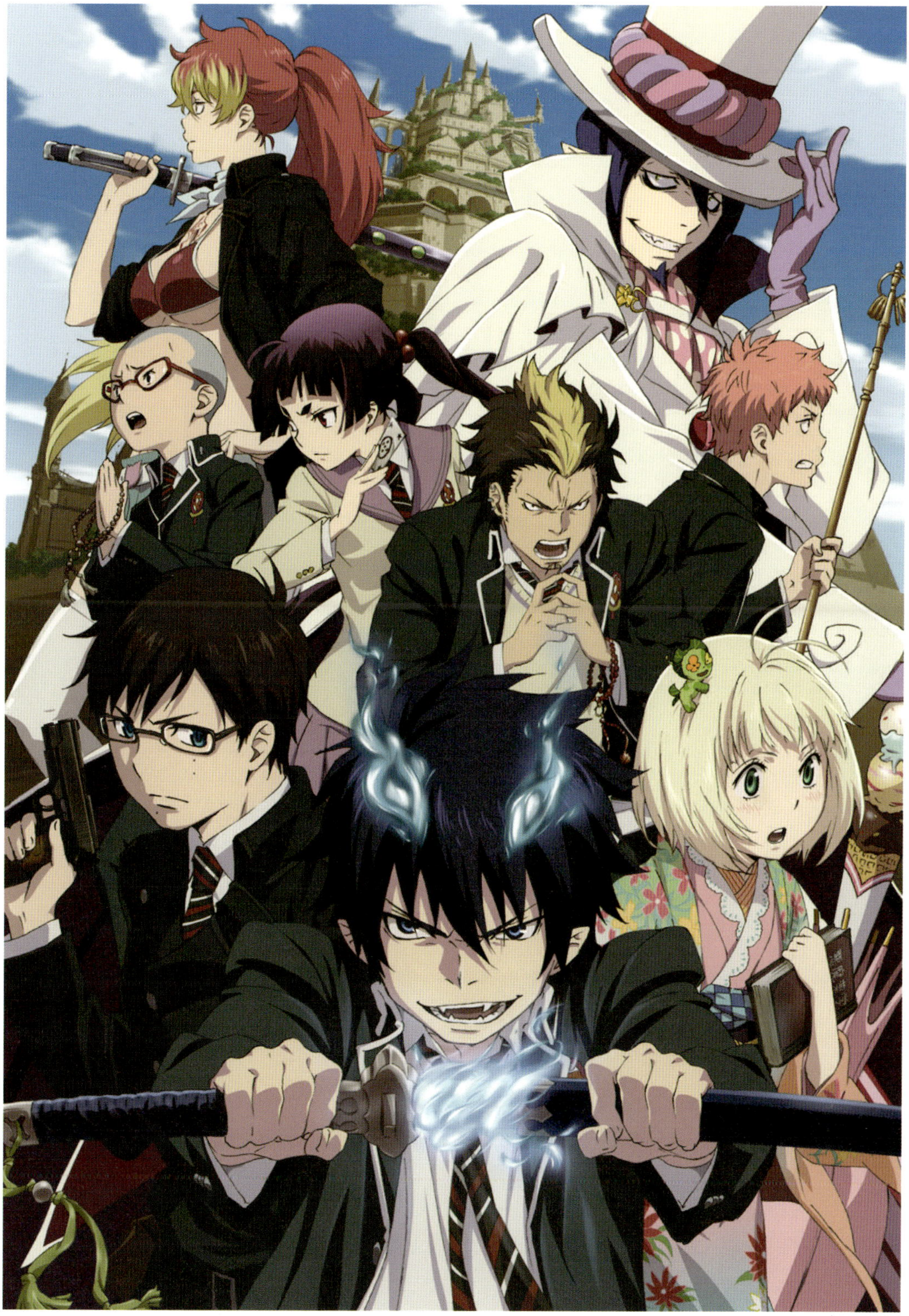

Animation 『戦国乙女～桃色パラドックス～』
● SENGOKU OTOME

キャラクターデザイン
山川宏治
Yamakawa Koji

[代表作]『ストライクウィッチーズ2』(キャラクター総作画監督)
『初恋限定。』(プロップデザイン)

戦国時代に似た、女の子しかいない世界に現代の女子中学生・ヒデヨシが飛ばされ、織田ノブナガら、戦国武将と出会う。甲冑や武具など、個々の戦国武将の特徴を取り入れながらも、露出は多く、女性らしい丸みのあるデザインに仕上げている。キャラクターデザイン原案は白組。山川宏治は総作画監督も務めている。

Hideyoshi, a girl attending junior high school, is sent to a world resembling the Period of Warring States in which there are only girls. Here she meets Oda Nobunaga and other Warring States Samurai. While the armor, weapons and other items worn possess the individual characteristics of the Warring States Samurai, they also expose a lot to create a rounded and feminine design. The character design proposal was made by SHIROGUMI. Yamakawa Koji also serves as the general animation director.

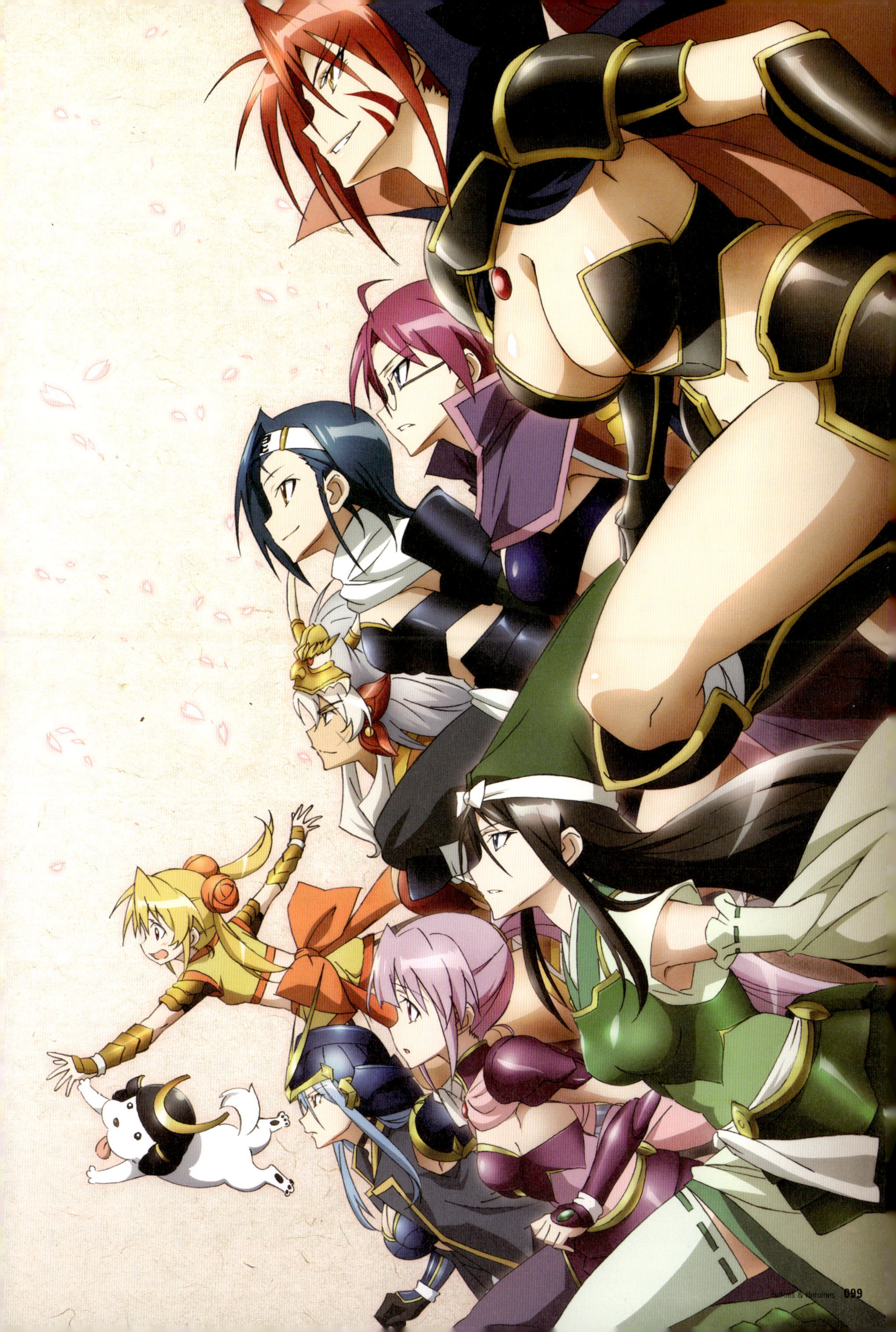

Game

『戦国BASARA3』
● SENGOKU BASARA3

キャラクターデザイン
土林誠
Tsuchibayashi Makoto

[代表作]『Devil May Cry』『Shinobi』『VANQUISH』

2005年にカプコンからシリーズ第1弾『戦国BASARA』が発売されると、爽快な操作性とともに、キャラクターデザインを務める土林誠の流麗な武将デザインが男女問わずゲームユーザーの心を掴んだ。本作品シリーズが近年の戦国ブームの一助となっていることは間違いないだろう。

The first title in this series, Sengoku Basara, was released by CAPCOM in 2005. Upon its release the refreshing controls and elegant warrior designs by character designer Tsuchibayashi Makoto grabbed the hearts of players regardless of gender. There's no mistake that this series contributed to the "Warring States" boom of recent years.

SENGOKU BASARA3

Heroes & Heroines | 101

| Game | 『戦律のストラタス』
● Stratus

キャラクターデザイン
エナミカツミ
Enami Katsumi

[代表作]『英雄伝説 零の軌跡』
　　　　『サモンナイトグランテーゼ 滅びの剣と約束の騎士』

キャラクターたちの人間ドラマを主軸とした連続アニメ形式で展開するドラマチック殲滅アクション。キャラクターデザインを担当するのは、人気ライトノベル『バッカーノ！』の挿絵等、洗練されたイラストで多くのファンを魅了するエナミカツミ。

This is a dramatic "annihilation" action game in which the story develops in the format of an anime series centered on the human drama of the characters. In charge of character design is popular light novel BACCANO! illustrator Enami Katsumi, whose refined illustrations have attracted many fans.

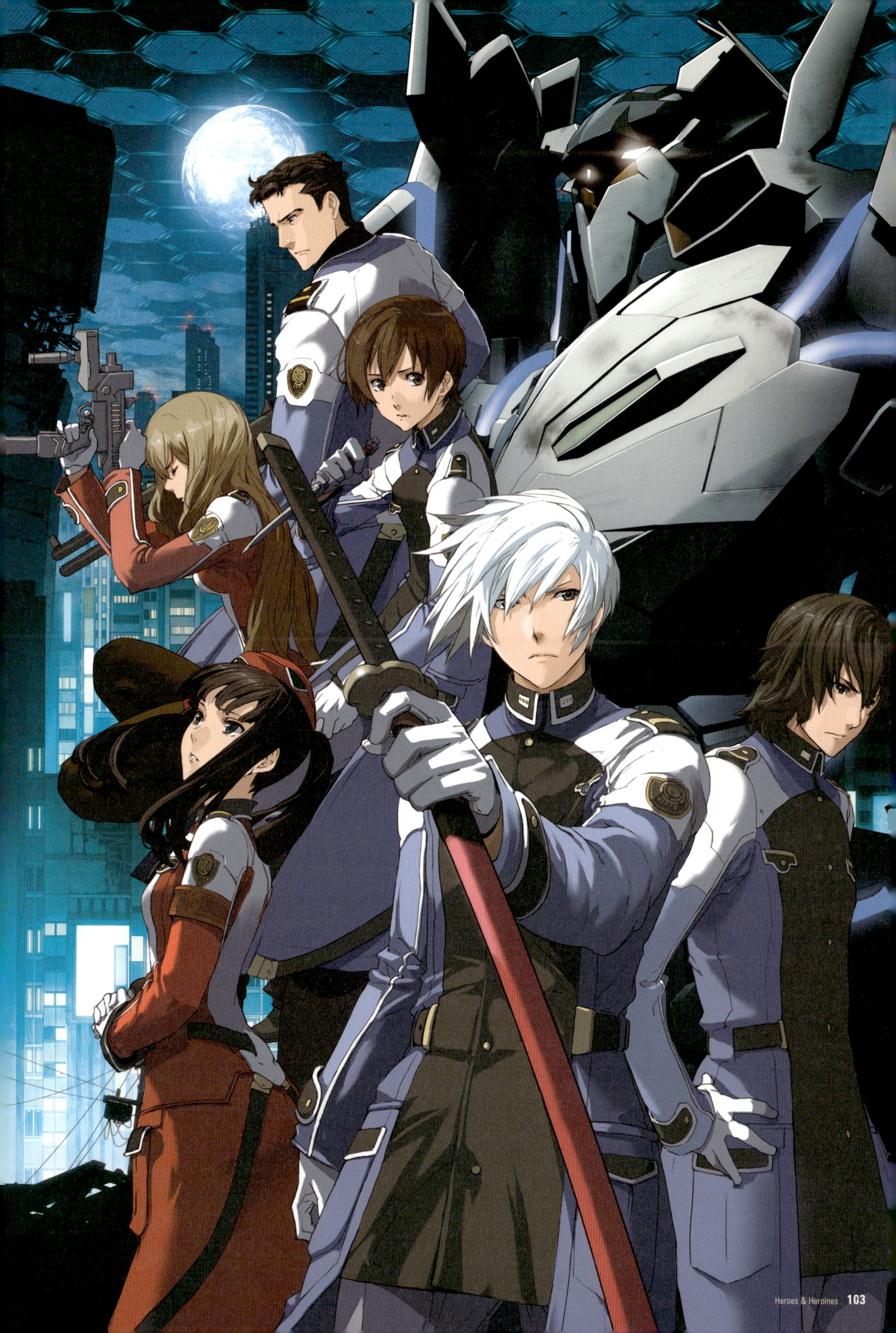

Game

『ソニコミ』
● COMMUNICATION WITH SONICO

キャラクターデザイン
津路参汰
Tsuji Santa

[代表作]『スマガ』（原画）『アザナエル』（原画）

ゲームメーカー・ニトロプラスのライブイベント専用のマスコットガールとして 生まれたキャラクター「すーぱーそに子」。その人気ぶりから、いよいよ恋愛コミュニケーションゲームとなって登場。むちむちふわふわとした女性らしいスタイルと愛くるしい笑顔で、発売前から多くのファンを獲得している。ゲーム化にあたっては、3Dポリゴンを同社3Dモデラー・オガタガクオ（ポリゴン番長）が制作している。

Super Sonico is a character created by the game maker Nitroplus to be the "mascot girl" for their live events. Its popularity has finally resulted in its appearance as a "love communication game." Her fluffy and plump feminine style and cute smile attracted many fans even before the game went on sale. The 3D polygons were created by Ogata Gakuo (Polygon Team Leader) for the game version.

オガタガクオ
（ポリゴン番長）

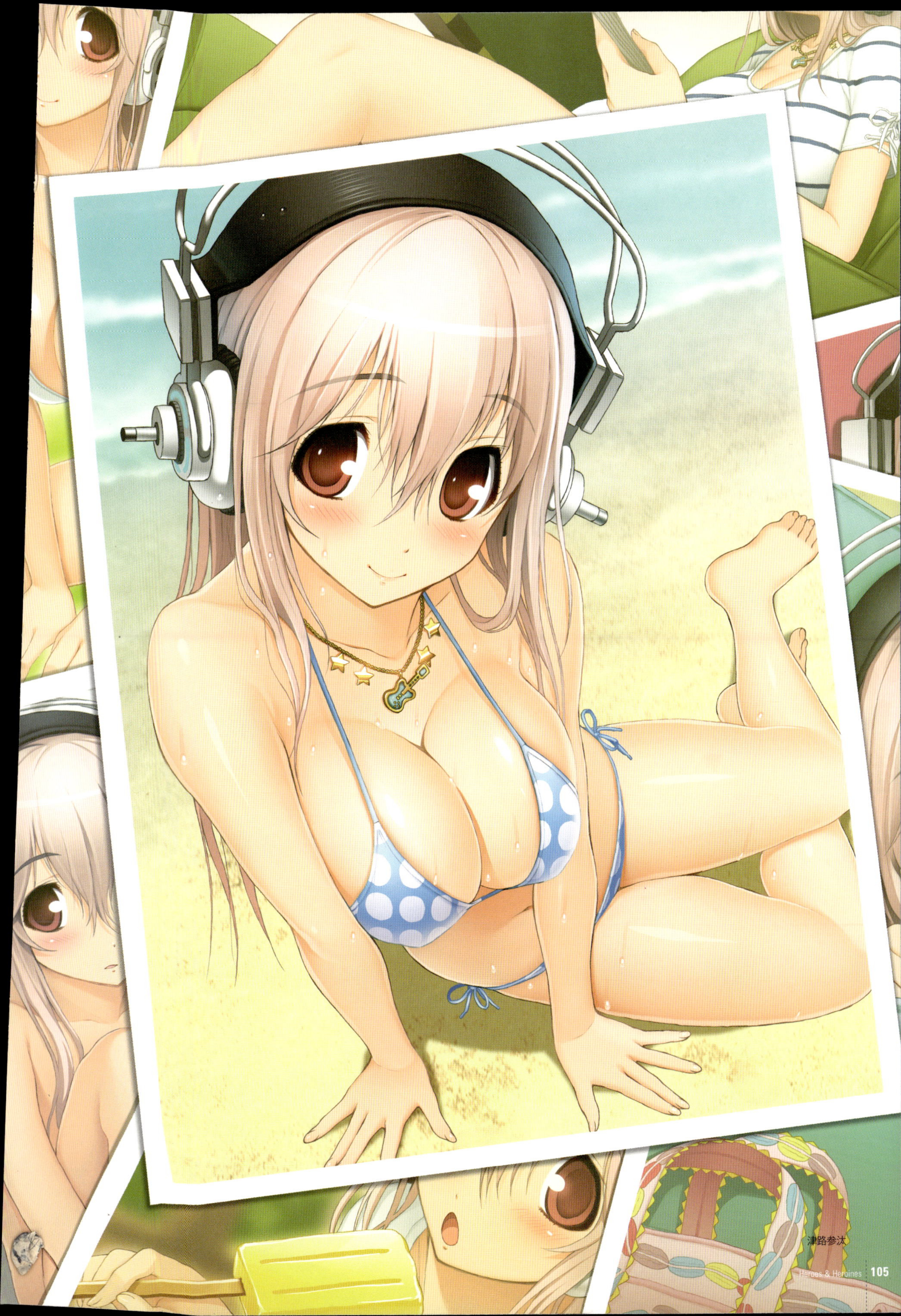

津路参汰

Animation 『それでも町は廻っている』
● And Yet the Town Moves

原作 石黒正数 / **キャラクターデザイン** 山村洋貴
Ishiguro Masakazu / Yamamura Hiroki

[石黒正数代表作]『それでも町は廻っている』『外天楼』(漫画)
[山村洋貴代表作]『かってに改蔵』(キャラクターデザイン・総作画監督)
『さよなら絶望先生』(キャラクターデザイン・総作画監督)

石黒正数の人気漫画をテレビアニメーション化。新房昭之監督作品には欠かせない山村洋貴がキャラクターデザインを担った。下町の商店街にあるメイド喫茶っぽい喫茶店「シーサイド」で働く女子高生・嵐山歩鳥を取り巻く、普通でちょっと変な人たちの日常を描くコメディー。

An anime based on Ishiguro Masakazu's popular manga. Features character design by Yamamura Hiroki, an integral part of director Shinbo Akiyuki's works. The show involves Arashiyama Hotori, a high school student who works at a maid café style café called Seaside downtown. It's a comedy about the ordinary lives of slightly off-beat people.

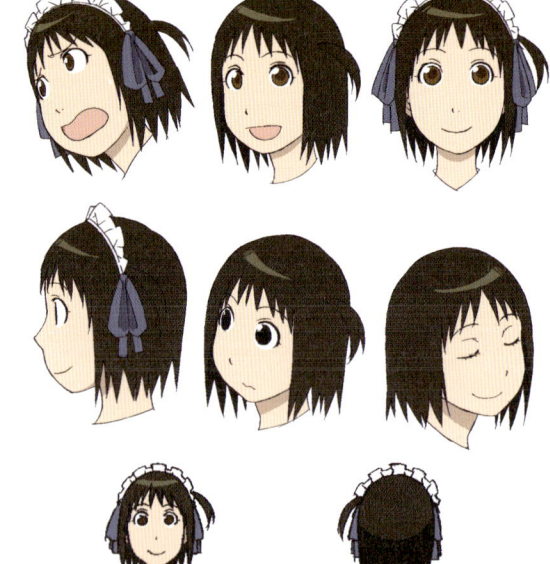

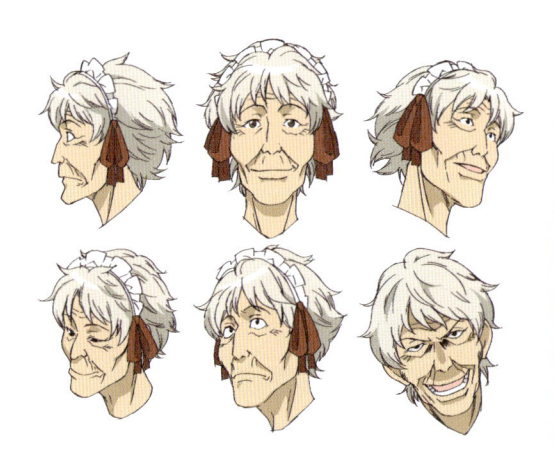

石黒正数

山村洋貴

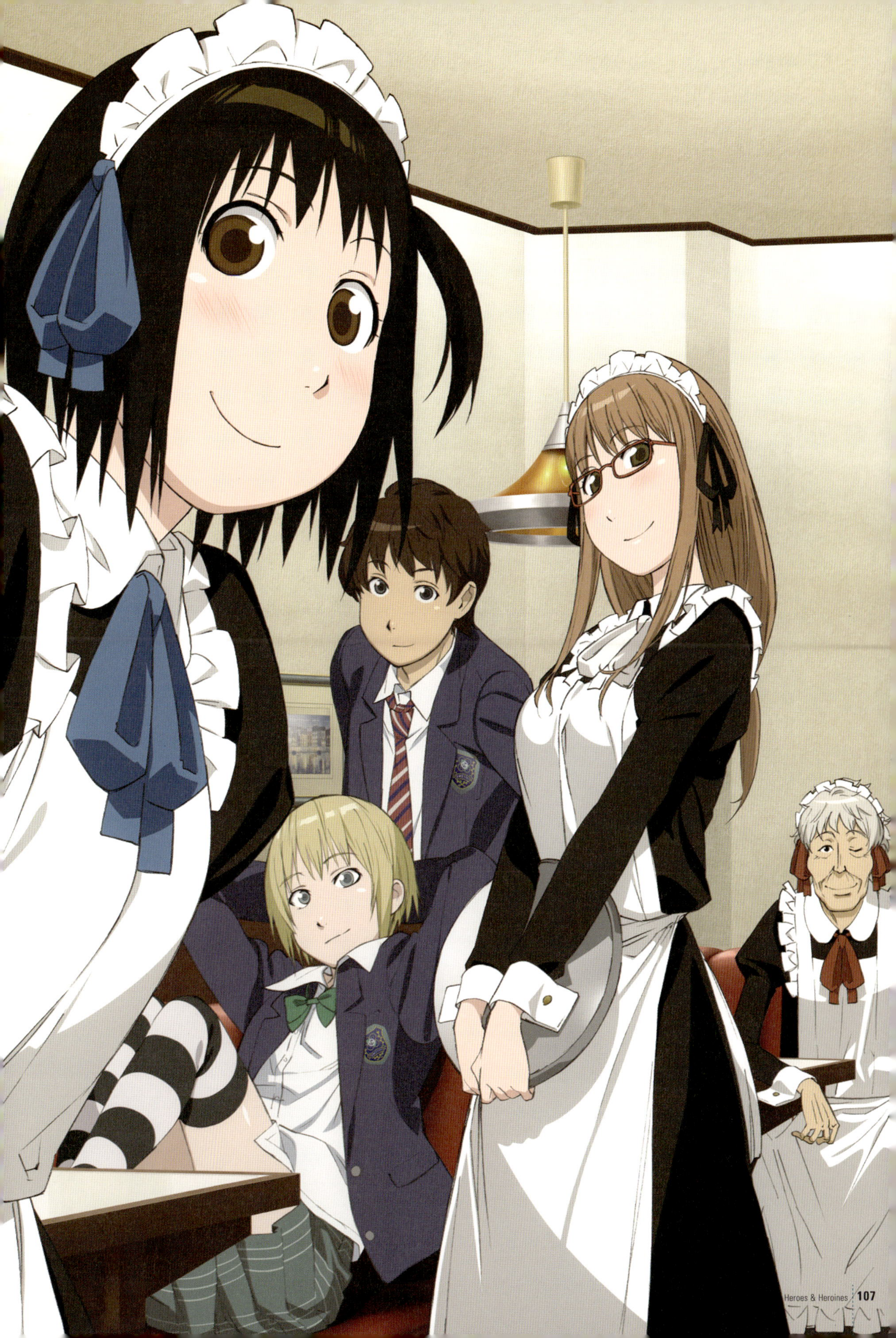

Game

『ダンガンロンパ 希望の学園と絶望の高校生』
● DANGANRONPA

キャラクターデザイン

小松崎類
Komatsuzaki Rui

[代表作]『ダンガンロンパ/ゼロ』小説（挿絵）

あらゆる分野で超一流の能力を持つ高校生15人が学級裁判の中で相手の矛盾を論破し、殺人事件の犯人を暴くハイスピード推理アクション。学園長と称する動くぬいぐるみ・モノクマの一見可愛らしいデザインが油断を誘う。

This is a high-speed reasoning action game in which 15 high school students with extremely first-rate abilities in every field refute the inconsistencies of their opponents during a class trial to expose a murderer. "Monokuma," the moving stuffed animal claiming to be the school headmaster, causes people to let their guard down at first glance with his cute design.

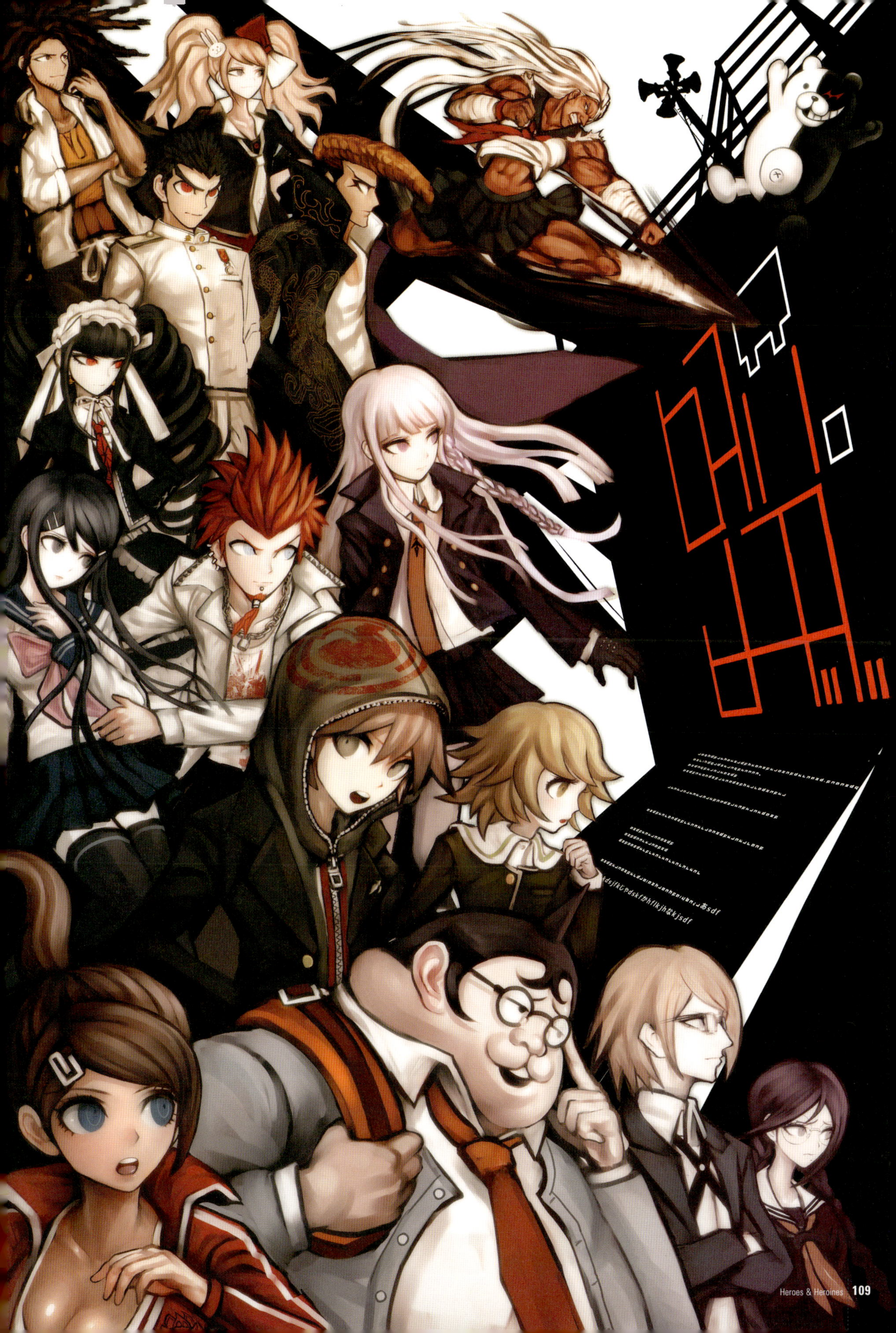

Game

『超次元ゲイム ネプテューヌmk2』
● Hyperdimension Neptuniamk2

キャラクターデザイン
つなこ
Tsunako

[代表作]『超次元ゲイム ネプテューヌ』
　　　　『超次元ゲイム ネプテューヌmk2』

ゲーム業界がモチーフになったユニークな世界観と架空のゲームハードが美少女に擬人化するRPG『超次元ゲイム ネプテューヌ』の続編。前作に続き、可愛いグラフィックと萌え要素がある本作。つなこがキャラクターデザインを担当。

This is the continuation of the game industry-motif RPG "Hyperdimension Neptunia," in which a unique world view and fantasy game hardware is personified in beautiful girls. As was the case in the previous entry in the series, Tsunako was in charge of character design. The work contains cute graphics and "moe" elements.

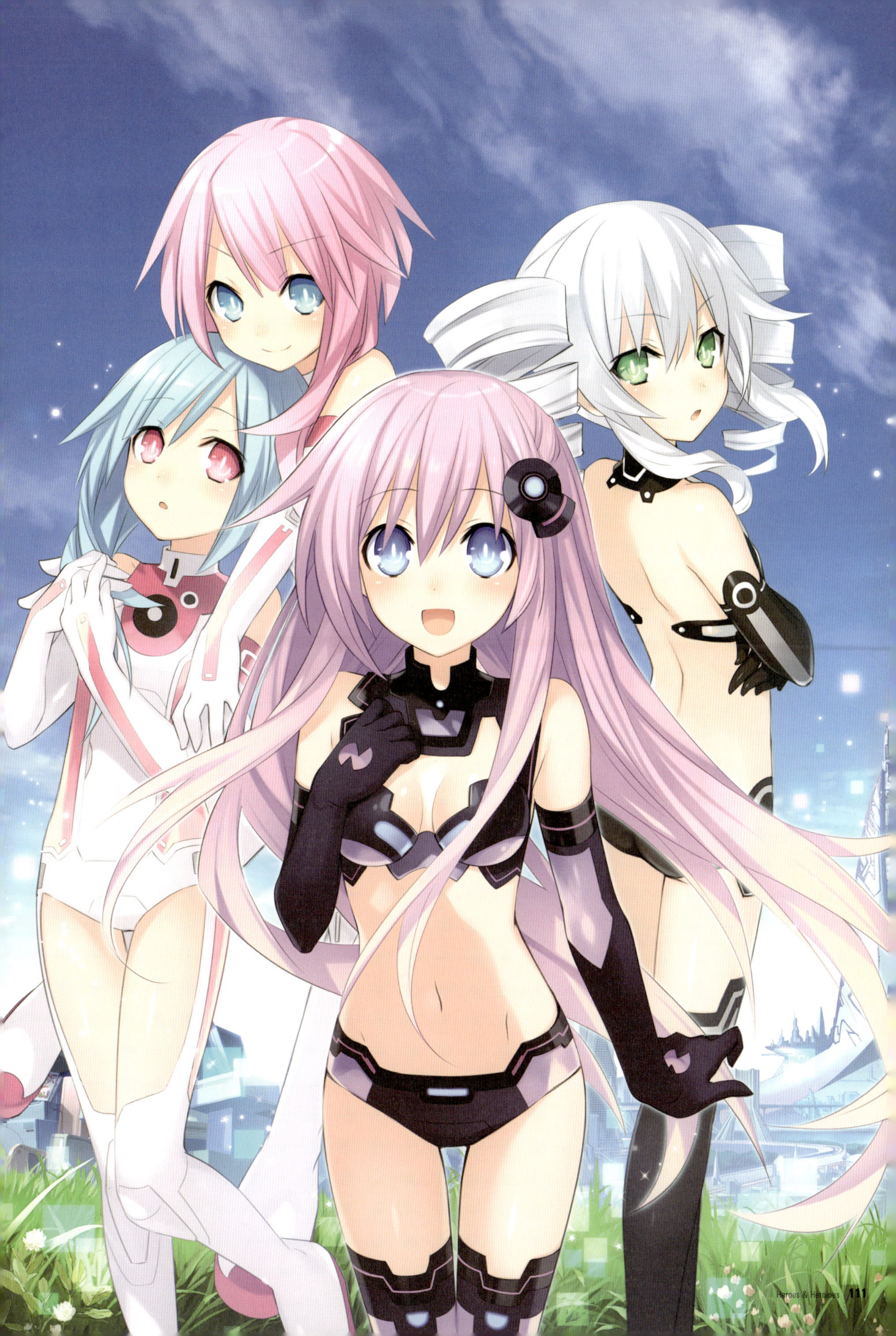

Game

『デビルサバイバー』シリーズ
● DEVIL SURVIVOR OVER CLOCK, DEVIL SURVIVOR2

キャラクターデザイン
ヤスダスズヒト
Yasuda Suzuhito

［代表作］『夜桜四重奏 ～ヨザクラカルテット～』（漫画）
『デュラララ!!』小説（挿絵）

極限状態の日本で悪魔と契約し、その強大な力を使って7日間を生き抜くシミュレーションRPG。プレイヤーの選択でいくつもの未来を切り開くことができるマルチエンディングシステムが特徴的。ヤスダスズヒトの描くスタイリッシュなキャラクターがドラマチックなストーリを色濃く演出している。

This is a simulation RPG set in a Japan experiencing extreme circumstances. Players enter into contracts with demons, and using their great power attempt to survive a period of seven days. Characteristic of this game is its multi-ending system, which opens up a number of futures based on the player's decisions. The stylish characters illustrated by Yasuda Suzuhito powerfully stage a dramatic story.

キービジュアルラフ

『DEVIL SURVIVOR OVER CLOCK』

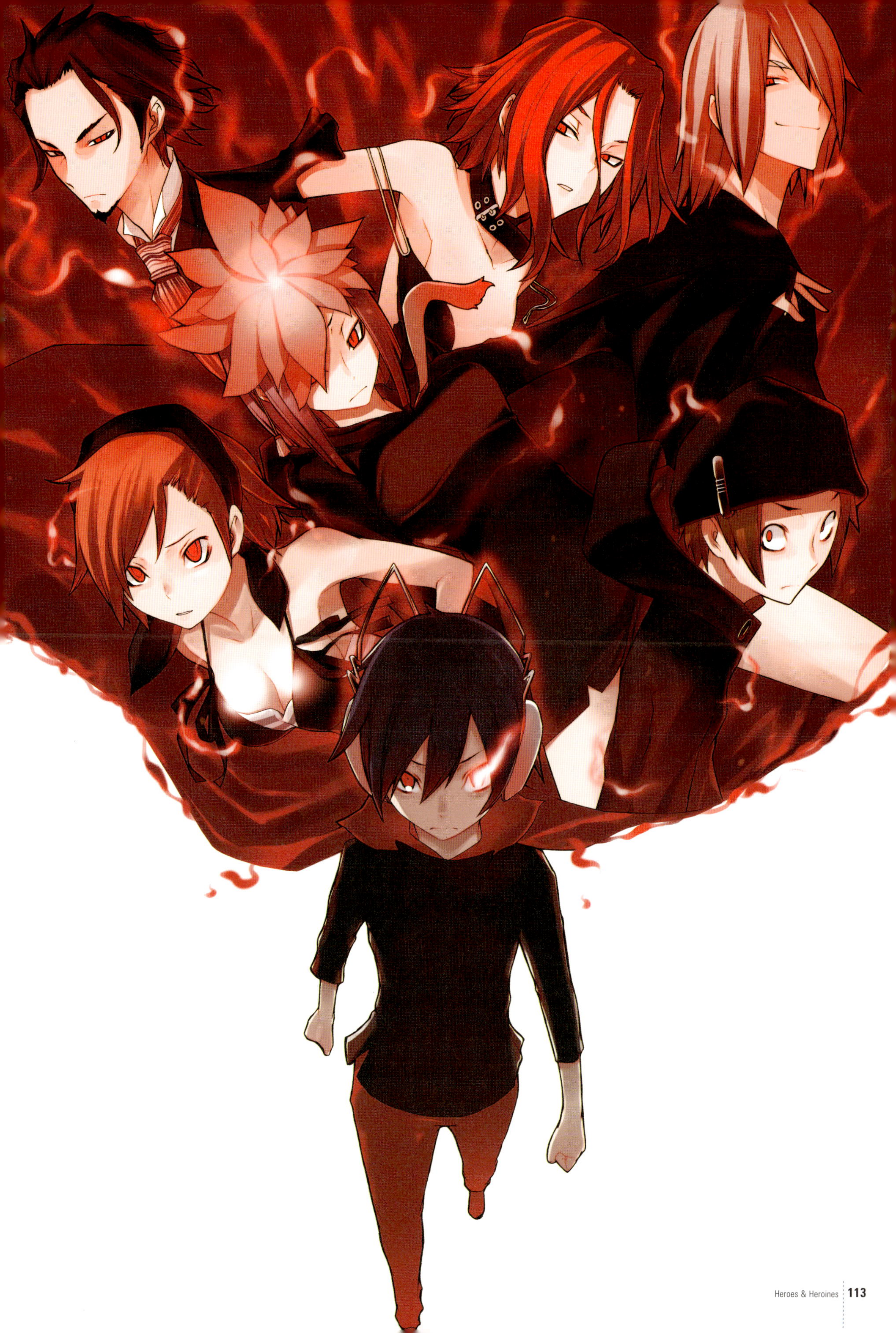

Game
『デビルサバイバー』シリーズ
● DEVIL SURVIVOR OVER CLOCK, DEVIL SURVIVOR2

『DEVIL SURVIVOR OVER CLOCK』

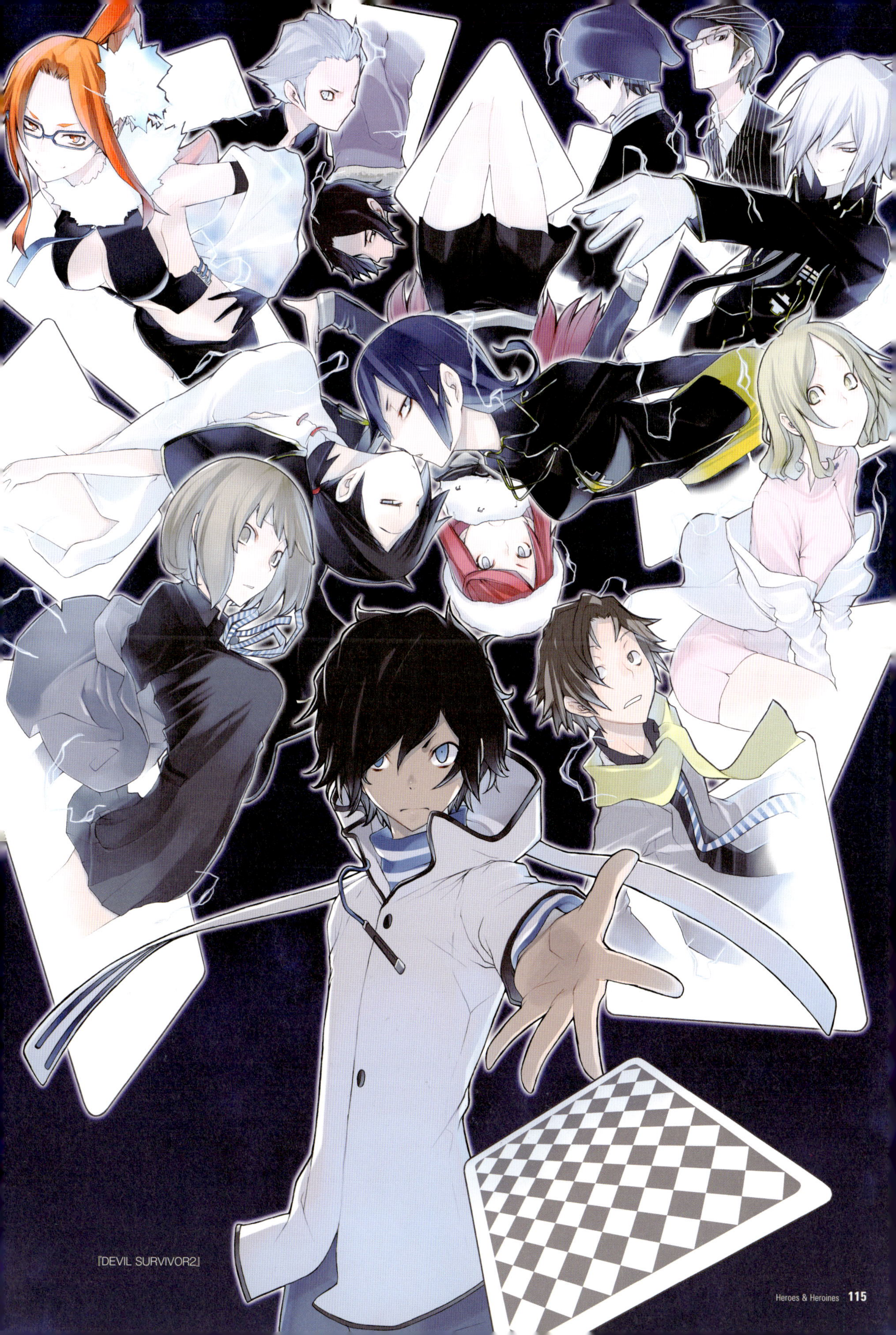

『DEVIL SURVIVOR2』

Game

『デビルサバイバー』シリーズ
● DEVIL SURVIVOR2

DEVIL SURVIVOR2

『DEVIL SURVIVOR2』

Game

『DUNAMIS15』
● DUNAMIS15

キャラクターデザイン
長浜めぐみ
Nagahama Megumi

[代表作]『プロジェクトケルベロス』『永遠の終わりに』

日本から離れた海の向こうにある学園島。一見平穏に見える学園島の実態とは……？ 平和な学園生活が一転するサスペンス・フィクションアドベンチャーゲーム。長浜めぐみの描く色気のある少年少女は女性にも人気。女子生徒の制服デザインが秀逸。

A campus island that lies in the ocean far from Japan. The campus island looks calm at first, but is it really? This is a suspense/fiction adventure game where a peaceful school life takes a dramatic turn of events. The charming young boys and girls drawn by Nagahama Megumi are popular among women too. The designs of the school uniforms for the female students are outstanding.

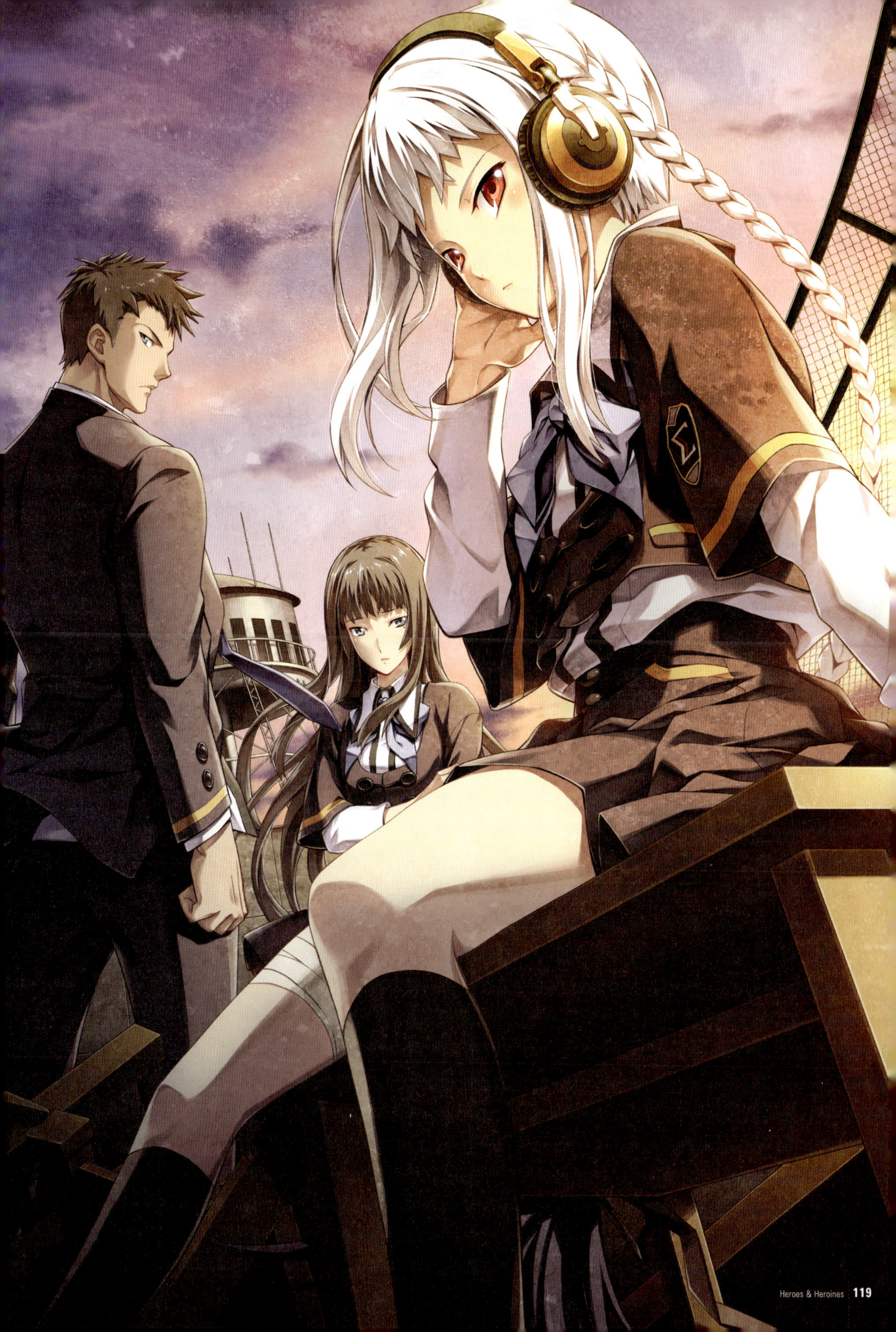

Animation

『とある飛空士への追憶』
● Toaru Hikuushi e no Tsuioku

キャラクターデザイン
松原秀典
Matsubara Hidenori

[代表作]『いばらの王 -King of Thorn-』『ああっ女神さまっ』シリーズ

犬村小六の小説を映画化。名もなき飛空士と皇妃となるお姫様との淡い恋と飛空戦を鮮やかに描いた。80年代からアニメーターとして活躍する松原秀典は『サクラ大戦』シリーズのキャラクターデザインや、『ヱヴァンゲリヲン新劇場版』シリーズの作画監督など、数々の名作に携わっている。

This is the movie adaptation of the novel by Inumura Koroku. The movie vividly illustrates an air war as well as the fleeting love between a nameless pilot and a crown princess. Matsubara Hidenori has been active as an illustrator since the 1980s, and has been involved in the creation of a number of famous works; he was the character designer for the "Sakura Wars" series, and the animation director for the "Rebuild of Evangelion."

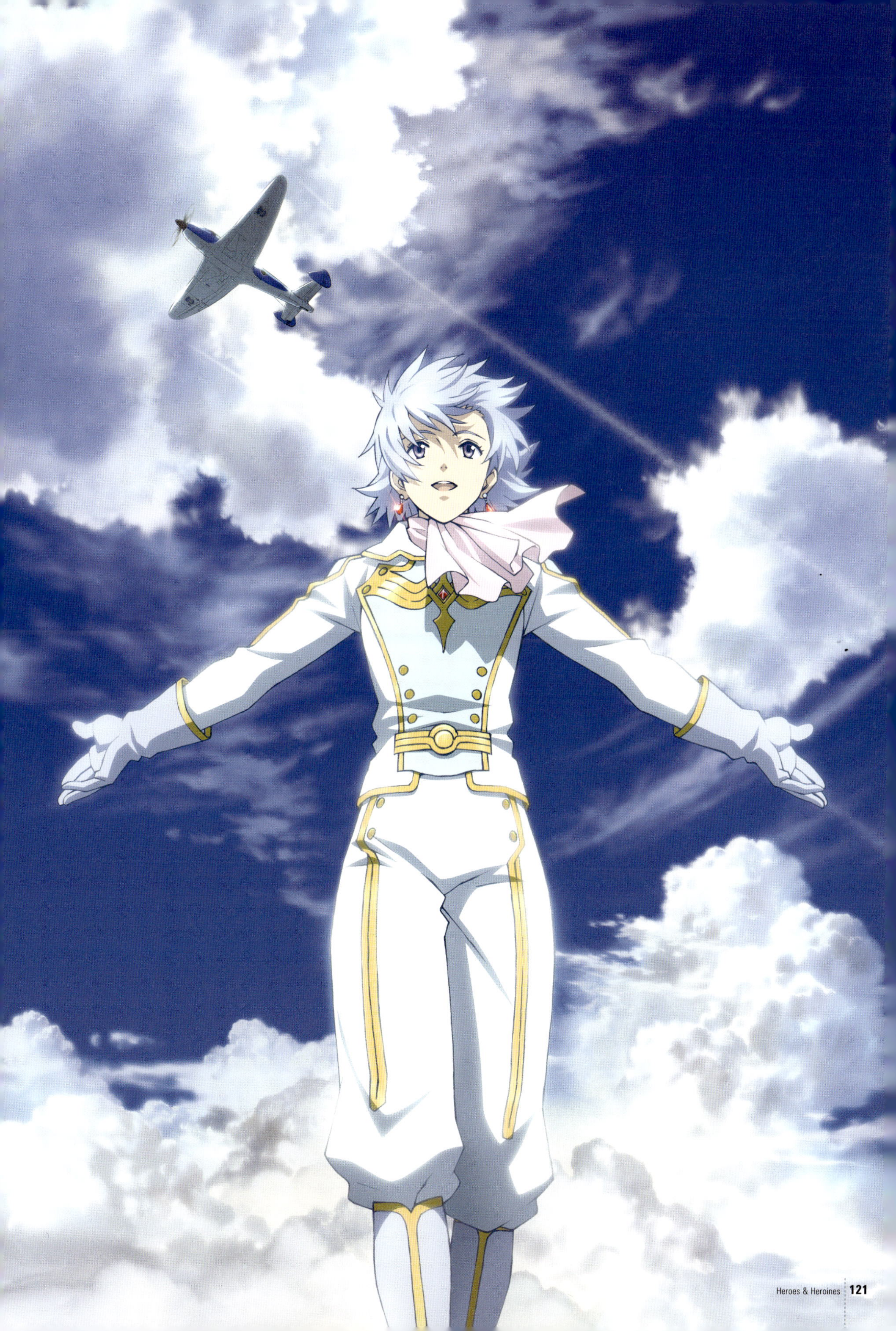

Animation 『NO.6』
● NO.6

キャラクター原案
toi8
toi8

キャラクターデザイン
石野聡
Ishino Satoshi

[toi8 代表作]『ソウルクレイドル 世界を喰らう者』
[石野聡代表作]『乃木坂春香の秘密』(アニメ)

あさのあつこの近未来SF小説が原作。過酷な状況下に置かれたふたりの少年が理想都市「NO.6」の本質を探っていく。鉛筆画風の繊細なタッチが人気のイラストレーター・toi8が原案、多くのアニメーションで原画、作画監督等を務める石野聡がキャラクターデザインを担当した。

Based on the SF novel set in the near future by Asano Atsuko. Two young boys in a pinch set out to find the truth behind the utopian city No.6. The original concept was by the popular illustrator toi8, known for his deft, detailed pencil work, with character design by Ishino Satoshi, key animation lead and director behind many anime.

toi8

Heroes & Heroines

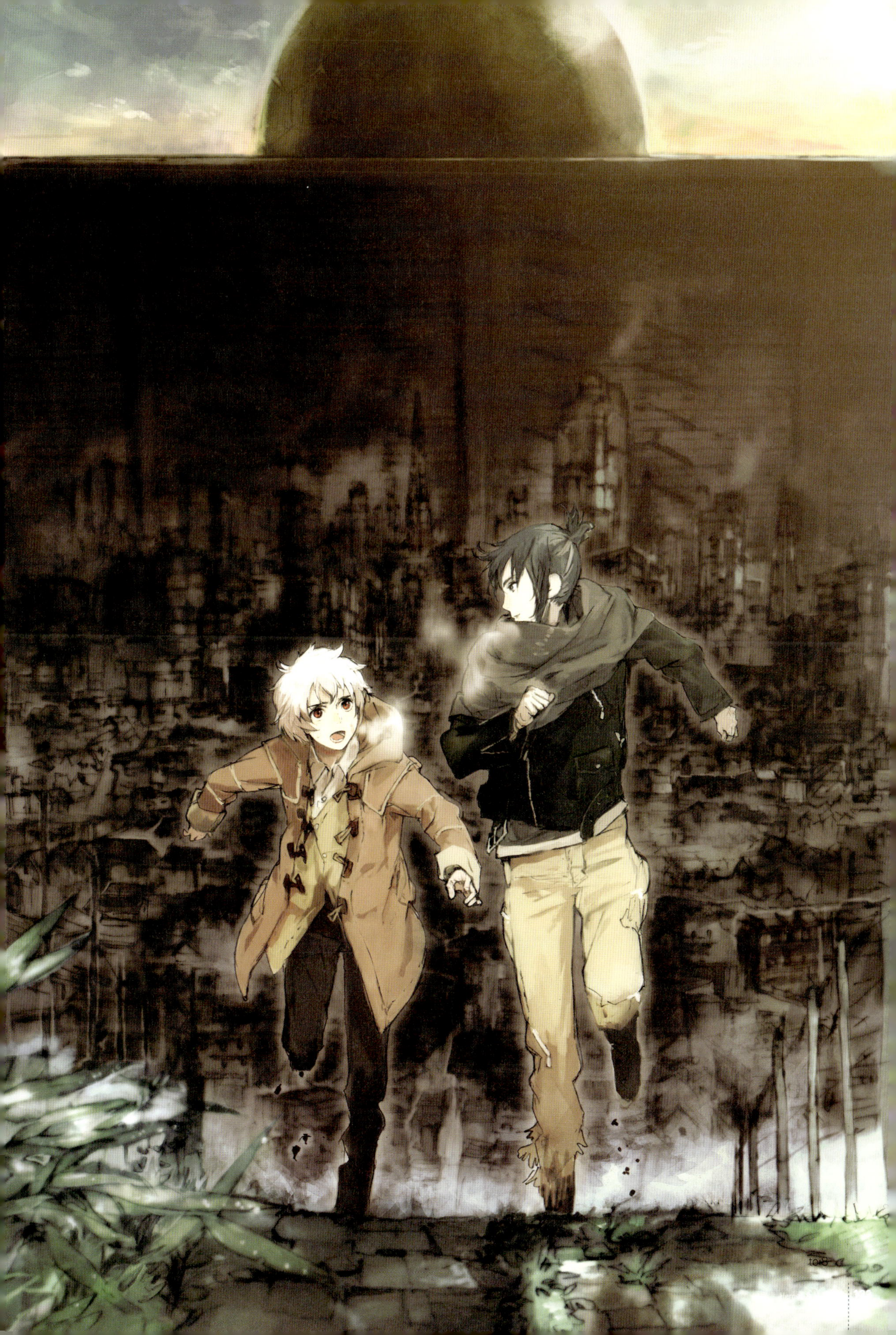

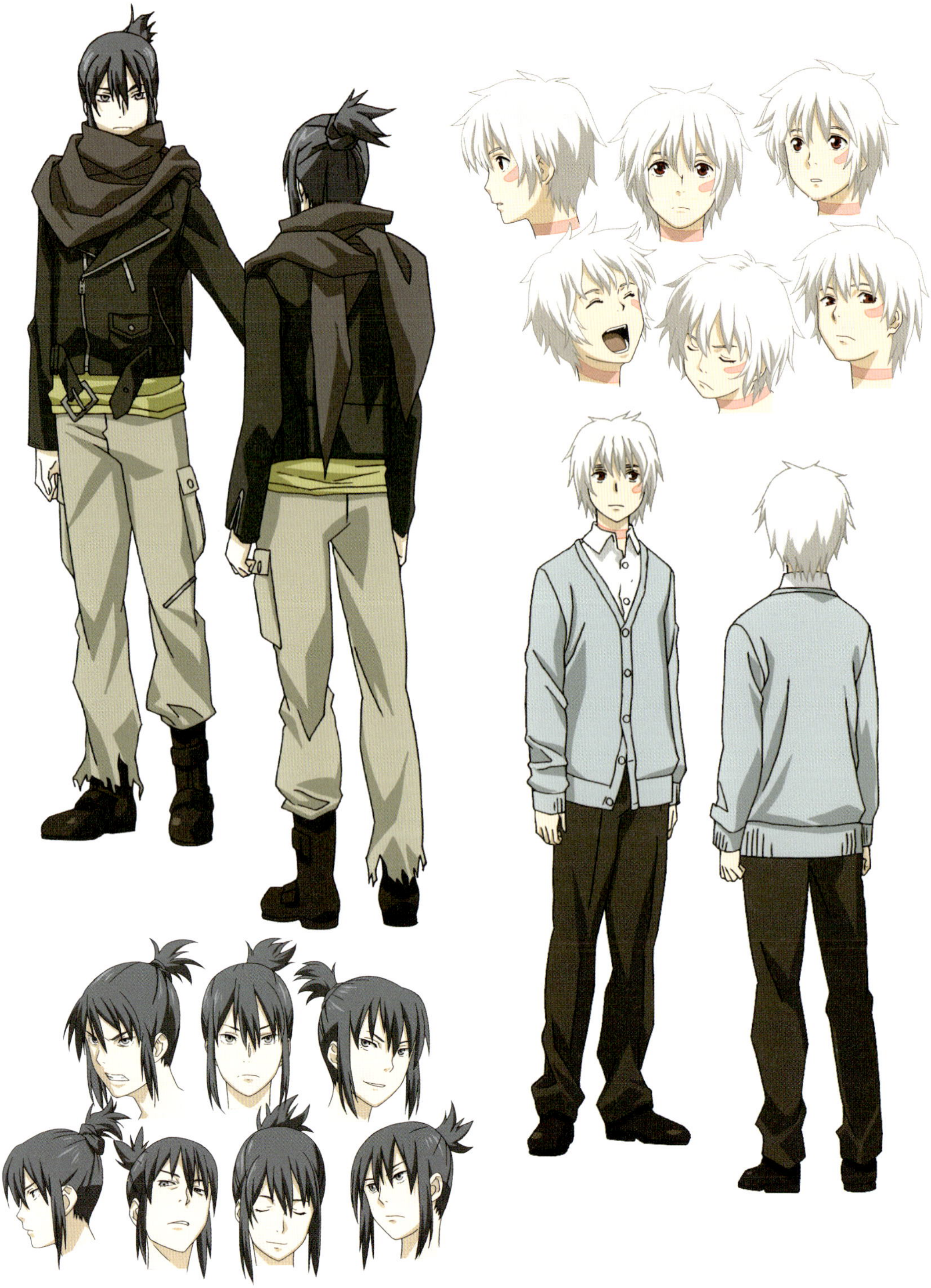

石野聡

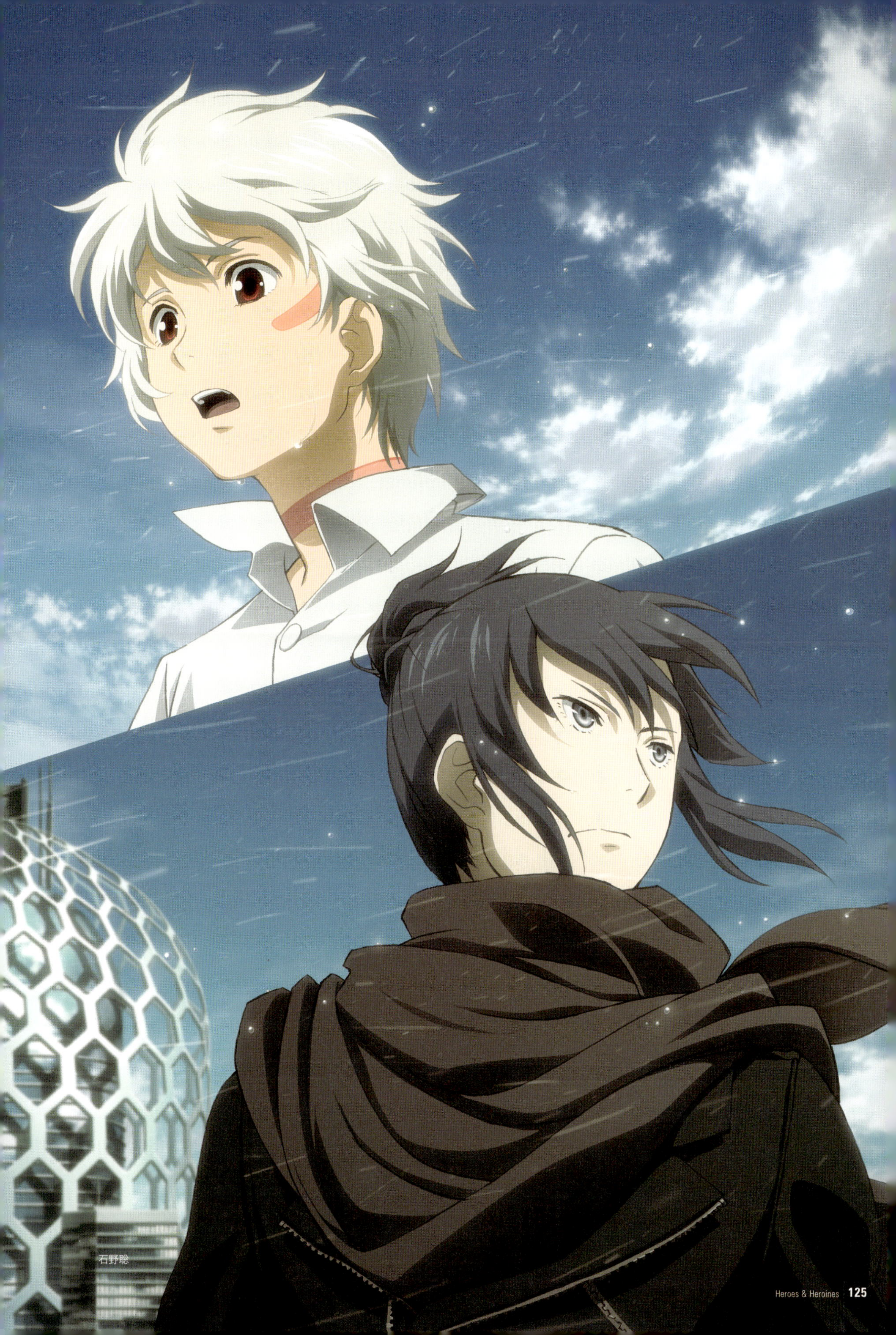

石野聡

Game
『NEWラブプラス』
● NEW LOVEPLUS

キャラクターデザイン
ミノ☆タロー
Mino☆Taro

[代表作]『ときめきメモリアル ONLINE』『ラブプラス』

2009年にシリーズ第一弾の『ラブプラス』が発売されるやいなや、従来の恋愛ゲームと異なる、恋人になってからの彼女との恋愛生活を楽しむ内容にユーザーの心は奪われた。ユーザーの心をとろかす3人の彼女を描くミノ☆タローは、シリーズを通してキャラクターデザインを務めている。

As soon as the first game in this series (LOVEPLUS) was released in 2009, players' hearts were stolen by its contents. These games differ from traditional dating simulations in that they allow players to enjoy a life of love with their girlfriends after they start dating. Mino☆Taro drew the three player heart-melting girlfriends, and he has been involved in character design throughout the entire series.

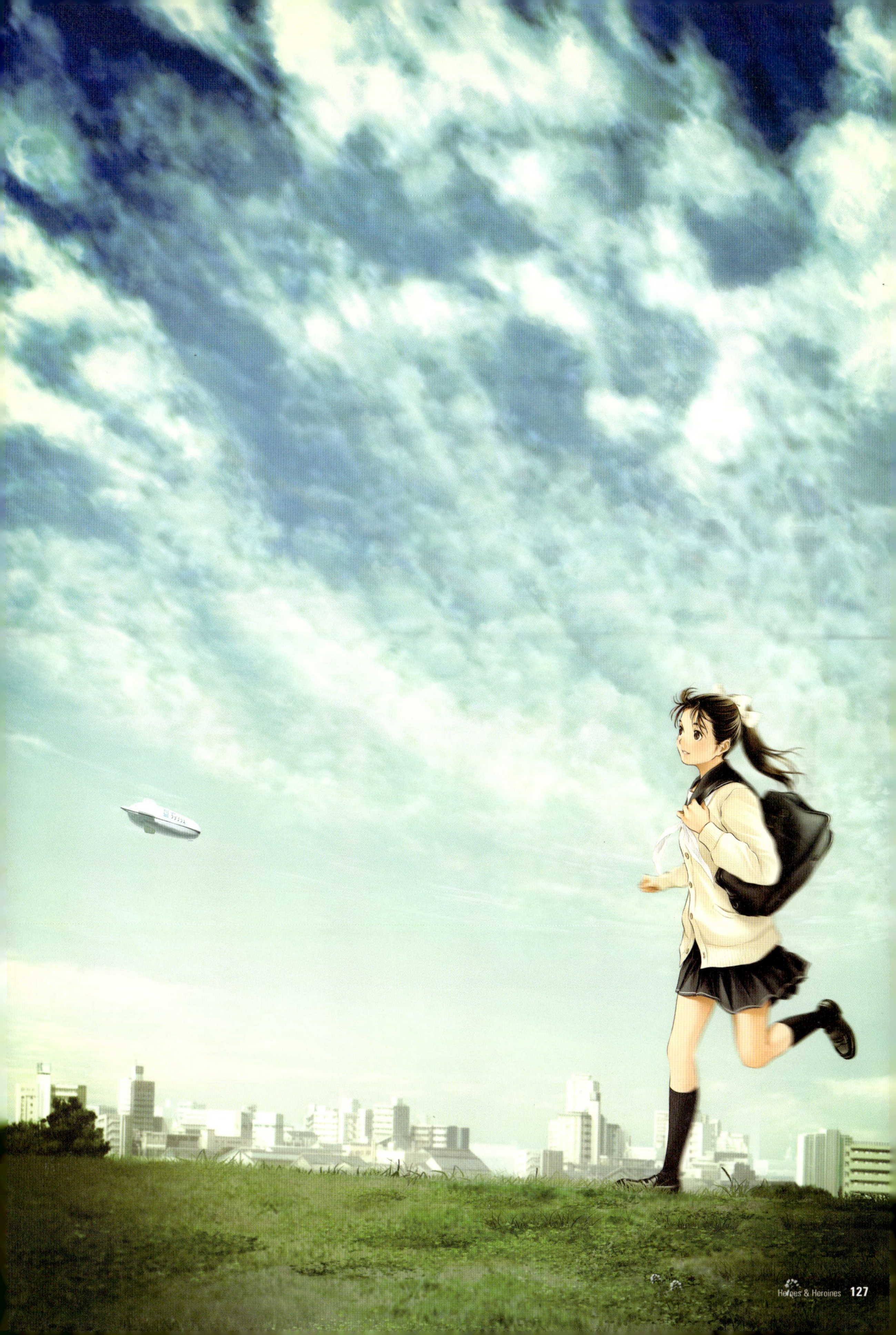

Game
『NO MORE HEROES 2 DESPERATE STRUGGLE』
● NO MORE HEROES 2 DESPERATE STRUGGLE

キャラクターデザイン
コザキユースケ
Kozaki Yusuke

[代表作]『幕末機関説 いろはにほへと』
『SPEED GRAPHER』(キャラクター原案)

全米No.1の殺し屋を目指すヒーローアクションゲーム。現代的でセクシーなキャラクター造詣はファンに熱狂的に迎え入れられた。コザキユースケは本作品の先着購入特典である『エロチカ★コミック』にオリジナル漫画も描き下ろしている。

A heroic action game where you try to become America's No. 1 killer. Its modern, sexy characters were wildly praised by fans. Kozaki Yusuke also draws original manga for Erotica★Comic, a special comic that was sold first come, first served.

NO MORE HEROES 2
DESPERATE STRUGGLE

Animation 『花咲くいろは』
● Hanasaku Iroha

キャラクター原案　キャラクターデザイン
岸田メル／関口可奈味
Kishida Mel　Sekiguchi Kanami

[岸田メル代表作]『メルルのアトリエ ～アーランドの錬金術士3～』
『ソ・ラ・ノ・ヲ・ト』(キャラクター原案)
[関口可奈味代表作]『CANAAN』『true tears』

松前緒花は、夜逃げした母と離れ、祖母の経営する温泉旅館の住み込み仲居見習いとして、高校2年生の春をスタートさせる。旅館で働く従業員たちとの触れ合いを通して描かれる少女のビルドゥングスロマン。活躍めざましい岸田メルの描く少女の可愛らしさが秀逸。

Matsumae Ohana's mother skips town and leaves her behind, so as she starts her junior year of high school she is living at her grandmother's onsen inn while learning to be a maid. It's a coming-of-age novel depicting a young girl as she interacts with the other workers at the inn. Of note is the extraordinary cuteness of the young girl as drawn by the up-and-coming Kishida Mel.

キャラクターデザイン　関口加奈味

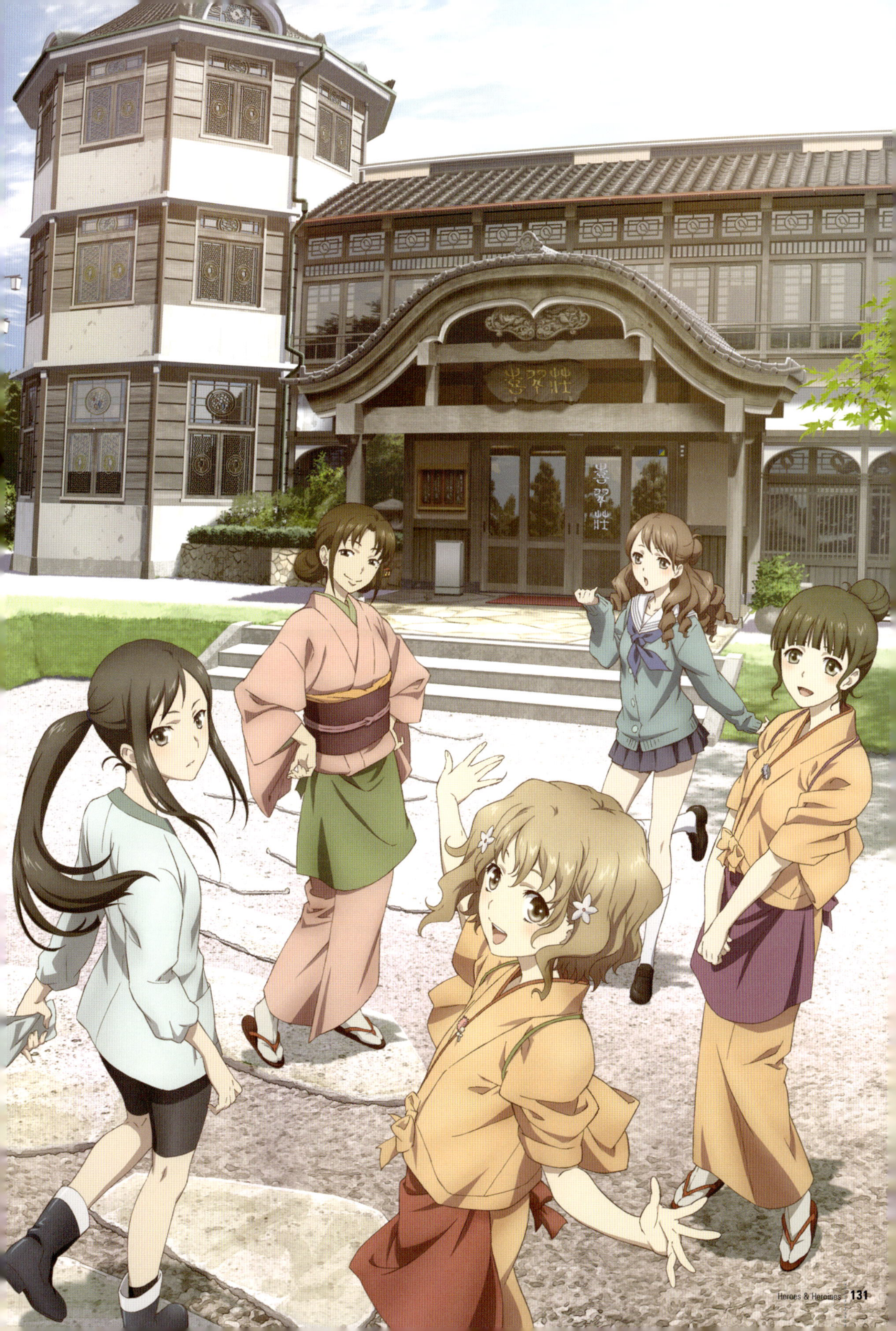

Animation

『花咲くいろは』
● Hanasaku Iroha

キャラクター原案　岸田メル

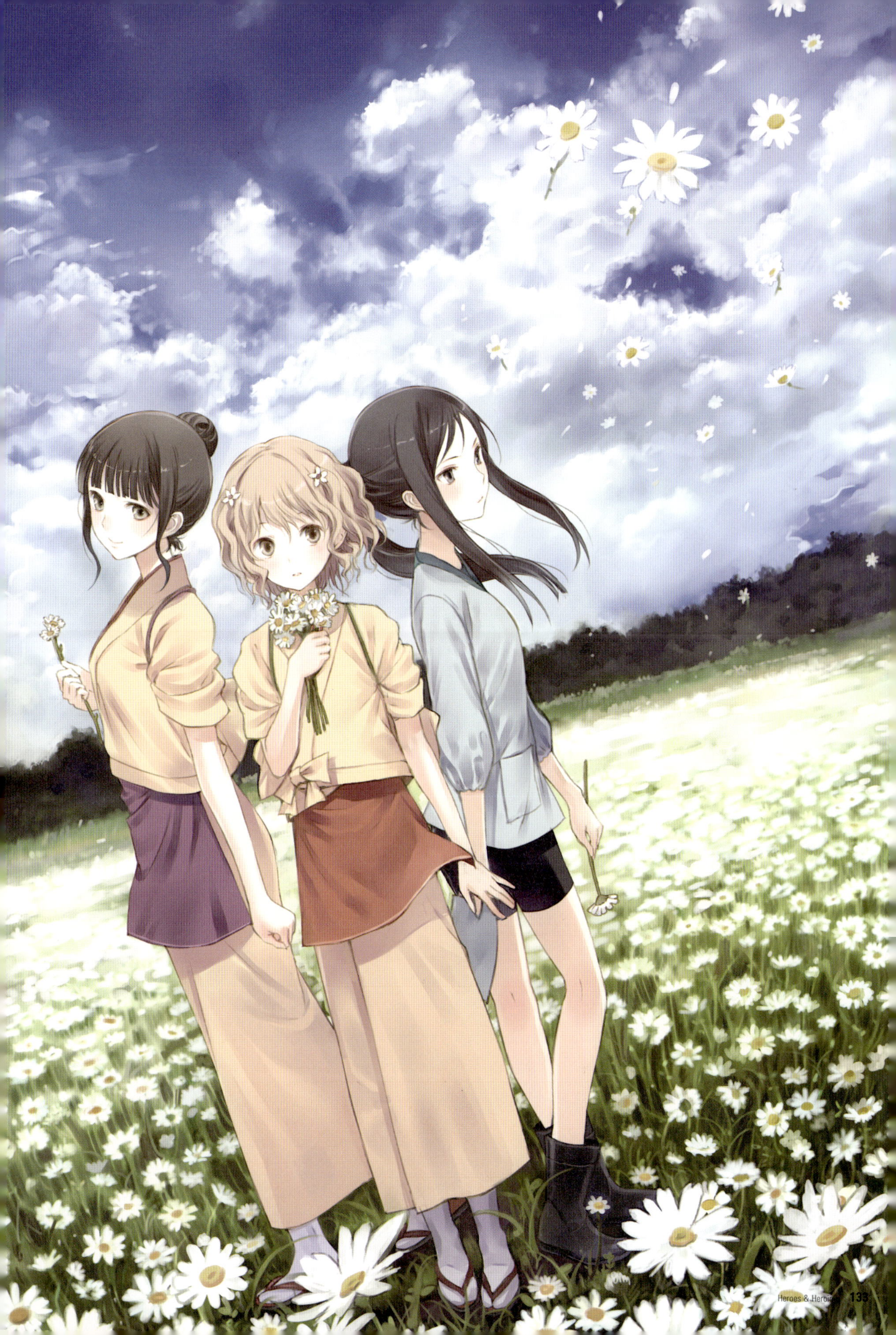

Game

『華ヤカ哉、我ガ一族』
● Hanayakanari Wagaichizoku

キャラクターデザイン
ユウヤ
Yuuya

[代表作]『華ヤカ哉、我ガ一族 キネマモザイク』

大正時代の日本。美しく個性的な6人兄弟のいる宮ノ杜財閥に使用人として働くことになった少女・はる。大正ロマンという言葉が合う、華美ながら気品ある洋装和装の6人兄弟たちに比べて、主人公・はるのオーソドックスで清楚に見えるメイド姿が好ましい。

It is Japan during the Taisho Period. A young girl named Haru comes to work as a servant at the Miyanomori Conglomerate, where there are six beautiful, individualistic brothers. These six brothers are the well suited to the term "Taisho Romance." The orthodox and clean maid figure of the heroine Haru is quite appealing in contrast to the cosmopolitan, magnificent and refined six brothers.

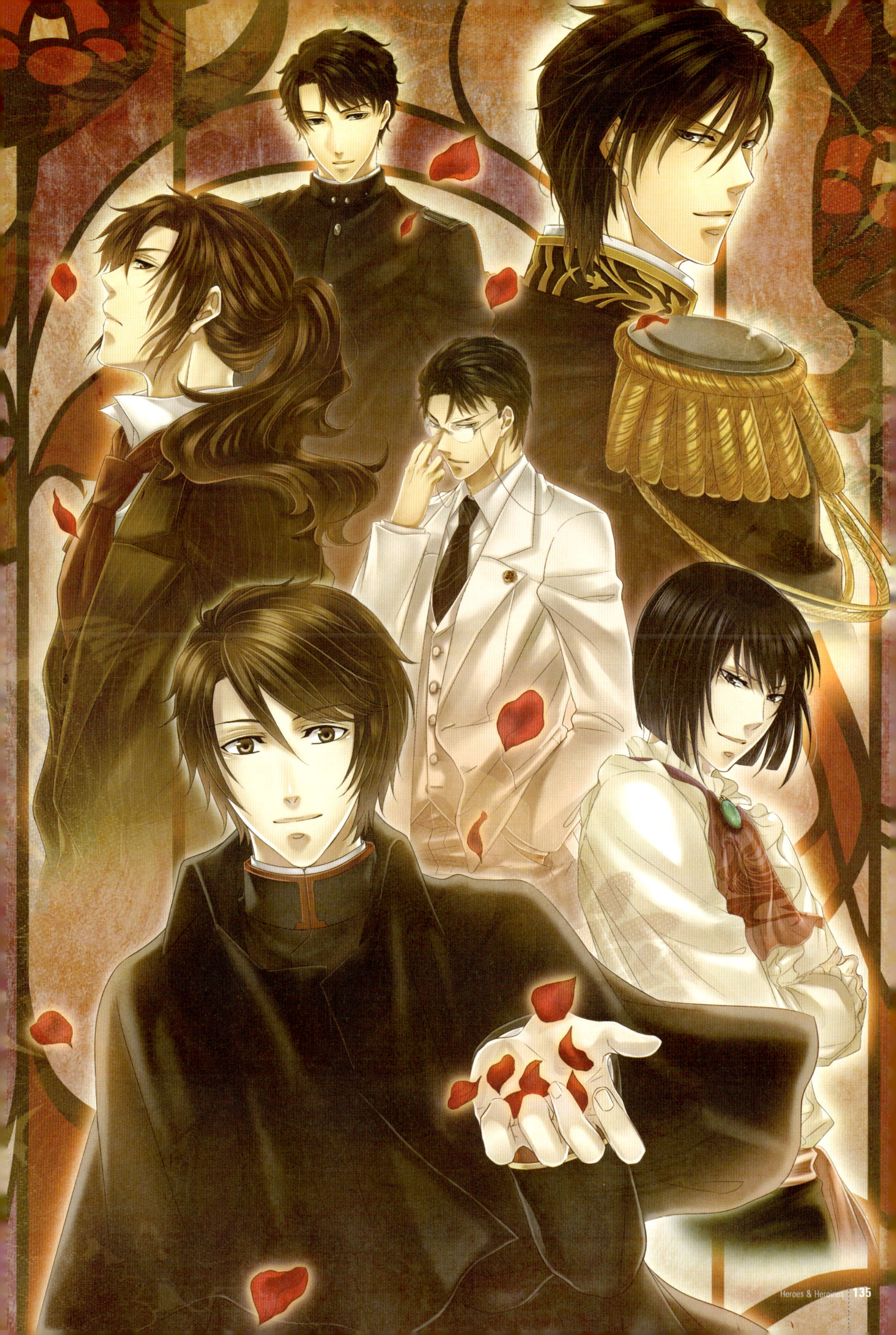

Game

『バレットソウル －弾魂－』
●Bulletsoul

キャラクターデザイン
渡辺明夫
Watanabe Akio

[代表作]『化物語』『神のみぞ知るセカイ』

強大な軍事力を駆使し、全宇宙を支配しようと企図するメッチャワール帝国に立ち向かう３人の勇者たちの物語。熱血縦スクロールシューティングゲーム。萌えの世界で一段と輝く渡辺明夫の描く女性キャラ・ユン、そして、DLC の追加キャラ・ループのデザインに注目。

A story of 3 brave characters that stand up against the Metchawaru Empire, which plans on conquering the entire universe using its massive military strength. An exciting side scrolling shooting game. Yun, a female character drawn by Watanabe Akio, a shining figure in the "moe" world, and the "moe" designs of the additional DLC character Loop are something to keep an eye on.

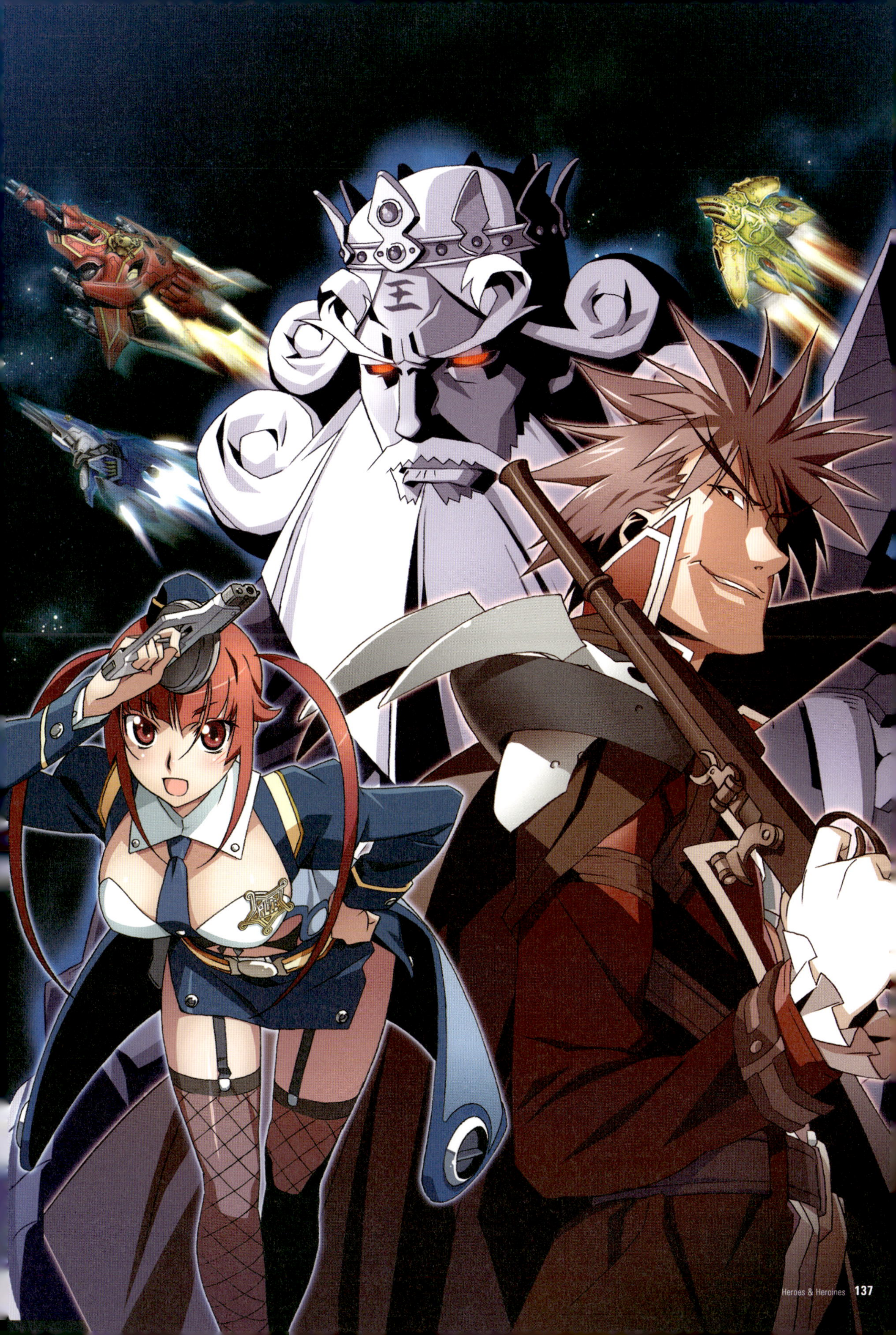

Animation 『東のエデン』
●Eden of The East

キャラクター原案　　　　　　キャラクターデザイン
羽海野チカ／森川聡子
Umino Chika　　　　Morikawa Satoko

[羽海野チカ代表作]『ハチミツとクローバー』(漫画)
[森川聡子代表作]『猫の恩返し』

フジテレビ「ノイタミナ」枠初のオリジナルストーリーアニメーションとして、テレビ放映から始まり、劇場版2作まで展開された。監督は『攻殻機動隊 S.A.C.』シリーズの神山健治。主要キャラクターの原案を羽海野チカ、アニメーションのキャラクターデザインを森川聡子が担当した。

An original anime story from the noitaminA framework on Fuji TV, the TV series has spawned two movies. The director is Kamiyama Kenji, who directed Ghost in the Shell:Stand Alone Complex Series. Main character concept is by Umino Chika, while Morikawa Satoko is in charge of animated character design.

森川聡子

羽海野チカ

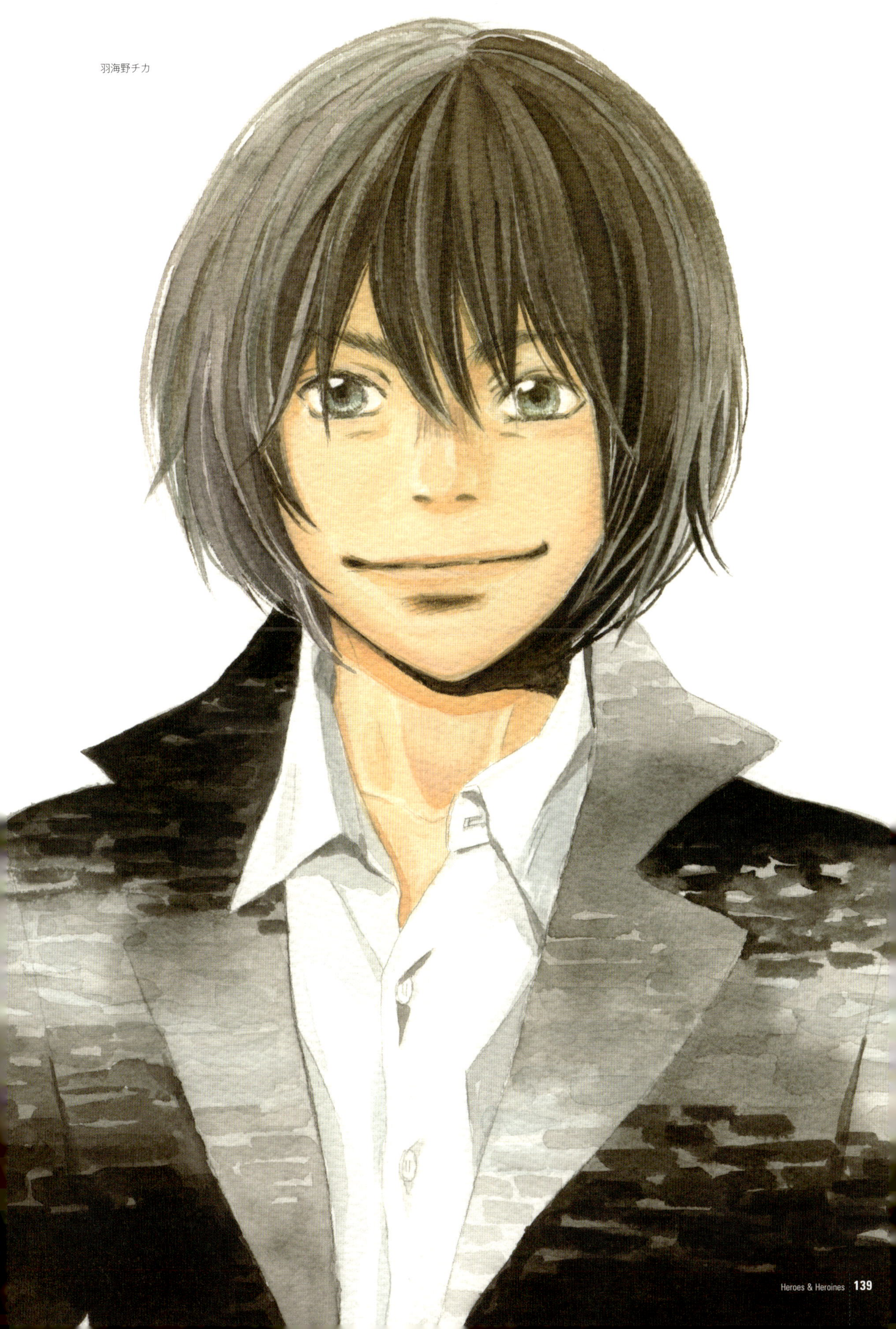

Game
『BEYOND THE FUTURE -FIX THE TIME ARROWS-』
● BEYOND THE FUTURE - FIX THE TIME ARROWS -

キャラクターデザイン
ギンカ
Ginka

［代表作］『ミスフィットの秘密』（小説）挿絵、『空と月の王』（小説）挿絵

剣や魔法が息づく、ファンタジックなRPGの世界観を持った乙女ゲーム。ユーザーは傭兵、魔術師、神殿騎士、格闘家ほか、様々なジョブの美青年とともに冒険へ旅立つ。個性あふれるセクシーな美青年と可愛らしい少女を描くギンカは、期待のイラストレーターである。

A girl game with a fantasy RPG worldview in which swords and sorcery come to life. Users set out on adventures with beautiful young men with various jobs such as mercenaries, sorcerers, temple knights, martial arts fighters and more. With his extremely unique, sexy, and beautiful young men and cute young girls, Ginka is a promising illustrator.

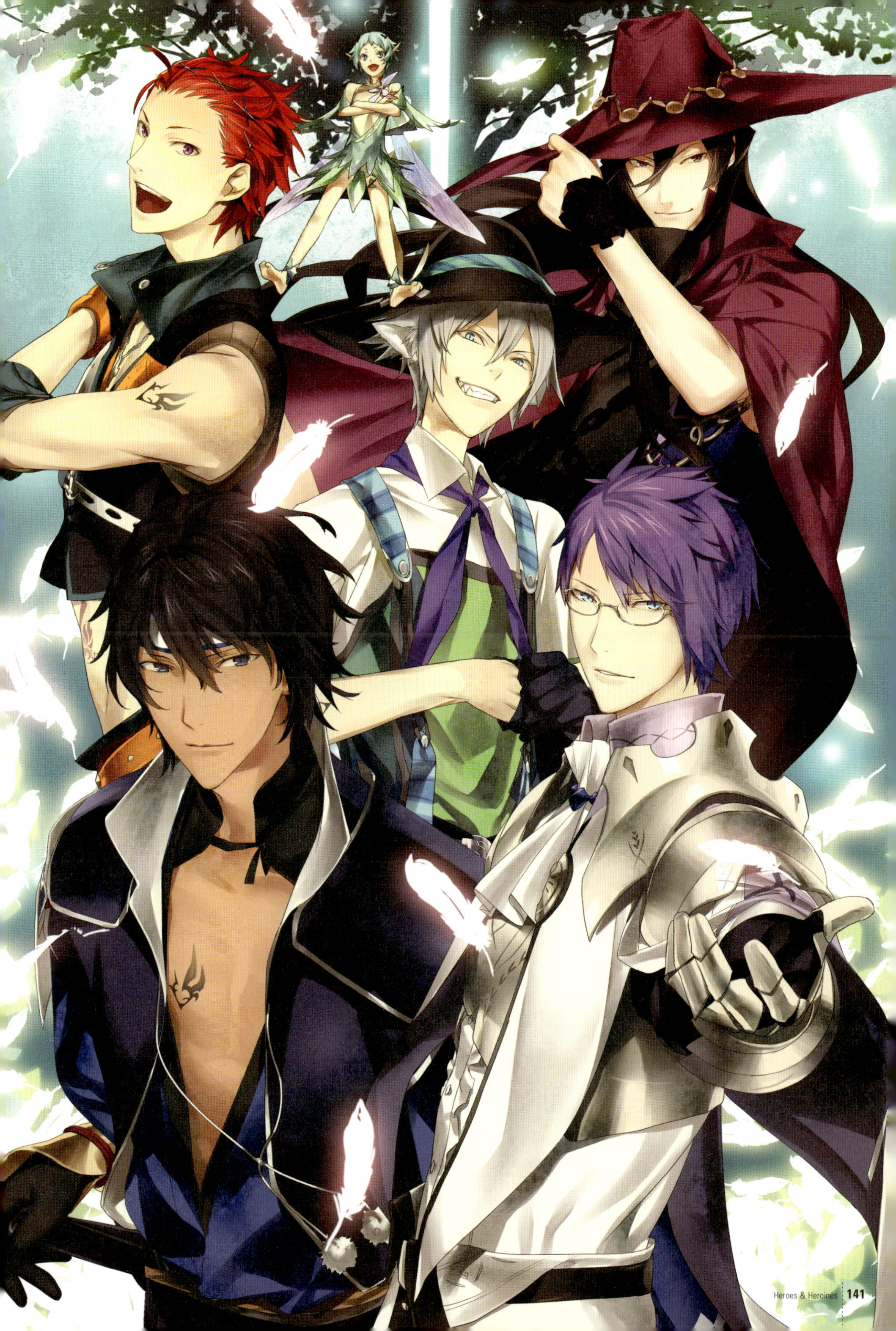

Game 『BEYOND THE FUTURE -FIX THE TIME ARROWS-』
● BEYOND THE FUTURE - FIX THE TIME ARROWS -

BEYOND THE FUTURE
- FIX THE TIME ARROWS -

Heroes & Heroines 143

🎮 Game 『ファントムブレイカー』
● PHANTOM BREAKER

キャラクターデザイン
鈴平ひろ
Suzuhira Hiro

[代表作]『Monochrome』『銀盤カレイドスコープ』小説（挿絵）

華麗な衣装をまとった美少女たちが可憐に闘う美少女対戦格闘ゲーム。女子大生、アイドル、忍者、巫女、メイドなど、様々なキャラクターたちがユーザーを楽しませる。鈴平ひろの描く美少女に萌えるのはもちろんのこと、凝ったデザインの衣装も見どころ。

A fighting game that pits beautiful girls dressed in luxurious costumes against each other. Various characters including co-eds, idols, ninjas, miko maidens and maids entertain the user. Not only will you "moe" at the beautiful girls drawn by Suzuhira Hiro, the elaborately designed costumes are also something to be seen.

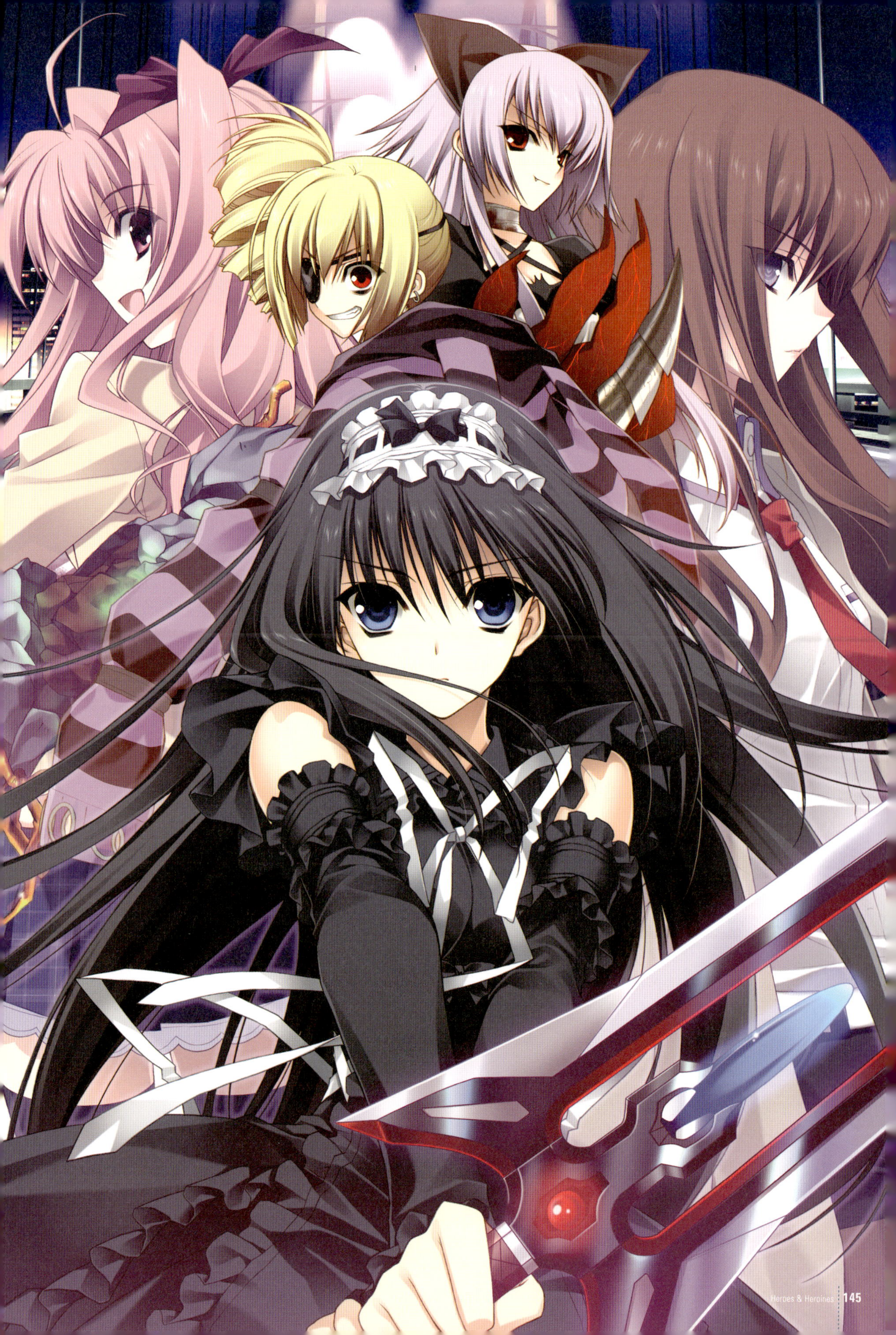

Animation 『Fate/Zero』
●Fate/Zero

キャラクターデザイン
須藤友徳／碇谷敦
Sudo Tomonori　　Ikariya Atsushi

[須藤友徳代表作] 劇場版『空の境界』
[碇谷敦代表作] 『武装神姫 Moon Angel』

奇跡を叶える「聖杯」の力を求め、7人の魔術師が7人の英霊を召喚し、最後のひとりになるまで戦いを繰り広げる究極の決闘劇。大人気ゲーム『Fate/stay night』では断片的に語られるのみだった第四次聖杯戦争の真実がアニメーションとなって明かされる。

Calling upon the power of the miraculous Holy Grail, seven magicians invoke the power of seven war dead for an on-going battle to the death. The popular game Fate/stay night told the story in bits and pieces, but the anime told the truth behind the Fourth War of the Holy Grail.

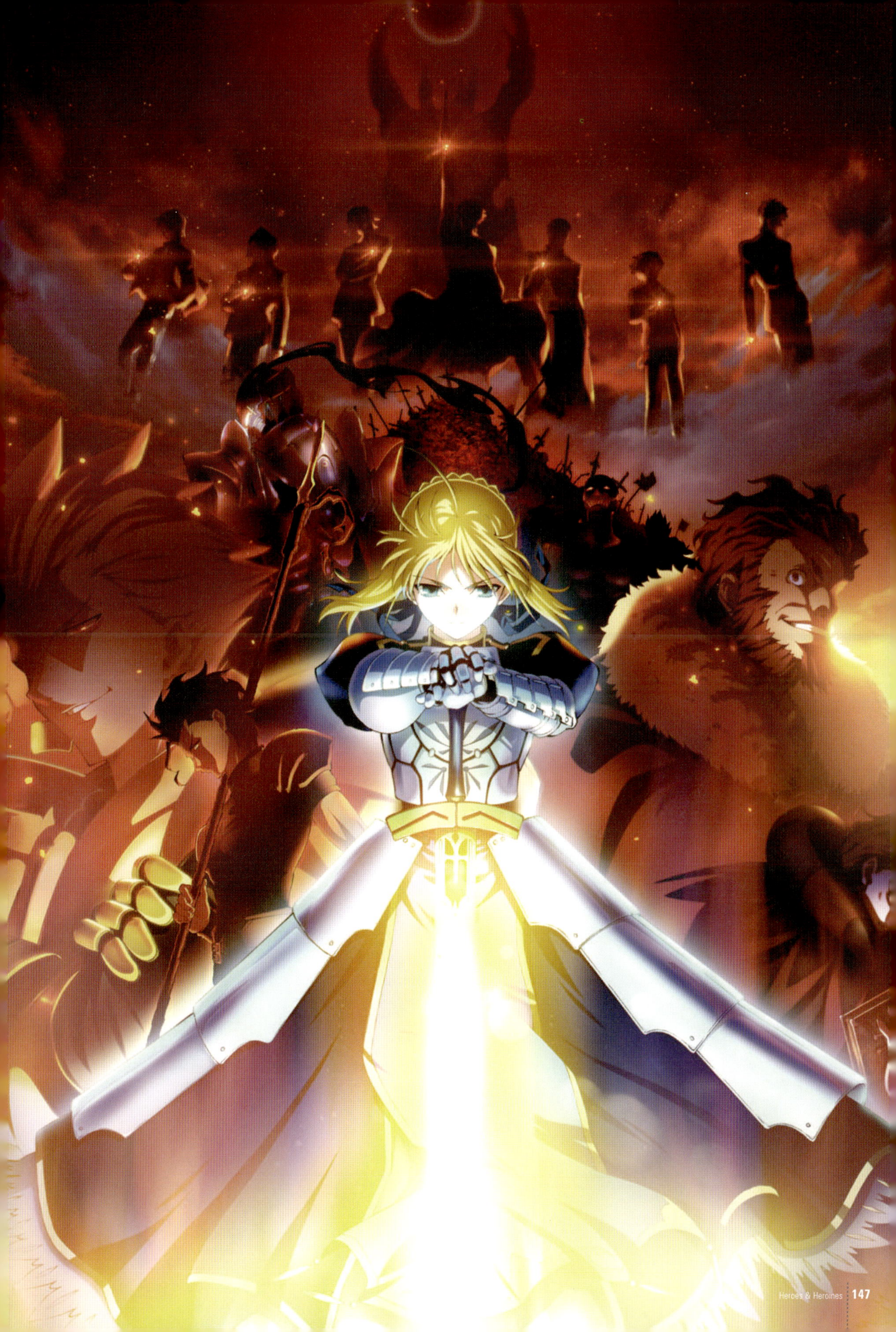

Game
『武装神姫 BATTLE MASTERS Mk.2』
● BUSOUSHINKI BATTLE MASTERS Mk.2

キャラクターデザイン
島田フミカネ
Shimada Humikane

[代表作]『ストライクウィッチーズ』(原作)
『スカイガールズ』(キャラクター原案)

ソーシャルゲームやフィギュアと連動して展開している大人気バトルゲーム『武装神姫』シリーズ。ユーザーによる思い思いの武器や装備で神姫をカスタマイズできる。キャラクターデザインを務める島田フミカネは、兵器少女のクリエイターとして、たいへんな人気を博している。

Busoushinki is a popular series of battle games in which the soldier games were developed together with the figures. Users may customize their "goddess-princess" as they please with preferred weapons and armor. Character designer Shimada Humikane enjoys great popularity as the creator of these "maiden weapons."

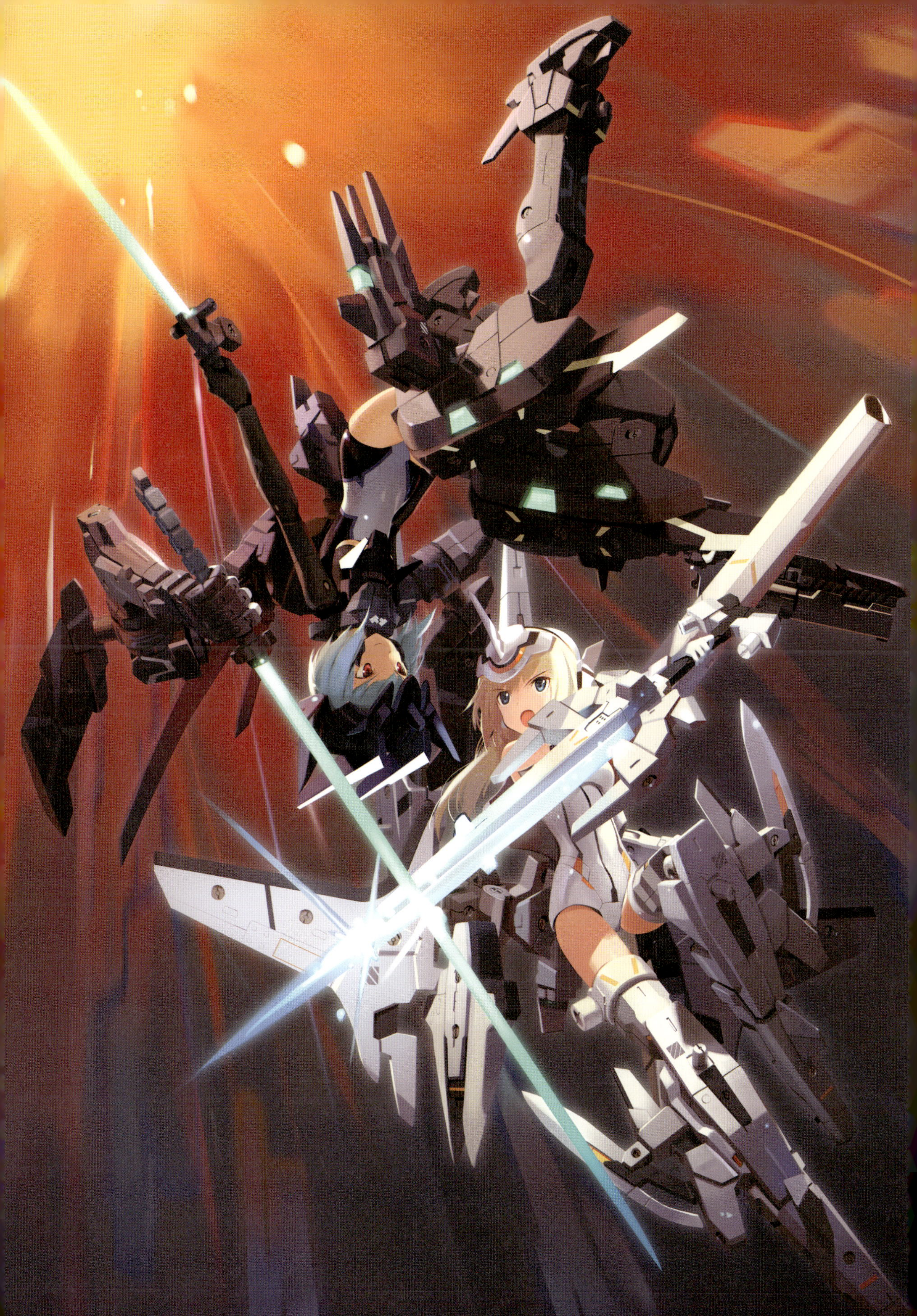

Animation 『フラクタル』
●FRACTALE

キャラクター原案

左
Hidari

[代表作]『雪語り』『Remember11 -the age of infinity-』

「終われない世界」に立ち向かう決意をした少年少女たちの壮大な冒険ファンタジー。左は『嘘つきみーくんと壊れたまーちゃん』等、数多くのライトノベルの挿絵を担当し、イラストレーターとしても幅広く活躍している。

This epic fantasy adventure focuses on the young girls who have decided to stand up against the world's end. Hidari has done the artwork for pulp novels such as Usotsuki Miikun to Kowareta Maachan, and is active as an illustrator as well.

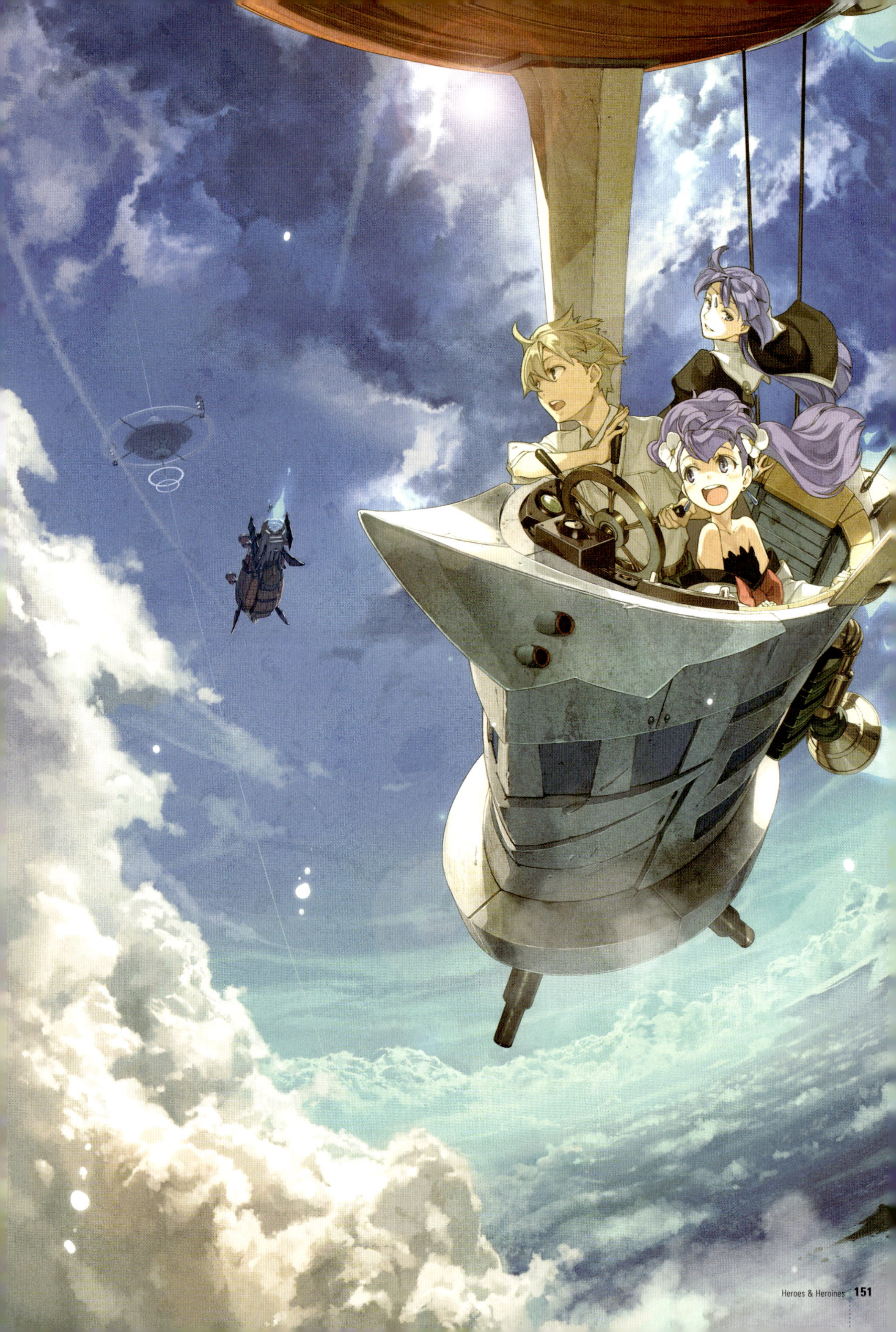

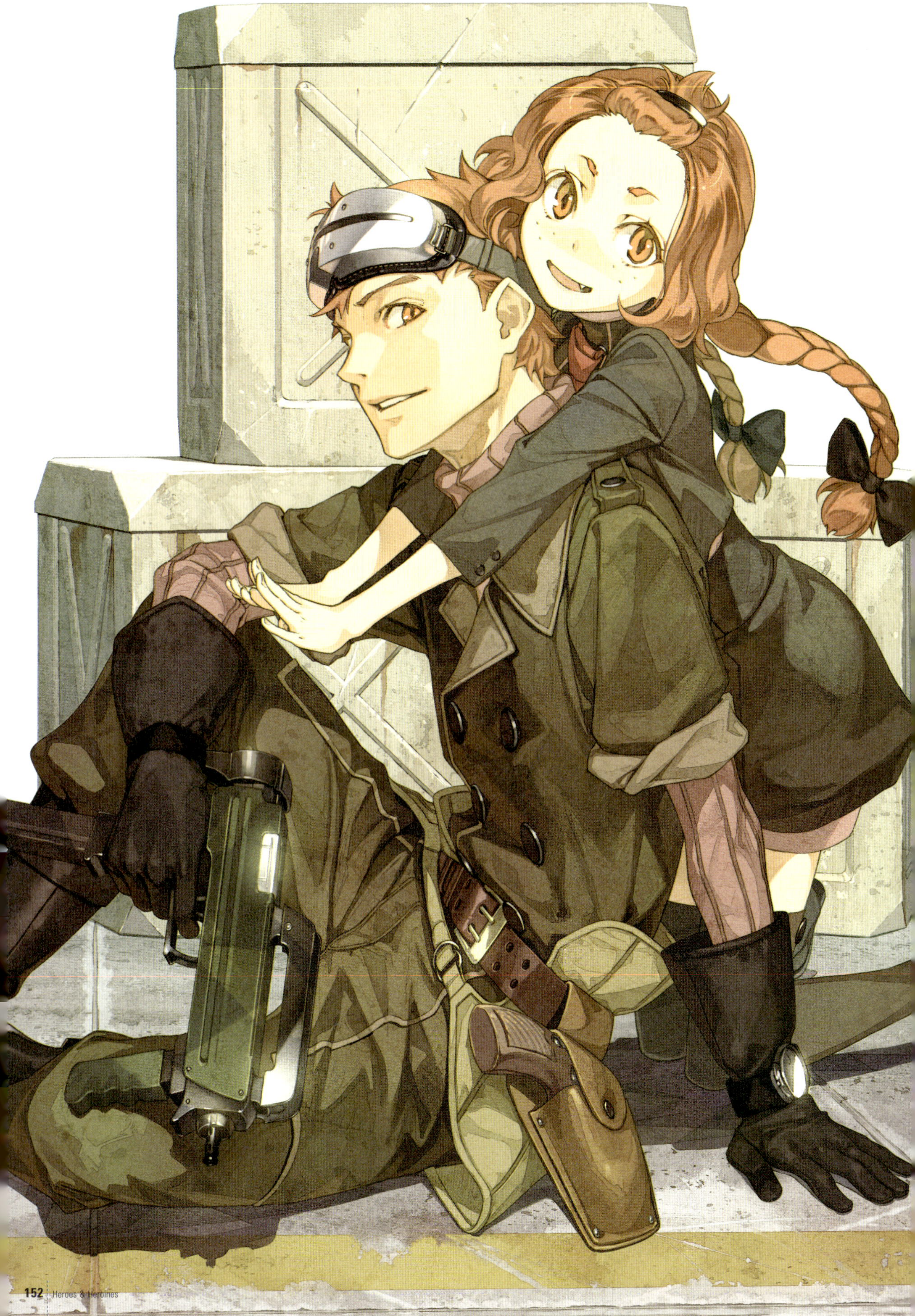

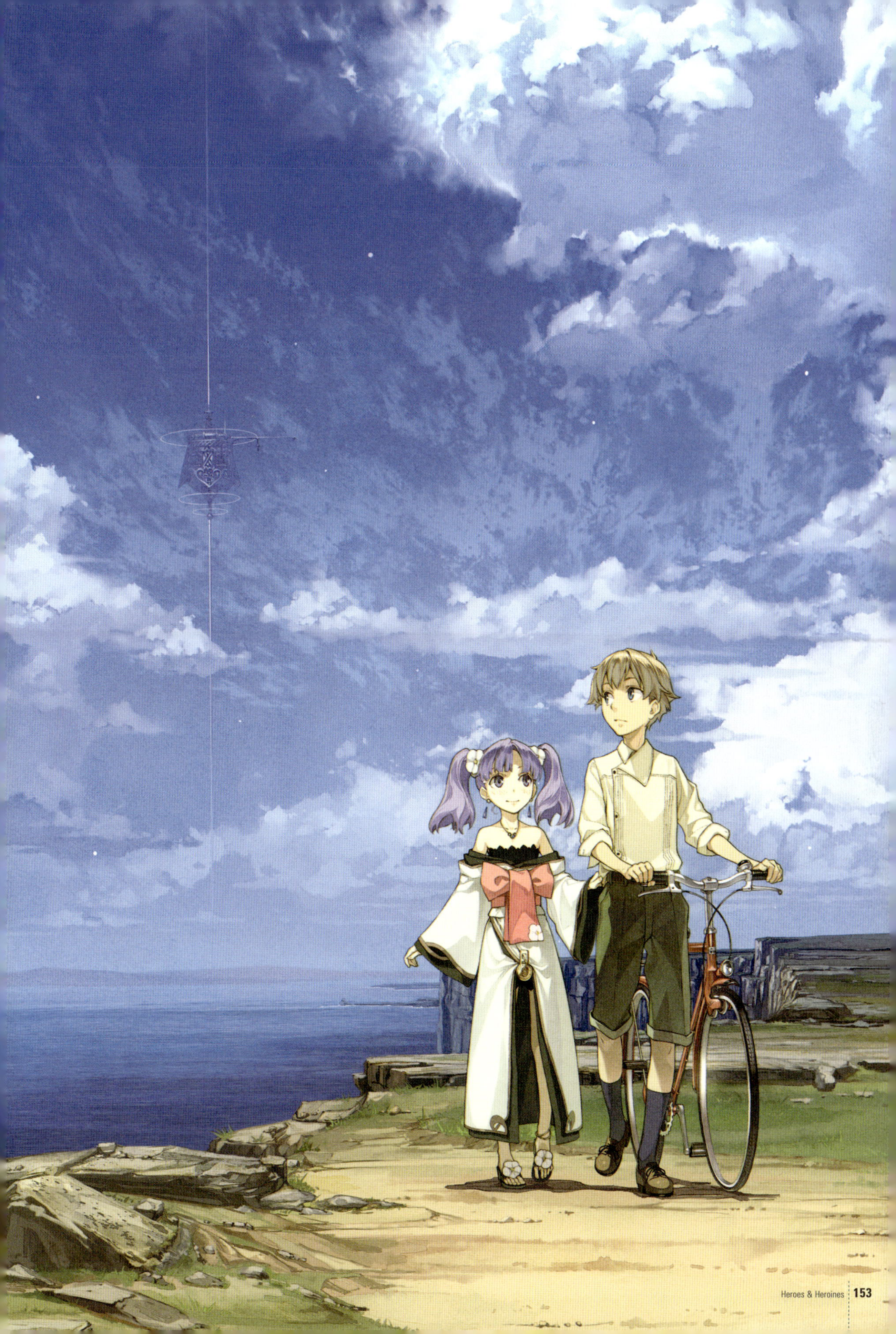

Animation
『フラクタル』
●FRACTALE

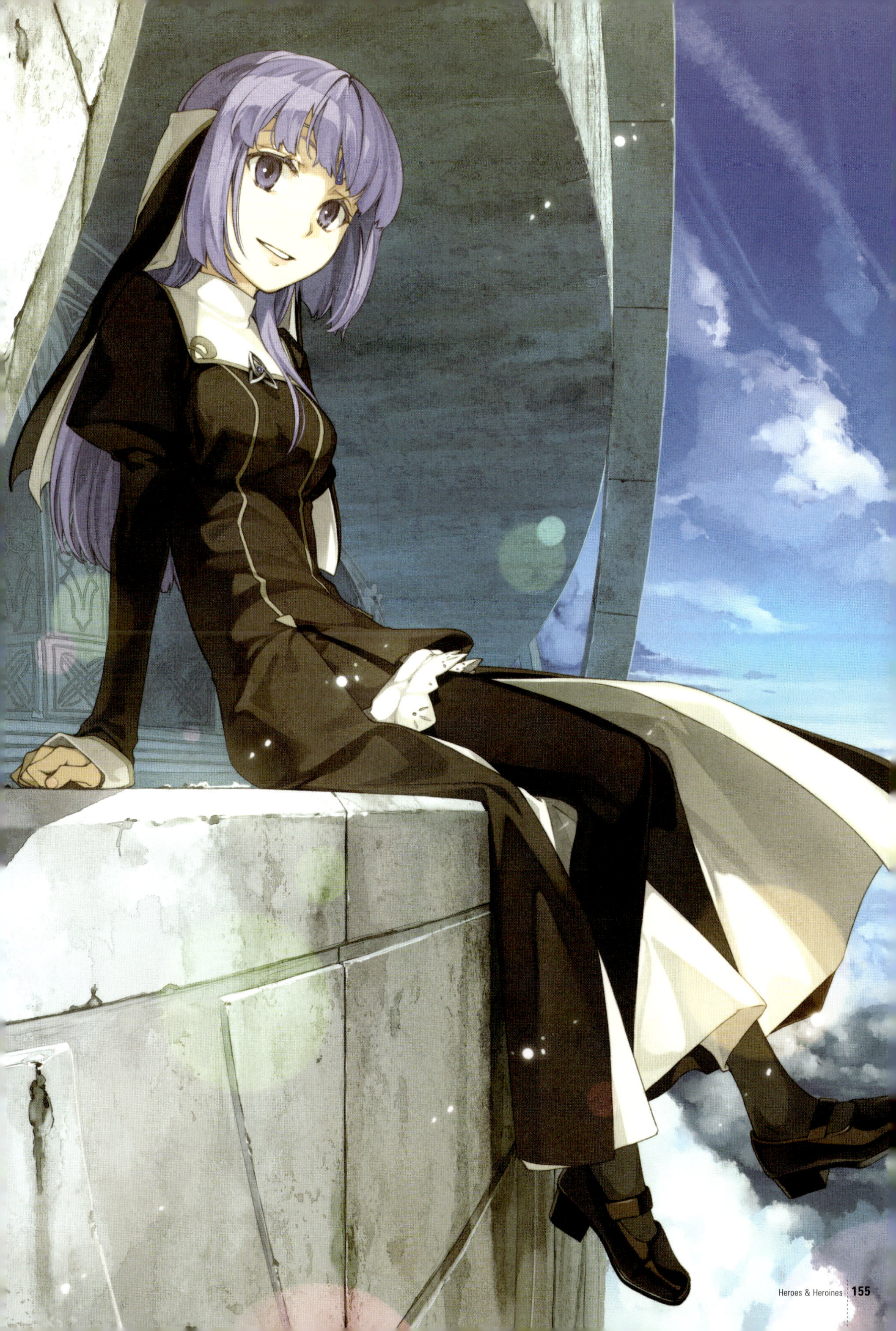

Game

『BAYONETTA』
● BAYONETTA

キャラクターデザイン

島崎麻里
Shimazaki Mari

[代表作]『大神』

『Devil May Cry』、『大神』等、大人気ゲームのディレクター・神谷英樹が新たに手がけたスタイリッシュガンアクション。島崎麻里が描く、メガネ、長身、ボディスーツと、大人の色香たっぷりの魔女・ベヨネッタは、ユーザーから「ベヨ姐」「ベヨ様」と敬称されている。

This is a new stylish gun action title from Kamiya Hideki, the director for a number of very popular games including "Devil May Cry" and "Okami." Shimazaki Mari draws the alluringly mature witch Bayonetta's glasses, tall figure and body suit in a way that causes Japanese players to refer to her as "Beyonee," "Beyosama" and other titles of respect.

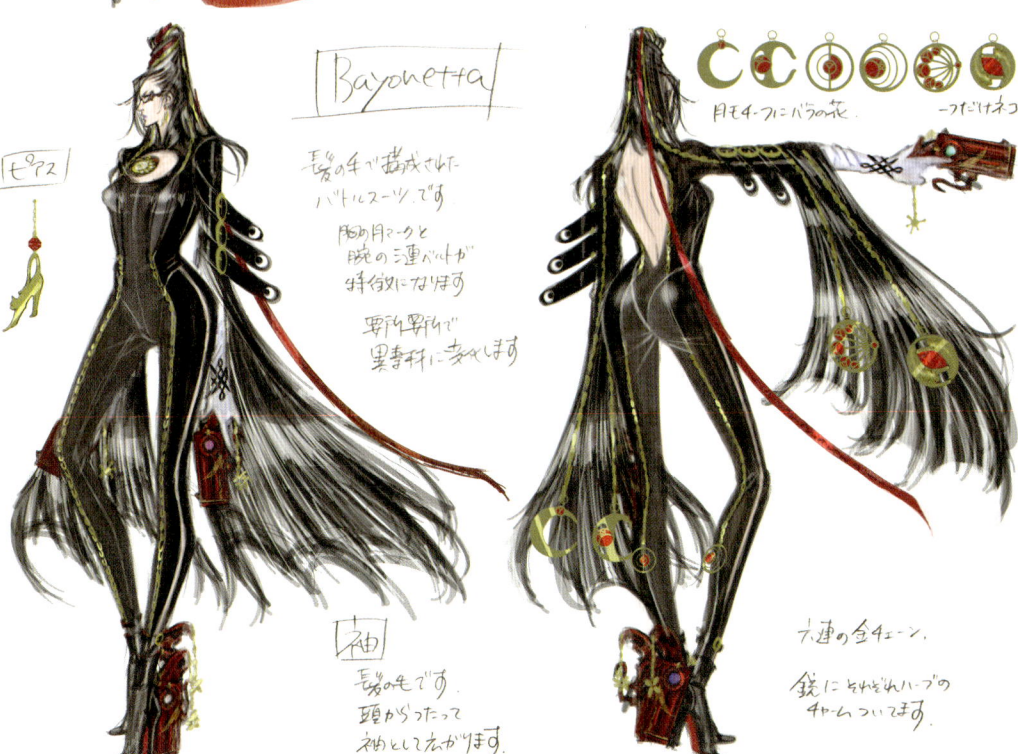

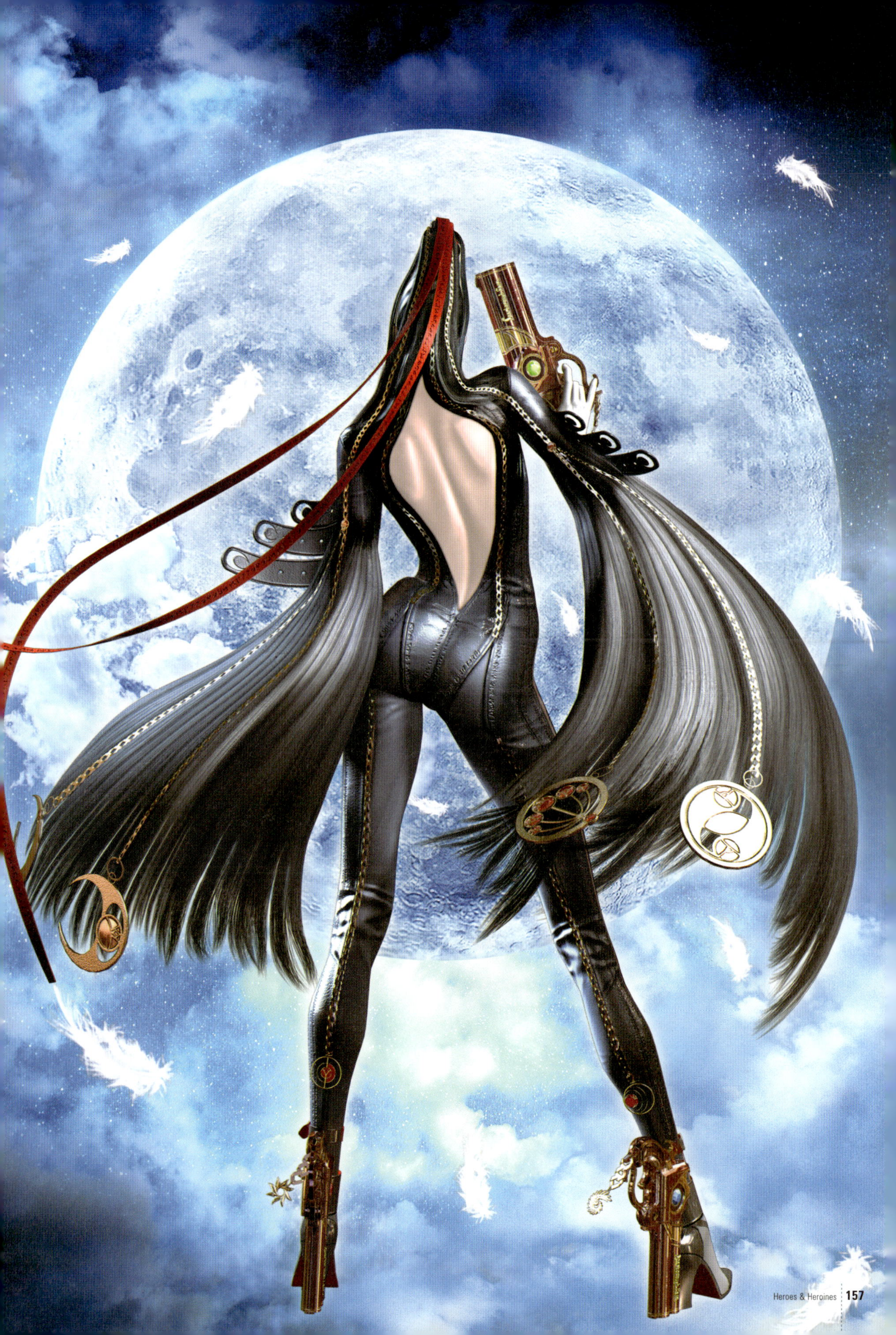

Game
『BAYONETTA』
- BAYONETTA

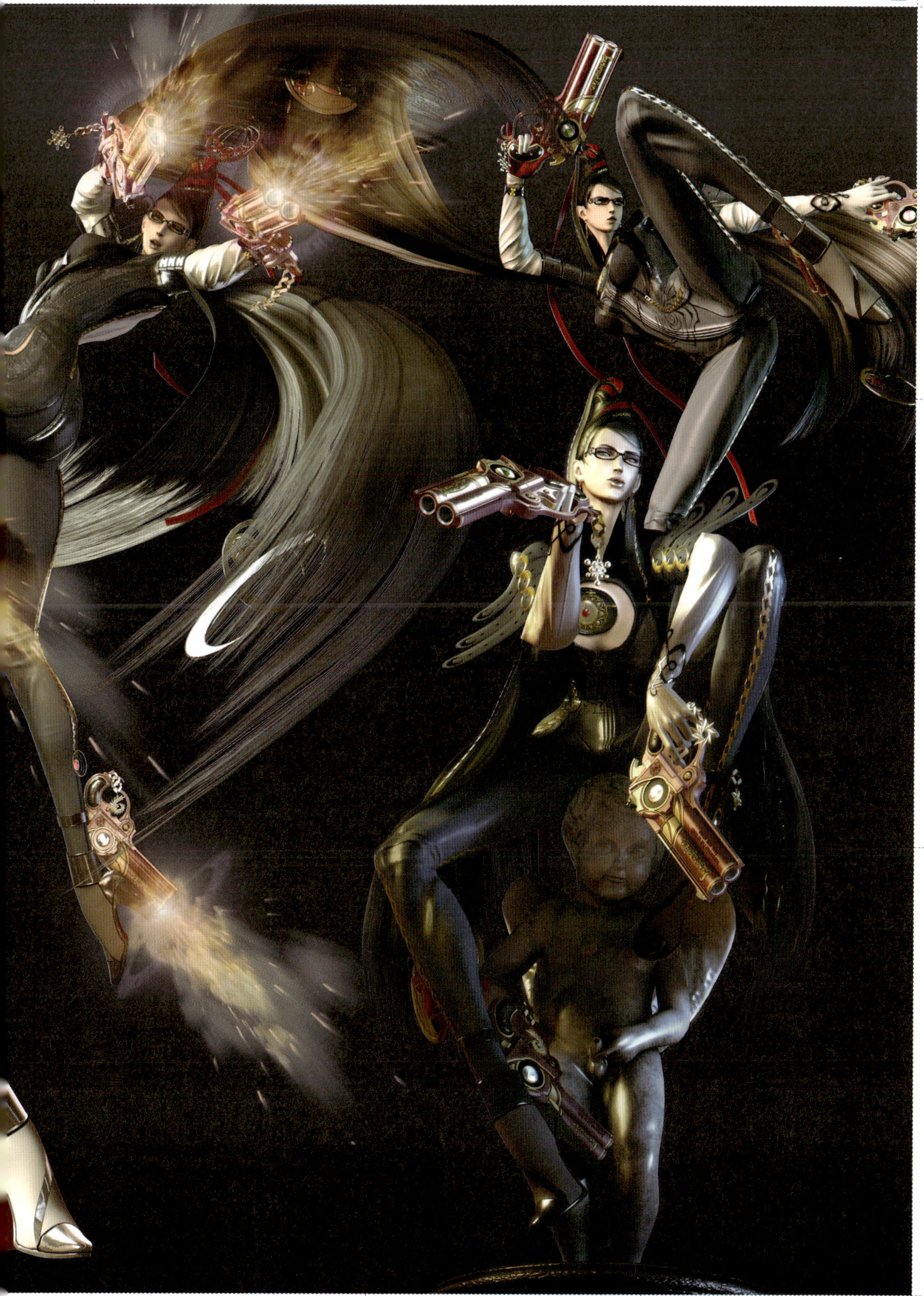

Game
『ボーダーブレイク エアバースト』
● BORDER BREAK AIRBURST

キャラクターデザイン・パブリシティイラスト
風間雷太
Kazama Raita

[代表作]『Coded Soul —受け継がれしイデア—』
『三国志大戦』シリーズ（カードイラスト）

アーケード業界初、最大20人の全国同時対戦を実現させたハイスピードロボットチームバトル。風間雷太の描くシステムオペレーター・フィオナ（オペ子とも呼称される）の美貌は、プレイヤーを発奮させるようである。どうもただのオペレーターではないようだ。

Originally an arcade game, it is a fast paced robot team battle where up to 20 people from all over Japan can play simultaneously. The system operator, Fiona (called Opeko), was designed by Kazama Raita to really excite players. She's not your normal operator!

BORDER BREAK
AIRBURST

Heroes & Heroines **161**

Game

『真剣で私に恋しなさい！』シリーズ
● Majide Watashini Koishinasai! / Majide Watashini Koishinasai!S

キャラクターデザイン
wagi
wagi

[代表作]『真剣で私に恋しなさい！』

ドタバタ学園青春コメディとして発表されて以降、アニメ化、そして続編ゲームが制作されるまでとなった大人気ゲームシリーズ。川神学園2年生の直江大和の周りには、現代の侍とも言える武芸達者な女の子ばかり。凛々しい侍娘たちに負けるな、日本男児！

Since debuting as a situational school comedy, this popular game series has been made into anime and has spawned game sequels as well. Naoe Yamato, a junior at the Kawakami Academy, is surrounded by modern female samurai warriors. It's time to take a stand against these femme fatales!

Majide Watashini Koishinasai!
Majide Watashini Koishinasai!S

Heroes & Heroines 163

Animation

TVアニメ『真剣で私に恋しなさい!!』
● Majide Watashini Koishinasai!!

キャラクターデザイン
渡辺真由美
Watanabe Mayumi

[代表作]『フリージング』『吉永さん家のガーゴイル』

大人気ゲーム『真剣で私に恋しなさい!』のアニメ化。2011年10月より放送を開始して以来、続編ゲームである『真剣で私に恋しなさい!S』共々話題に。アニメ版のキャラクターデザインを行った渡辺真由美は数々のテレビアニメーション、OVA等で作画監督やキャラクターデザインを務める実力派。

The anime version of the popular video game. Since its debut in October 2011, it's encompassed both the original game, Maji de Watashi ni Koi Shinasai as well as its sequel, Maji de Watashi ni Koi Shinasai S.Watanabe Mayumi, lead character designer for the anime, is a key animation director and character design who has worked on numerous anime shows and OVA.

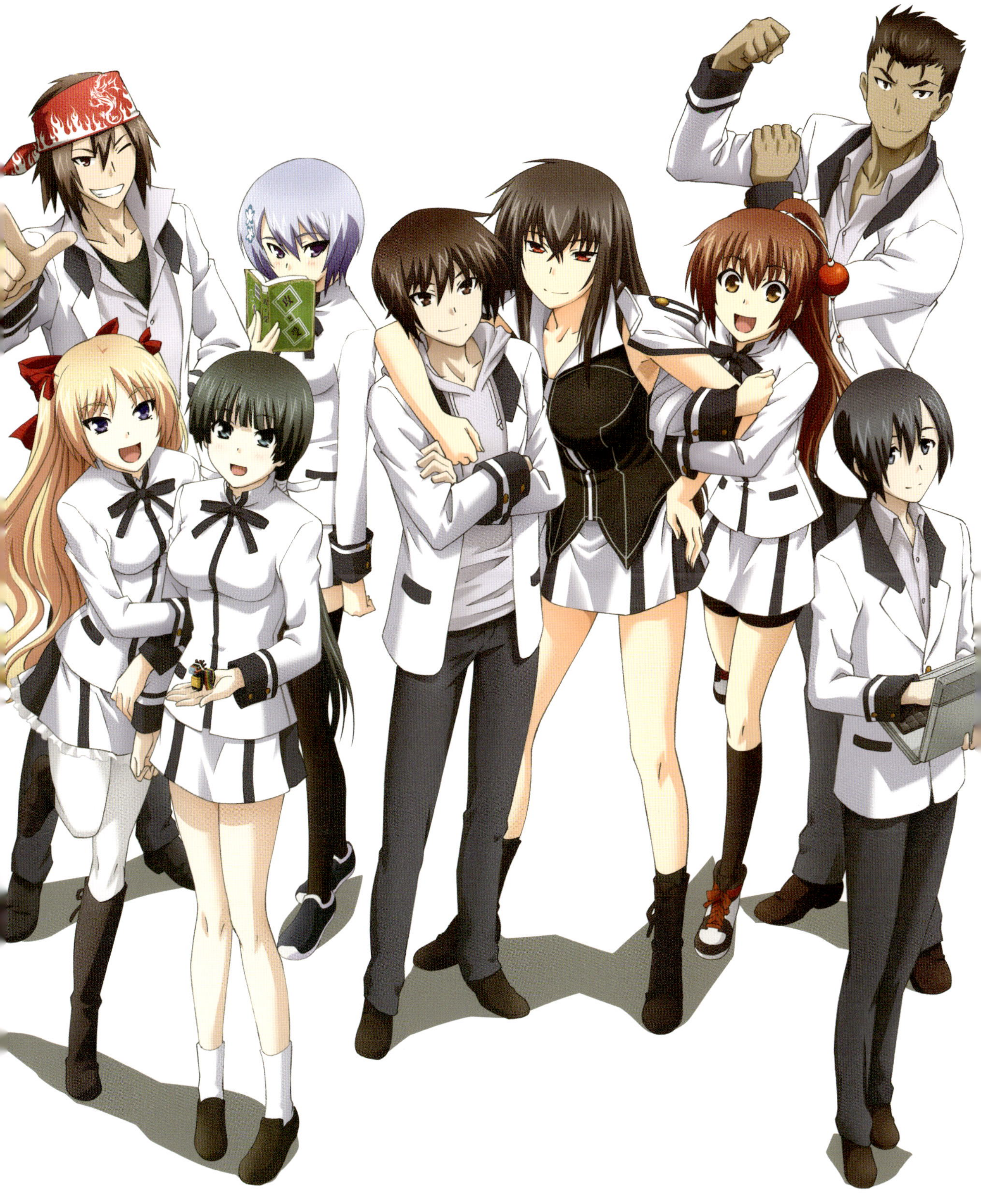

Animation
『魔法少女まどか☆マギカ』
●PUELLA MAGI MADOKA MAGICA

キャラクター原案　蒼樹うめ　／　キャラクターデザイン　岸田隆宏
aokiume　／　Kishida Takahiro

[蒼樹うめ代表作]『ひだまりスケッチ』(漫画)
[岸田隆宏代表作]『デュラララ!!』

2011年の社会現象になったとも言われる人気作。蒼樹うめの描く少女の可愛らしいキャラクターデザインからは想像もできない驚愕のストーリー展開は、若年層向けの「魔法少女もの」とは一線を画し、メルヘンホラーとも形容された。

The popular animation that became a social phenomenon in 2011. With aokiume's cute young girl character designs you wouldn't believe the startling story she has in store. PUELLA MAGI MADOKA MAGICA is a world of fairy tale horror that is a fresh departure from normal young adult fare.

岸田隆宏

岸田隆宏

蒼樹うめ

166　Heroes & Heroines

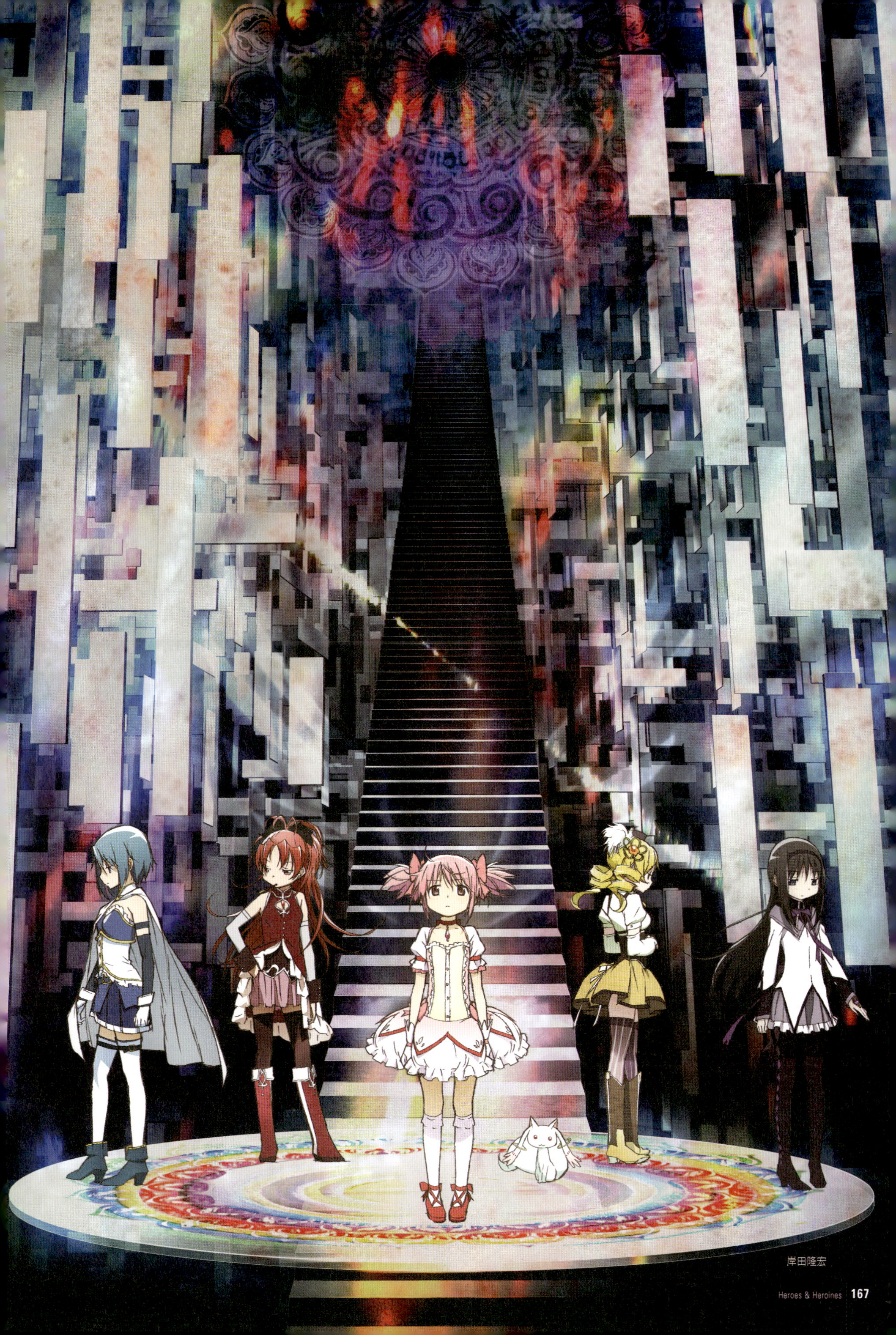

岸田隆宏

Animation 『宮本武蔵―双剣に馳せる夢―』
● Miyamoto Musashi Souken ni haseru yume

キャラクターデザイン
中澤一登
Nakazawa Kazuto

[代表作]『キル・ビル Vol.1』(アニメパート監督)
『サムライチャンプルー』

宮本武蔵の著した「五輪書」をもとに、武蔵の生涯と剣法「二天一流」の謎に迫る歴史アニメドキュメンタリー。制作は Production I.G、キャラクターデザインを担う中澤一登は、数々のアニメーション作品に携わっているが、剣劇アクションにも造詣の深さがうかがえる。

Based on Gorinnosho by Miyamoto Musashi, this historical anime documentary gives clues to the life of Musashi and his treatise on swordsmanship, Niten Ichiryu. Created by Production I.G, with Nakazawa Kazuto in charge of character design. While he has been involved with many other animation projects, Nakazawa is a virtuoso of sword fighting action.

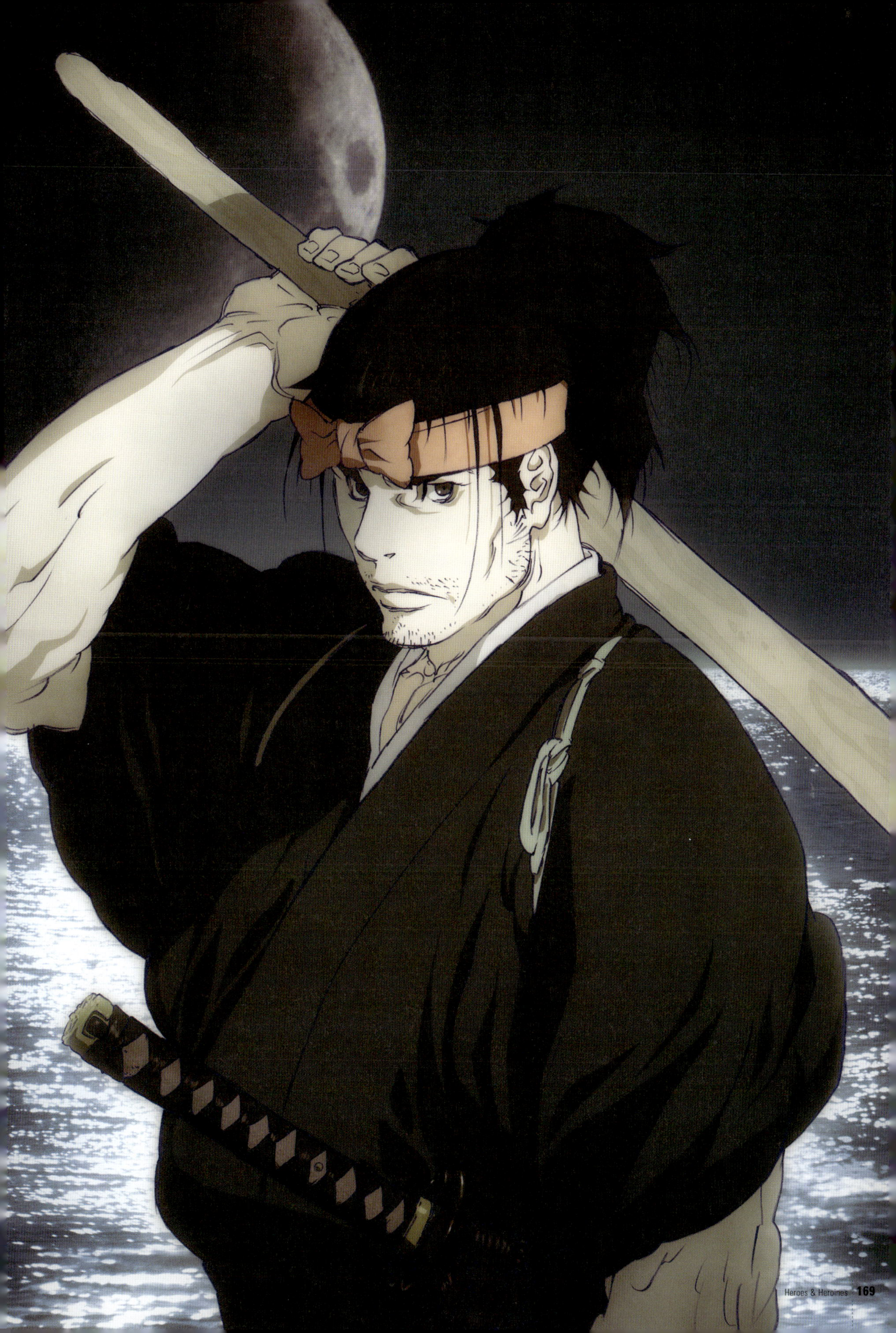

Game

『METAL GEAR SOLID PEACE WALKER HD EDITION』
METAL GEAR SOLID PEACE WALKER HD EDITION

キャラクターデザイン

新川洋司
Shinkawa Yoji

[代表作]『メタルギアソリッド』シリーズ

言わずと知れた世界的名作『メタルギアソリッド』シリーズ。主人公・スネークは他メーカー作品にもよくカメオ出演するほど、多くのゲームユーザーに敬愛されている。立っていても隠れていても様になる男なのである。新川洋司は今作品のアートディレクターでもある。

The Metal Gear Solid Series is a worldwide phenomenon. The hero, Snake, is a favorite among game fans, and is famous enough to make cameos in other games as well. Whether in the shadows or in the limelight, Snake makes for a dashing hero. Shinkawa Yoji is now art director for the series as well.

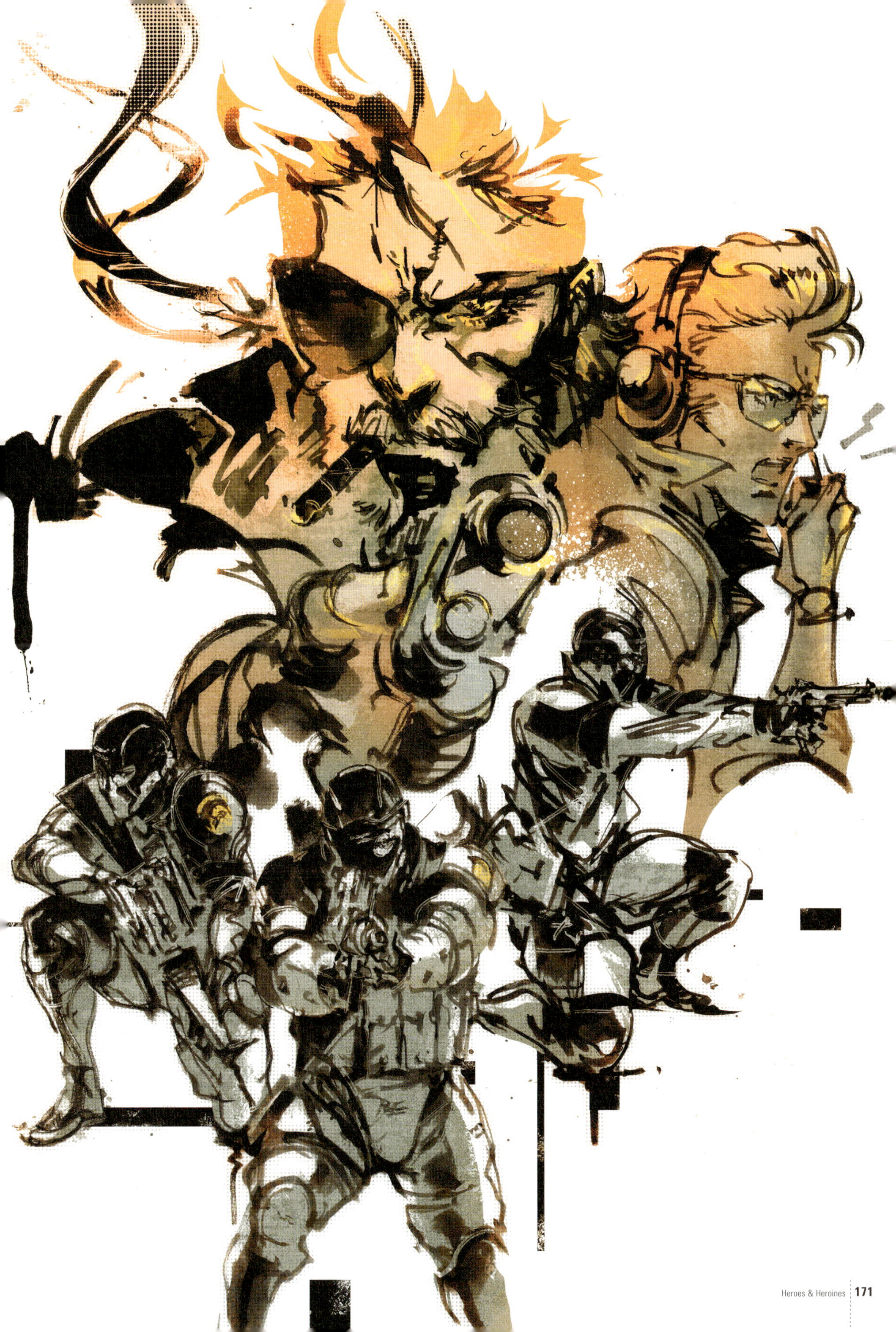

『メモリーズオフ ゆびきりの記憶』

● Memories off Yubikiri no Kioku

キャラクターデザイン

森井しづき

Morii Shizuki

［代表作］『金魚鉢ホロスコープ』（漫画）、『ダブルクロス』小説（挿絵）

『Memories Off』シリーズ7作目の恋愛アドベンチャーゲーム。前作までのキャラクターイメージを一新し、コミックやライトノベル等のイラストで活躍中の森井しづきがキャラクターデザインを担った。繊細な描線で描かれたキャラクターが奥深い世界観を表現している。

A romantic adventure game, the seventh in the Memories Off series. The character images that were used up until the previous game were completely renewed and the new characters were designed by Morii Shizuki, active in Comic and illustrating light novels. The characters, drawn with detailed lines, express a unique and deep world view.

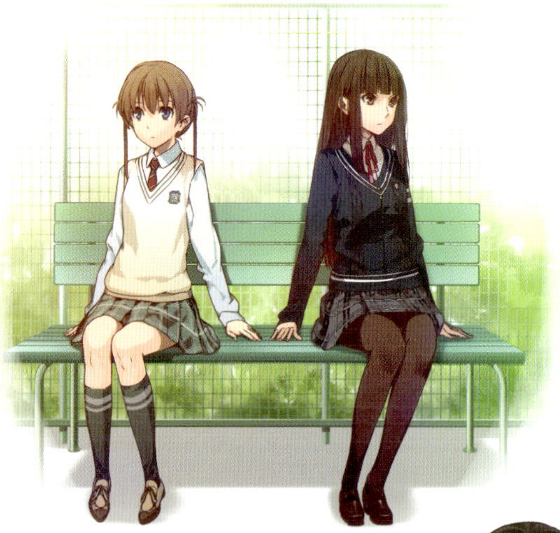

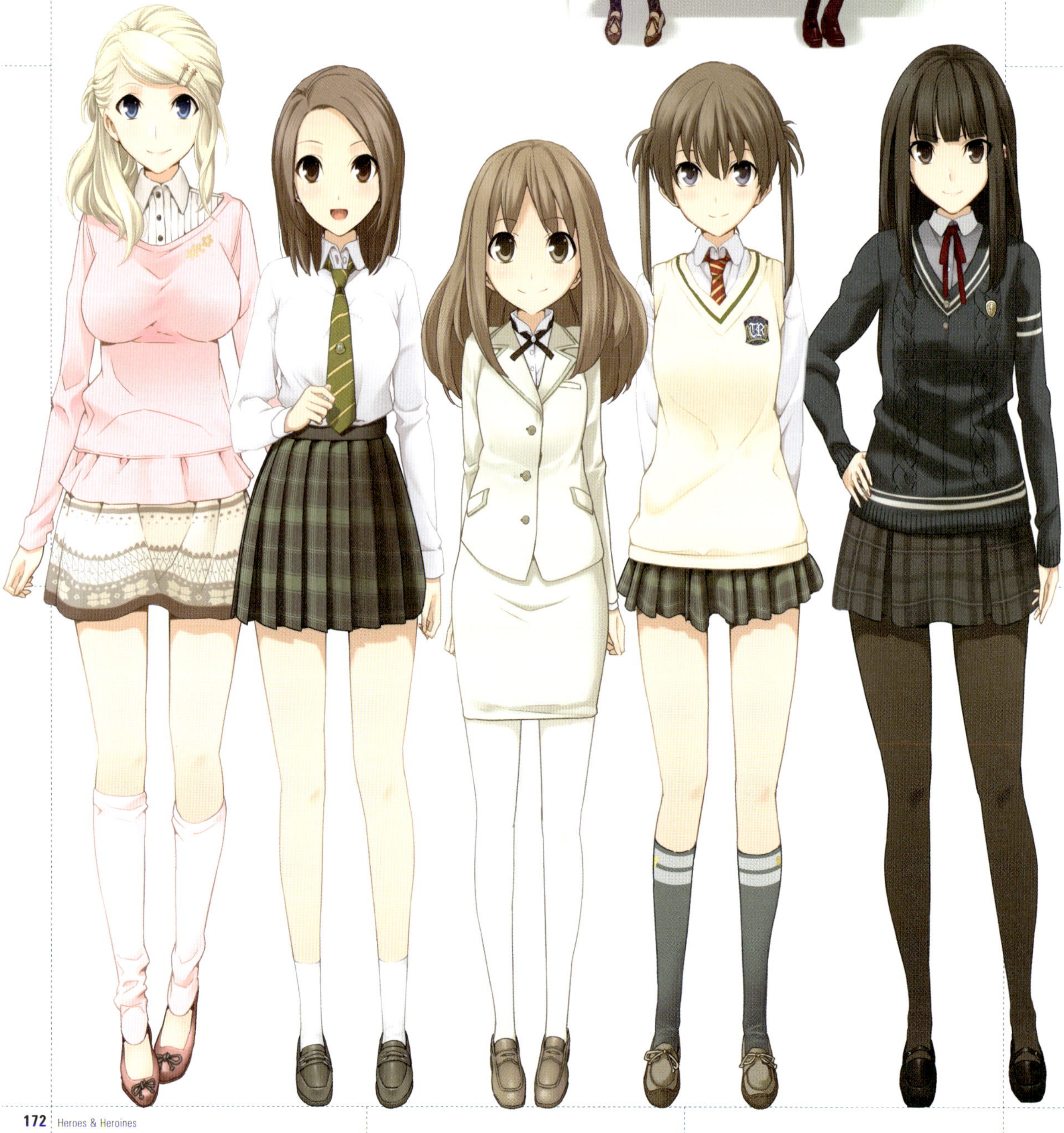

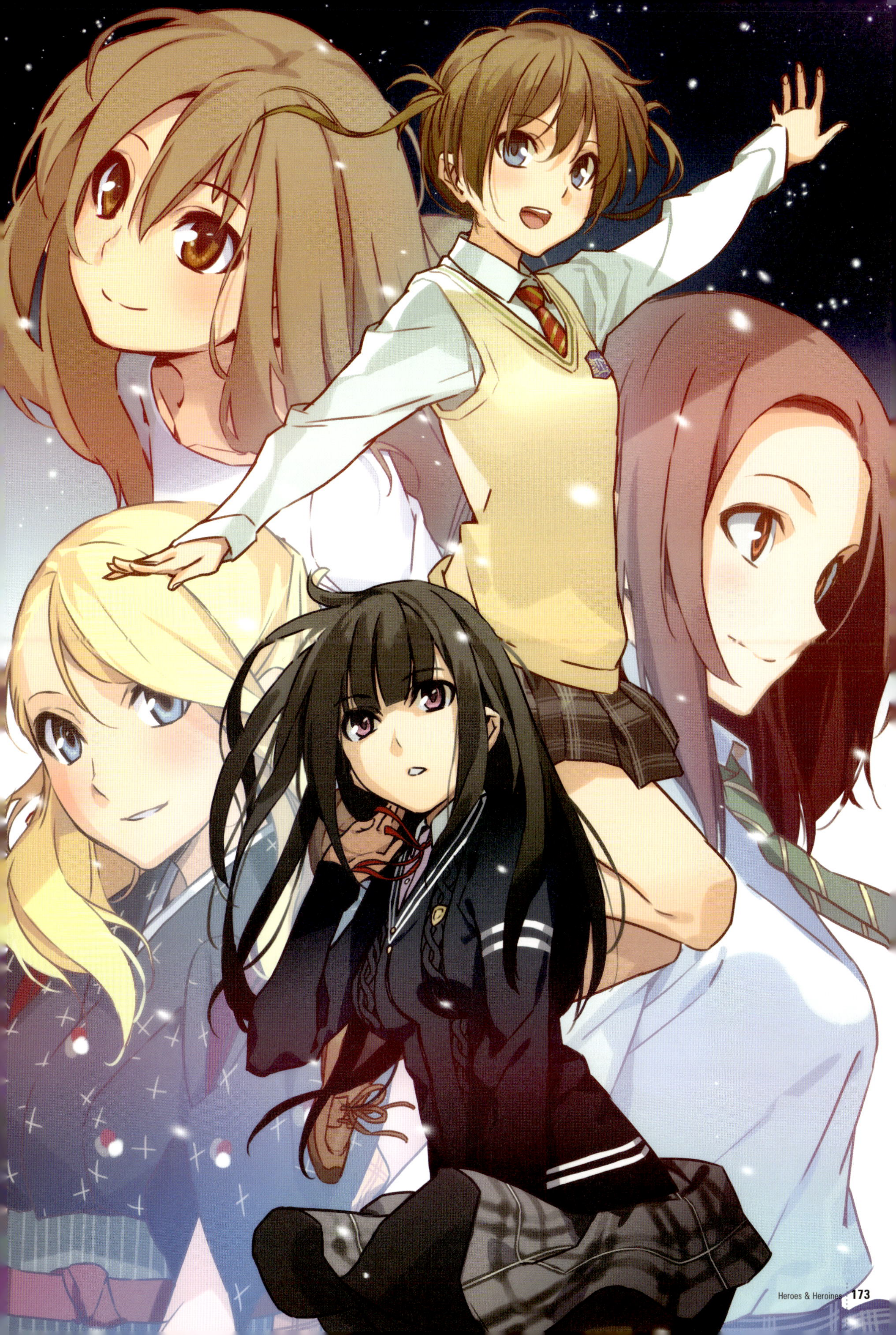

Animation

『四畳半神話大系』
● The Tatami Galaxy

キャラクター原案　キャラクターデザイン
中村佑介／伊東伸高
Nakamura Yusuke / Ito Nobutake

[中村佑介代表作] ASIAN KUNG-FU GENERATION CD/DVD（ジャケットイラスト）

[伊東伸高代表作] 『カイバ』

京都を舞台に四畳半のおんぼろ下宿屋に住む男子大学生「私」が織りなす、妄想と不毛と愚行の青春奇譚。キャラクター原案に、ノスタルジックなイラストで人気の中村佑介、キャラクターデザインに湯浅政明監督作品には欠かせない伊東伸高が起用された。

Watashi, a male college student living in a tiny, run-down boarding house in Kyoto, weaves a fantastic tale of delusion, folly, and stupidity. Character concept was by the popular, reliable Nakamura Yusuke, while character design was by Ito Nobutake, an indispensible part of direct Yuasa Masaaki's works.

中村佑介

伊東伸高

174　Heroes & Heroines

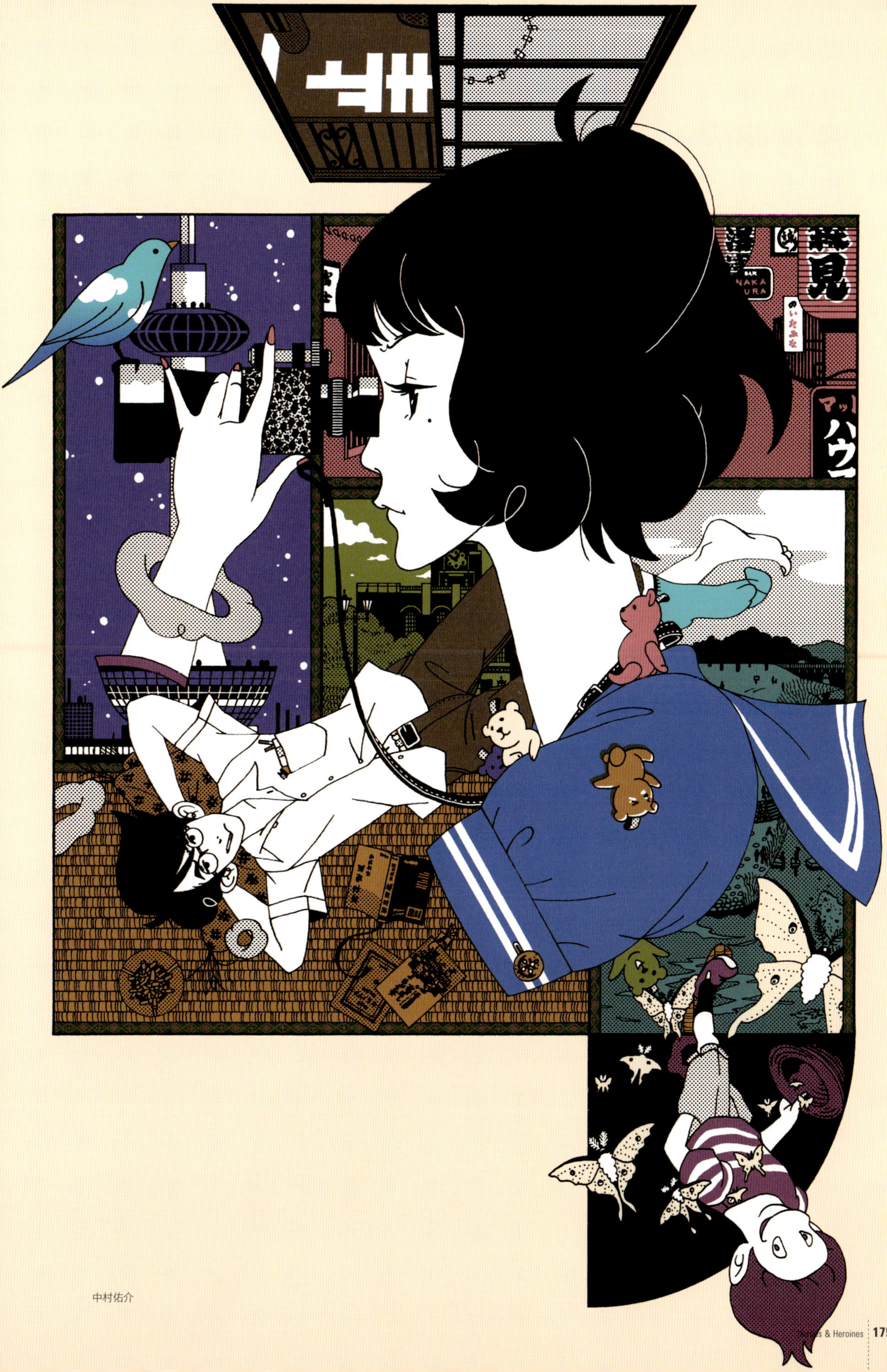
見
BAR
NAKA
URA
のいたあな
ハウ

中村佑介

Game 『REZELCROSS』
● REZELCROSS

キャラクターデザイン
金田榮路
Kaneda Eiji

[代表作]『創聖のアクエリオン』(キャラクター原案)
『ファイナルファンタジーXI』シリーズ小説 (挿絵)

「覚醒」した人間たちが10章からなるストーリーを進めるオリジナルRPG。シナリオは『弟切草』などを手がけた山崎修、個性的なキャラクターを『創聖のアクエリオン』や数多くのトレーディングカードのイラストで人気の金田榮路が繊細に表現した。

An original 10 chapter RPG of "awoken" people. Yamazaki Osamu, who worked on Otogirisou, created the story, while individual intricate character design was by Kaneda Eiji, the popular illustrator behind Genesis of Aquarion and many trading cards.

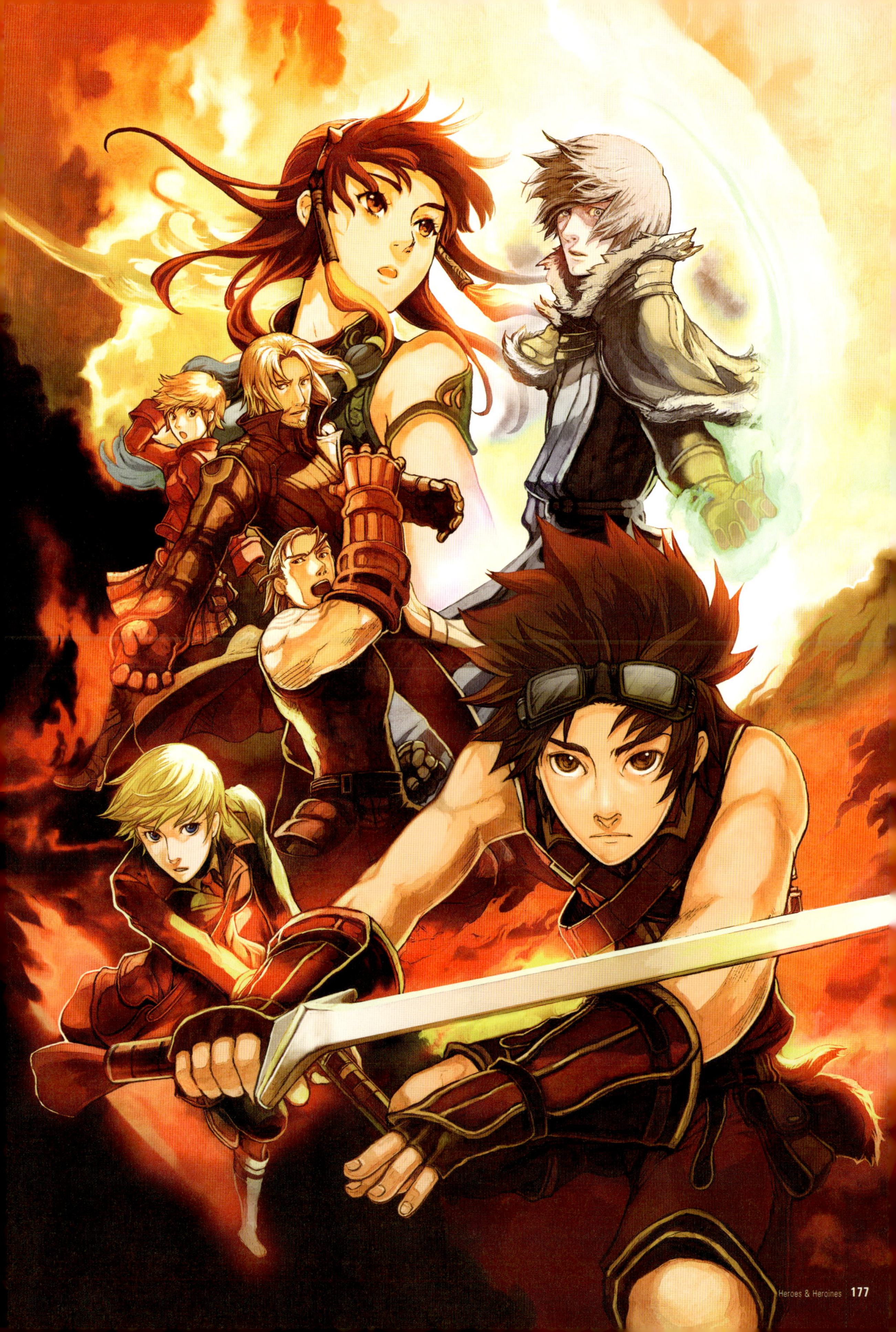

Game

『Lucian Bee's』シリーズ
● Lucian Bee's RESURRECTION SUPERNOVA / Lucian Bee's JUSTICE YELLOW / Lucian Bee's EVIL VIOLET

キャラクターデザイン
前田浩孝
Maeda Hirotaka

[代表作] 『TOKYO ヤマノテ BOYS』シリーズ
『Vitamin』シリーズ

全世界のダメ男ダサ男を容貌性格ともに、麗しい男性に磨き上げていく恋愛アドベンチャーゲーム。出自や素顔は悪くないのに、勘違いな性格、残念なファッションセンス等、むしろ涙を誘う人生を邁進している個性的なダメ男を前田浩孝が愛嬌たっぷりに描きあげている。

A romance adventure game where you change and refine the appearances of hopeless, unattractive men, into beautiful, attractive men. They don't have bad backgrounds and their real selves aren't bad but they have misguided personalities and sad tastes in fashion. Maeda Hirotaka illustrates, in a lovable manner, these unique hopeless men who push forward with their tear jerking lives.

『Lucian Bee's RESURRECTION SUPERNOVA』

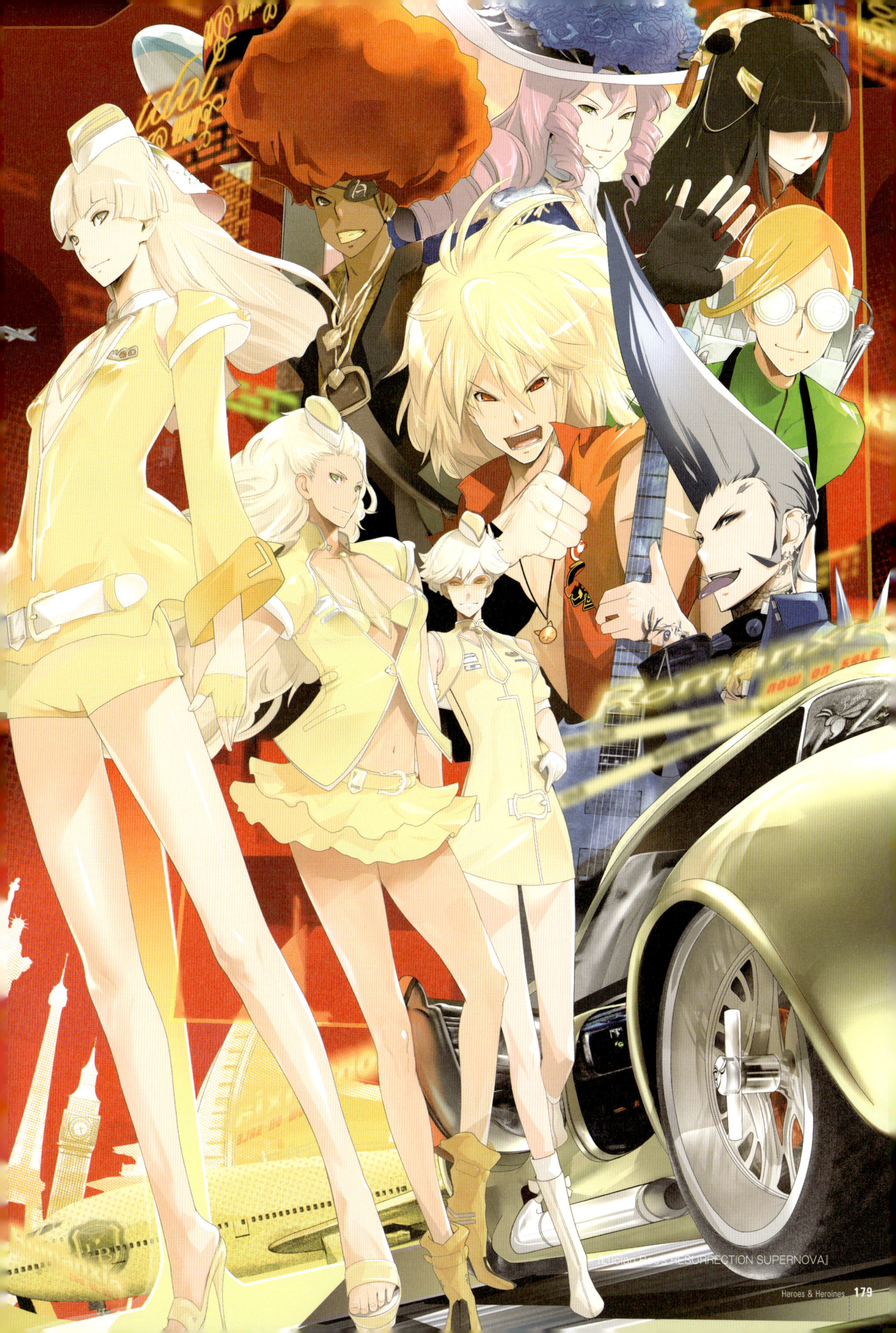
idol

『Lucian Bee's RESURRECTION SUPERNOVA』

Game

『Lucian Bee's』シリーズ
● Lucian Bee's RESURRECTION SUPERNOVA / Lucian Bee's JUSTICE YELLOW / Lucian Bee's EVIL VIOLET

『Lucian Bee's RESURRECTION SUPERNOVA』

Lucian Bee's JUSTICE YELLOW

181

Game

『Lucian Bee's』シリーズ

● Lucian Bee's RESURRECTION SUPERNOVA / Lucian Bee's JUSTICE YELLOW / Lucian Bee's EVIL VIOLET

『Lucian Bee's EVIL VIOLET』

「Lucian Bee's EVIL VIOLET」

Game

『ROBOTICS;NOTES』
● ROBOTICS;NOTES

キャラクターデザイン
福田知則
Fukuda Tomonori

[代表作] 『ROBOTICS;NOTES』

『CHAOS;HEAD』、『STEINS;GATE』に続く科学アドベンチャーシリーズ第3弾。キャラクターCGを3D化し、キャラクターの魅力を引き立てる演出になっている。キャラクターデザインを担当する福田知則は、5pb.気鋭のイラストレーターである。

The third in the science adventure series after CHAOS;HEAD and STEINS;GATE. The character CGs are now 3D and are depicted to accentuate the appeal of the characters. Fukuda Tomonori, who is in charge of character design, is the spirited illustrator for 5pb.

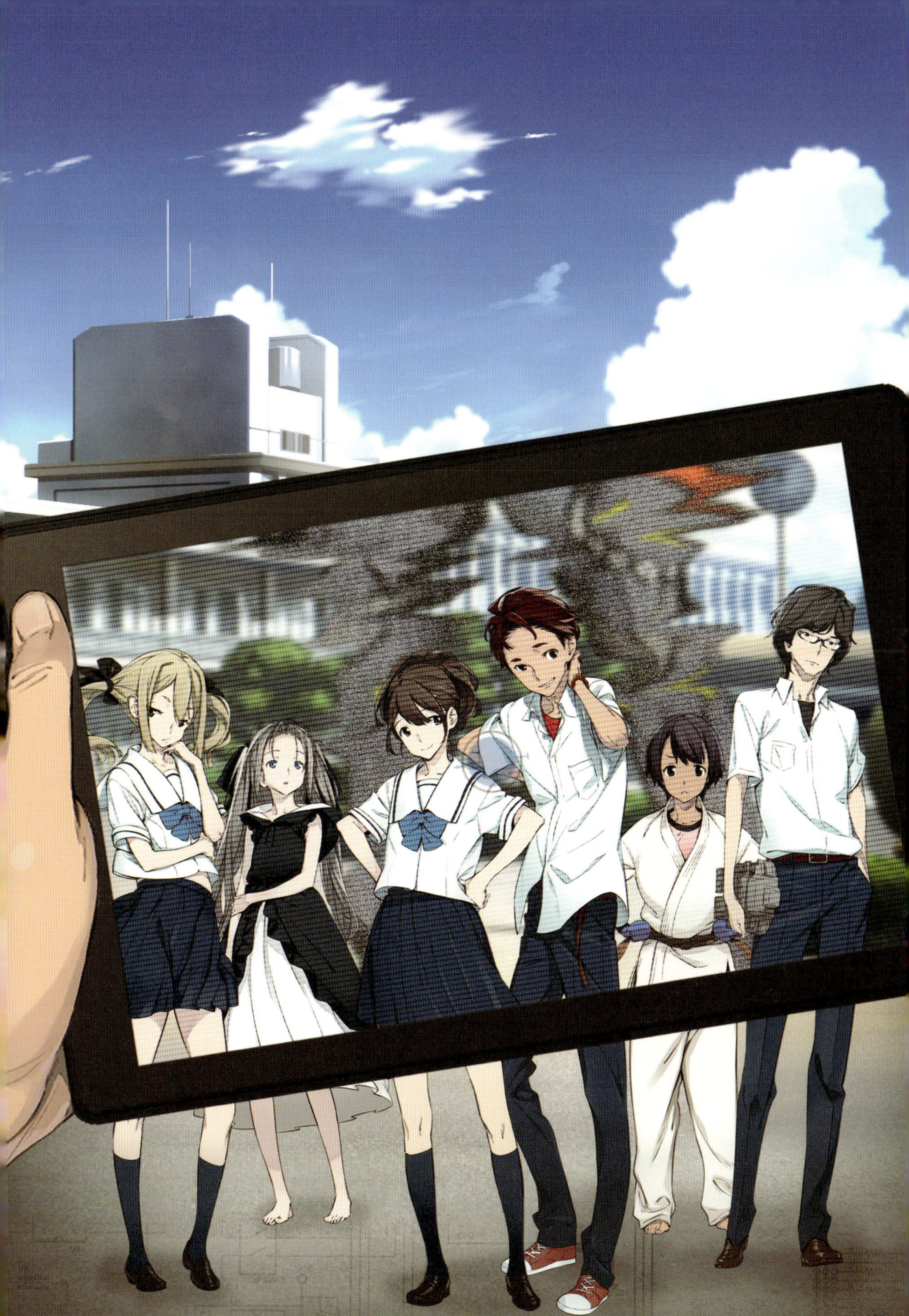

Game

『ロリポップチェーンソー』
● LOLLIPOP CHAINSAW

メインキャラクターデザイン

猫将軍
Nekoshogun

[代表作]『GuitarFreaks』
『DrumMania』シリーズ（クリップイラスト）

アメリカ西海岸のハイスクールに通うキュートなチアガール・ジュリエットがチェーンソーを武器に次々とゾンビを天国へ導いていく。ゲームのジャンルとしては確立しているゾンビアクションもの特有の陰鬱さはなく、ゾンビまでも明るく、キュートでキラキラしい絵作りだ。

Juliet, a cute cheerleader attending a high school on America's west coast, uses a chainsaw as a weapon to send one zombie after another back to heaven. While the genre of this game is zombie action, a well-established genre, the game does not have any characteristic somberness; even the zombies are illustrated to be bright, cute and sparkling.

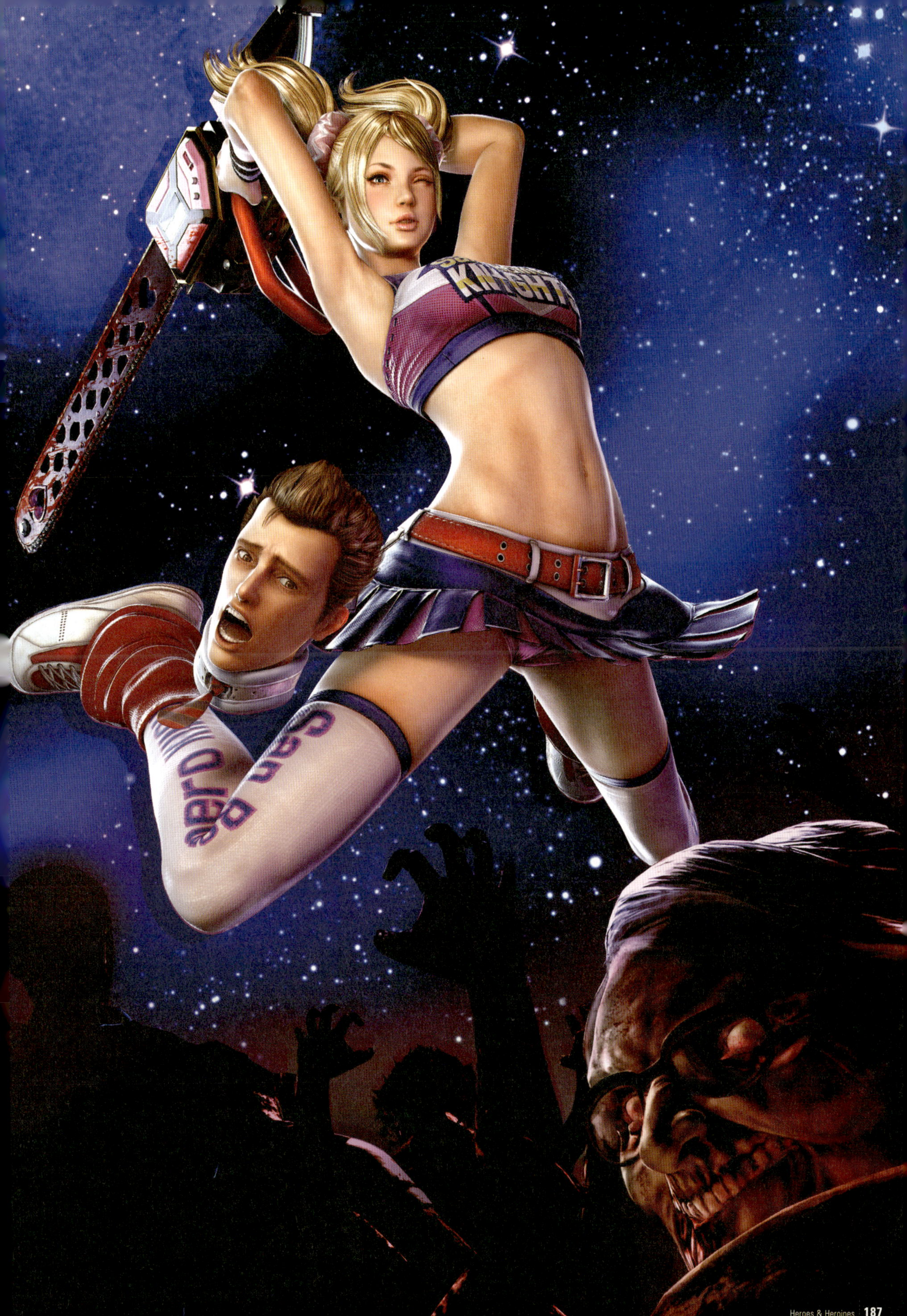

Animation 『WORKING!!』シリーズ
● WORKING!!

キャラクターデザイン
足立慎吾
Adachi Shingo

[代表作]『流星のロックマン』『流星のロックマン トライブ』(アニメ)

北海道にあるファミリーレストラン「ワグナリア」でアルバイトをする個性的すぎる店員たちが元気に危険に活躍するファミレスバイトコメディー！ 高津カリノ原作の人気漫画をアニメーション化。

A family restaurant comedy where the unique staff at Wagnaria, a family restaurant in Hokkaido, get into fun and danger! Originally a popular manga by Takatsu Karino, now a popular anime series.

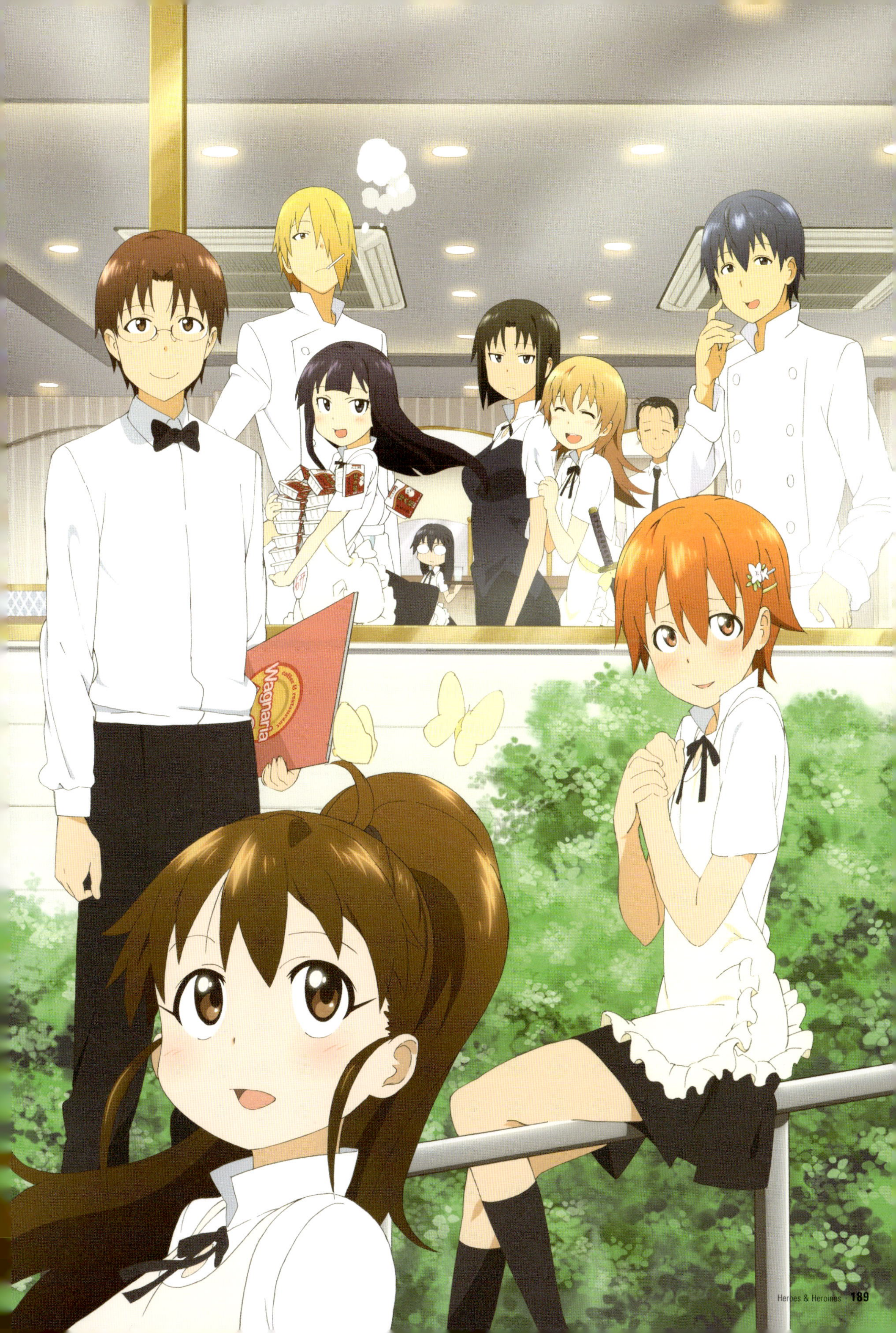
Wagnaria
coffee & restaurant

【デザイナーインタビュー2】
『REZELCROSS』
キャラクターデザイナー 金田榮路

ゲームからアニメまで、キャラクターデザイナー、イラストレーターとして活動を続ける金田榮路と、『リゼルクロス』プロデューサー・ソニー・コンピュータエンタテインメントの吉澤純一氏に『リゼルクロス』制作のお話を伺った。（※作品は本書p.176に掲載）

シナリオ先行で制作されたオリジナルRPG。

——どういった形で『リゼルクロス』のキャラクターデザインのご依頼があったのでしょうか？

金田 メールで依頼がありました。

——それは金田さんのホームページ経由で？

金田 そのあたりは詳しく聞かなかったんですけど（笑）。

吉澤 『リゼルクロス』は、弊社で発表するオリジナルRPGの新規タイトルでしたから、新しいRPGの顔となるキャラクターデザインをしてくださる方をうちのスタッフが探していたんです。そのなかで、金田さんが魅力的なキャラクターを描かれているというので、連絡させていただいたんです。

——『リゼルクロス』の発売が2007年ですが、金田さんにキャラクターデザインのご依頼があったのはいつ頃ですか？

金田 2004年頃でしょうか。

吉澤 ちょうどPSP「プレイステーション・ポータブル」が発売されたのが2004年の年末なんですよ。その当時発表するタイトルはある程度制作が仕上げてきていて、そこから次のオリジナルタイトルを作っていこうというなかの1本が『リゼルクロス』でした。ただ、『リゼルクロス』自体はそれこそ、私がまだ弊社にいない10年くらい前にプロットだけは存在していたんです。『アークザラッド』等を書かれていたシナリオライターの山崎さんがプロットを書かれていて、それをいつか実現しようとしているうちにPSPが出て、これをPSPでやろうということで立ち上がったんです。その当時はシナリオありきでRPGを作ろうというタイトルが少なかったんです。新しいゲームシステムがあって、そのシステムや企画に則ったもので進んだりするものなんです。それをシナリオ先行で重厚長大というか、深みがある、感動できるシナリオを用意してからそこにシステムを載せていこうというコンセプトで進行した作品です。この世界観を描けるのは金田さんしかいないだろうというのが当時の担当者の判断でした。

——そうすると、最初に依頼があってシナリオが届いたんでしょうか？

金田 そうですね。シナリオを見せていただいて、キャラクター設定はもう全員分ありましたね。それを絵で形にし

Kaneda Eiji, Rezel Cross character designer
I'm talking about the creation of Rezel Cross with Kaneda Eiji, a character designer and illustrator active in everything from video games to anime, and producer Yoshizawa Junichi from Sony Computer Entertainment. (Rezel Cross is shown on pgs. 176-177.)

An original RPG that started with the story first.

–How were you approached about the character design for Rezel Cross?
Kaneda:I got a request through email.
–Was that through your website?
Kaneda:I didn't get all the details. (Laughs)
Yoshizawa:Because Rezel Cross is a new, original RPG title we launched, our staff were looking for a character design with a face that was new to RPGs. Since Kaneda draws such fascinating characters, we decided to contact him.
–Rezel Cross was launched in 2007. When did you contact Kaneda about the character designs?
Kaneda:Around 2004.
Yoshizawa: It was at the end of 2004, just as the PSP was being launched. At the time we had just about finished creating the titles that would launch with the PSP, and one of the next original titles we were looking to make was Rezel Cross. But the plot for Rezel Cross itself was from around ten years before I started with the company. It was written by Yamazaki, a story writer who wrote Arc the Lad. We were looking for a chance to make this game, and that's when the PSP came out, so we decided that we would start on this. There weren't a lot of titles at the time where we had the story

もともと男性キャラだったが、女性が少ないという理由で変更となったライザ。とはいえひじょうに魅力的なキャラクターに仕上がっている。

Laiza, who was originally a male but was changed to a female due to a lack of female characters. Even so, they've created a remarkably attractive character.

ていく作業です。個々の髪形や衣装は私がデザインしました。
──描いたキャラクターに対して大幅な変更の依頼などはありましたか？
金田 それほど大きなものはなかったです。ラフの段階でお見せして、「ここはもっとこうして欲しい」という話は当然ありますよね。マリオンが二転三転した気がします。それから、レイファの顔は最初、女優の小西真奈美さんをイメージしていたんです。和風な顔立ちにしたいと思って。最終的には変更しましたけど。あと、アイルが決まらなかったですね。
吉澤 アイルの雰囲気はあるんだけど、この服装が明朗快活な彼の性格に合っているのかいないのかとか、結構やり取りしていましたよね。それから、ライザって最初の設定では男だったんですよ。でも登場人物に女性がいなさすぎる、男ばっかりで殺伐としてるって話になって、女性に変更していただいたんです。
──逆にすんなり決まったキャラクターは？
金田 セシルは早く決まりましたね。ショートカットの女性が好きなんですけど、シナリオを見て彼女は勝手にショートカットにしました（笑）。そうしたらすんなり決まったのを覚えています。
──クリーチャー的な要素もある敵のキャラクターは描きやすいですか？　描きにくいですか？
金田 私は敵のキャラクターは描きやすいです。「すごい美人を描いて」と言われると、逆に悩みますね。美人の感覚って人によって違うじゃないですか。誰が見てもかっこいい、誰が見ても可愛い人というのは難しいですね。ガソは気に入っています。動きがかっこいいんですよ（笑）。
──『リゼルクロス』のキャラクターを描く上でこだわったところはありますか？
金田 セシルはイギリスの女の子っぽくしたかったんです。そんな感じである程度、敵・味方ともにヨーロピアンな雰囲気を出したかったんです。それは設定を見て、敵方が軍事国家のような感じだったので、そっちは昔のドイツのイメージで、味方はトラッドな感じで。あとは寒い国という設定もあったので、ユリウスは厚着なんです。ロシア人をイメージしています。
──衣装を描く際に参考にしているものはありますか？
金田 実際の軍服は見ますね。あとはいろいろなところに行って制服の資料等は集めます。銃はモデルガンを買ったりしています。日本刀もうちにありますよ（笑）。描くのに困って、しょうがないと思って買いました。最近は3D素材とか便利なものがありますけど、昔はなかったので、ものひとつとっても違う角度から見たら、どう見えるだろうかとか検証したいし、衣装も資料を参考にしたりはしますけど、なるべく実物を見て、着方脱ぎ方を確認します。

寒い国ということでロシア風の軍服＋コートという流れで描かれたユリウス。このような衣装もきちんと実物をさわり、構造も知ることが大事という。
Julius, who comes from a cold region and so was drawn first with a Russian style military uniform and coat. Of course, this kind of clothing looks absolutely authentic ? it's important to know its basic structure.

so we wanted to make it an RPG. We had this new game system, so we were working on something to go along with that system and the new plans it brought. So Rezel Cross was a game that went forward as one that placed major emphasis on story first. We wanted a deep, moving story before we would launch it with the system. The lead manager at the time thought that only Kaneda could draw with that sort of world view.

–So, first you got the request, and then you got the story?

Kaneda:Right. They showed me the story, and all the characters had already been established. My job was to flesh them out in drawings. I designed each character's hairstyle and clothing.

–Did you have any requests for major changes after you drew the characters?

Kaneda:Nothing really major. During the rough drafts I would show them my work and they would tell me they want something a little more like this or that, of course. I think Marion was changed over and over. And Leifa's face was originally modeled after Konishi Manami, the actress. I wanted to give her Japanese features. I ended up changing it though. Isle hadn't been decided on yet either.

Yoshizawa: We had the feel for Isle, but there was a lot of back and forth about whether his clothing matched his cheerful, laid-back personality. And Laiza was a man at first, but there weren't enough female characters ? some said that an all male game seemed barbaric, so we changed Laiza into a female.

–So what characters were easy to decide on?

Kaneda:Cecile we decided on quickly. I like women with short hair, so when I saw the story I just drew her with short hair. (Laughs) I remember that's when we just landed on her.

–Are enemy characters with creature-like qualities easy to draw? Or are they difficult?

Kaneda:I find enemy characters easy to draw. Conversely, if you tell me to draw a really beautiful woman, I have trouble. Beauty is in the eye of the beholder, right? It's hard to draw someone that everyone is going to find handsome or cute. I like Guso. I think he looks cool walking. (Laughs)

–Was there any Rezel Cross character you obsessed on?

Kaneda:I wanted to make Cecile look like a British

画材はずっとフォトショップ。宣材によって適宜変更できるのがCGデータの強み。

——『リゼルクロス』のキャラクターはどういう画材で描かれたのですか？

金田 全部フォトショップです。下絵の下絵は手描きですけど、あとはフォトショップですね。ペインターも使ってないです。

——もともとフォトショップで絵は描かれるのですか？

金田 そうです。デビュー時からですね。2000年くらいから活動を始めたんですけど、そのときからフォトショップです。ラフの段階では手描きのほうが線がまとまって見えるので、手描きのものを送ったりしますが、ふだんの絵は最初からフォトショップですね。アナログはもうできない（笑）。学生のときはアナログで描いていましたが、CGを見つけてからはもうずっとそうです。96年頃からCGで描いていますが、その当時はこういう絵でCGで描いている人はまだあまりいませんでしたね。

吉澤 2004年〜2005年頃なので、グラフィックデータがすごく大きいんですよ。500メガくらいのデータが来て、当時のプロデュースグループのスタッフが持ってるパソコンでは開けないんです（笑）。デザイングループのほうに持って行って開いてデータをJPGにしてもらって確認していました。

金田 その節はご迷惑をおかけしました（笑）。昔は本当にデータが大きかったですよね。メインビジュアルのイラストはキャラクターが動かせるように全部レイヤーを分けていたんです。

吉澤 そうそう。金田さんはデータの作り方がすごいんですよ。ちゃんとレイヤーで分かれていて、全部分けて納品してくださるんです。それを弊社でパッケージ化粧して、サイズが違うものとか、レイアウトを変えたものとか、こちらでの最終的な調整がしやすいんですよ。

金田 ゲームのメインビジュアル等は、レイヤーで分けておいて、タイトルが入ってからあとでキャラクターをちょっと横にずらすとか、結構ありますね。

吉澤 よそのメーカーさんはわからないですけど、弊社は例えばPSPのパッケージだとA4の長方形でも、もっと横幅が狭いんですよね。それに合わせてキャラクターの位置を変えたりとかはしますね。

——では、当時から金田さんのパソコンのスペックは相当高かったんですね。

金田 兄がプログラマーでして、複雑なものを組んでくれるんです。そんな環境でしたから、昔から家にパソコンはあって、それでCGに入るのも早かったんですね。

——金田さんがイラストレーターになろうとしたきっかけは？

金田 小さい頃から絵を描くのが好きだったんですけ

ひじょうに悩んだというレイファ。意外とキャラクターデザインをする上で難しいのがこのような誰もがわかる美少女キャラだそうだ。

A lot of thought went into Leifa. She's a beautiful young girl whose character design shows how difficult the process can be.

girl. In doing so, to a degree I wanted to give the enemies and allies a European feel to them. Once I decided on that, the enemies had a sort of military state feeling behind them, so I gave them an old German look, while the friends had a more traditional feeling. And it took place in a cold region, so I gave Julius thick clothing, like a Russian.

–Do you have something you refer to when you're drawing clothing?

Kaneda:I look at actual military uniforms, and I also go here and there to gather material on reference. For guns I'll buy models. I own my own samurai sword! (Laughs) I was having trouble drawing them, so I thought my only recourse was to buy one. Lately there are 3D materials and other conveniences that we didn't have before. I want to see for myself what something looks like when you look at it from a different angle. I refer to different material on clothing, but I try to look at the real deal as much as possible to see how it's put on and taken off.

It was all done with Photoshop. One strength of CG data is that you can change it to suit the promo material.

–What did you draw Rezel Cross characters on?

Kaneda:They were all drawn with Photoshop. The rough, rough design was done by hand, but afterward it was done on Photoshop. I don't use Painter either.

–Have you always drawn with Photoshop?

Kaneda:Yes. I used Photoshop from the very beginning. I first got active around 2000, and that's when I started using Photoshop. At the rough stage, lines hold together better though when hand drawn, so I would send hand drawn sketches. But usually I did drawings in Photoshop. I can't do analog. (Laughs) When I was a student I drew in analog, but since I discovered computers I've always used them. I started using computers from around 1996. There weren't a lot of people at that time drawing with computers.

Yoshizawa:It was around 2004 or 2005, so graphic data was huge. I would get data that was about 500MB ? the computers that my producing staff had couldn't open it. (Laughs) I would take it to the

美大に行ってるときに普通の絵を描いててもつまらないなと感じて。漫画家になろうと思ったんですけど、学生時代の周りの友達がみんなすごい漫画を描いていたんです。今現在活躍中の漫画家さんばっかりです。周りの友達の描く漫画のレベルが高すぎて、私には無理だって思いまして（笑）。それでイラストレーターになろうと思ったんです。

――アニメのキャラクター原案なども担当されていますが、ゲームとの違いはありますか？

金田　『創聖のアクエリオン』は企画の最初の段階から参加させていただいたので、キャラクターは何もない所から起こしました。イメージを掴むためにシナリオの打ち合わせ等にも参加させてもらいました。「自由に描いていいよ」という部分が多く、楽しい反面大変でした（笑）。既にシナリオとある程度の設定が決まっていた『リゼルクロス』とは違いましたね。

キャラクターはシンプルにストレートに、一番押したいところを描ききる。

――絵を描く上で金田さんが気をつけているところは？

金田　目線というか、目力ですかね。キャラクターの強さが出ればいいなと思って。キャラクターを描きたいと思ったときから、それは気をつけています。

――キャラクターを描くときに最初に描く箇所は決まっていますか？

金田　鼻です。普通は輪郭から描いたりするんでしょうけど（笑）。鼻を描いて眉毛、目の順番です。顔の中心を描いてから輪郭を描きます。個々の顔にもよるんですけど、つるっとした雰囲気の女の子の輪郭は最後に描きます。みんなに「変なところから描くね」って言われます。昔、ゲームの仕事で、目と口は動くから別レイヤーで描いていたんです。今は3Dに発展しているので、目パチロパクだけのゲームってあまりないですけど、そのときのクセなんでしょうね。

――キャラクターデザイナーやイラストレーターを目指している方へ、こんな勉強をしておくといいということはありますか？

金田　勉強ですか？　うーん。ものはよく観察してから描いたほうがいいですね。構造を知っていて描くのと、知らないで描くのとでは、まったく違うと思います。動物もよく見て描いています。自宅が獣屋敷なんですよ（笑）。今は犬が2匹、猫が11匹います。動物が本当に好きで本当は馬も飼いたいくらいです。昔、人物のキャラクターを描く前は動物しか描いていなかったくらいです。

吉澤　モンスターも描いていらっしゃいますよね？

金田　はい。モンスターも好きで、よく描きます。

吉澤　『リゼルクロス』をお願いさせていただく選考の要素のなかに、魅力的なキャラクターを描けるというのとあわせて、特徴あるモンスターを描ける方ということで、金

design group to open, and they would change it to JPG for me to check.

Kaneda: Sorry for all the headaches back then. (Laughs) Data really was huge at the time. The main illustration visuals were all layered so the character could move.

Yoshizawa: Yeah. Kaneda had a great way of creating data. Everything was always layered, and each layer sent individually. We would then repackage it together, which would make it easier for us to do final adjustments on different sizes or layouts.

Kaneda: The game's main visuals and other aspects are layered because once the titles are inserted the characters are often moved to the side or whatever.

Yoshizawa: Other manufacturers may not know this, but even if we do a PSP package on A4 rectangular paper the width is smaller. So we have to change character positions to match it.

–So, Kaneda's computer has always had relatively good specs then?

Kaneda: My brother was a programmer, so he would put in a lot of elaborate stuff. So I grew up with a PC in the home, and so I started using it to draw early on.

–What made you decide that you wanted to be an illustrator?

Kaneda: I loved drawing since I was little, but even when I was going to art school I thought that drawing normal pictures was boring. I wanted to be a manga artist, but all of my friends at school drew superb manga art. They're all successful manga artist now. They all drew manga so well that

すぐに描いた3人衆。特に金田のお気に入りはガソ。3Dキャラクター時の動きがまた好きというが、このようにイラストが3D化されたときの監修も行うのがキャラクターデザイナーの仕事のひとつ。

The three main characters, who were easy to draw. Then there's Guso, who Kaneda especially likes. Even though he likes the movement of 3D characters, one job of character designers is supervising how these illustrations are brought to life in 3D.

田さんにお願いしたんです。『リゼルクロス』は作品の経緯で、金田さんにはキャラクターに寄っていただかないと、ボリュームや時間が間に合わなかったので、モンスターデザインは他の方にお願いしたんですけど、それはよく動物を描いているところからきているんでしょうね。

——プロデューサーの吉澤さんから見た金田さんはどういう方でしょうか?

吉澤 金田さんは個性ある画風で、絵自体が金田さん独自の世界観があるんですけど、メーカーのこちらが「こういうことがしたい、こういうものが欲しい」という要望に対して、すごく柔軟に受けとめて、それを返してくださる方です。ご自分の持っているひとつの世界観のなかで描かれる方ではなく、仕事に合わせて臨機応変にキャラクターのデザインや、仕事の仕方を変えていただける方という印象でした。弊社の『リゼルクロス』はスチームパンクをイメージしていますが、アニメのお仕事ではSFだったり、色々なカードイラストも描かれていますよね。非常に幅広い絵を描き分けられるので、絵の幅や奥の深い方ですよね。

——プロデューサーさんから、キャラクターデザイナーを目指す方へ一言いただけますか?

吉澤 金田さんの仕事を見ろ! もしくは、鼻から描く! (笑)。私はクリエイターの後輩にもよく言ってますが、とにかく夢を持つことだと思います。これをやりたいというしっかりしたビジョンを持つこと。これに尽きると思います。

——金田さんから、キャラクターデザイナーを目指す方へアドバイスをいただけますか?

金田 最近の若い子の絵を見ると、ちょっと盛りすぎかなと思うんですよ。もっとストレートに一点集中でバーンと表現すればいいのになと思います。やりたいことがいっぱいあるんだろうな、というのは感じるんですけど、詰め込みすぎですね。描けば描くほど、いろいろなアイデアがわいてきて、描き込んじゃうんだろうなと。それはいいことで、私も羨ましいんですけど、そこをぐっと我慢して、シンプルにここ一番というものを強く押し出したほうがいいと思います。でも、最近は高校生くらいでも、絵がめちゃくちゃ上手いですよね。pixivを見るとみんな上手くてもう見るのやめようとか思います(笑)。

——今後、こういう仕事をしたいという願望はありますか?

金田 さきほど言ったように、学生時代に一度諦めた漫画にまた挑戦したいですね。完全オリジナルなものを描きたいと思っています。

I thought it would be impossible for me to become a manga artist. (Laughs) So I thought, " I'll be an illustrator."

You also do a lot of anime character concept work. Are there differences with video games?

Kaneda:I started from the planning stage of Genesis of Aquarion, so I started with no characters whatsoever. I would participate in the story meetings so I could get an idea of them. There were a lot of times where I could just draw whatever I wanted, so it was fun, but tough also. (Laughs) It was different from Rezel Cross, where the story had already pretty much been set.

Draw your characters simple and straight, and focus on drawing what you want to stand out the most.

–What do you worry about the most when you're drawing?

Kaneda:The line of sight, or what draws the eye. It's good if the character's strengths come out. When I want to draw a character, I worry about that the most.

-Do you always start from a certain point when you first start drawing a character?

Kaneda:The nose. Normally you start with the silhouette, right? (Laughs) I start with the nose, then the eyebrows, then the eyes. Once I draw the face, I draw the silhouette. While it depends on each face, for a woman with a pretty face I draw her silhouette last. Everyone tells me I should start with strange parts first. Before, when I worked with video games, the eyes and mouth would move so I would draw them in a separate layer. With the advances of 3D, there aren't a lot of games where just the eyes and mouth move. So it's a throwback from earlier times.

–Is there anything you would recommend aspiring character designers or illustrators to study?

Kaneda:To study? Hmm. You should observe things before you draw. Knowing the structure of something when you draw and not knowing are totally different. You should really look at animals before you draw them. My house is like a menagerie. (Laughs) I have two dogs and 11 cats. I really love animals, and I would love to have a horse. Before I started drawing human characters all I drew was animals.

Yoshizawa:You draw monsters too, right?

Kaneda:Yes, I like monsters so I draw them a lot too.

Yoshizawa:Of all the elements I wanted for Rezel Cross, I wanted someone who could draw appealing characters and unique monsters, so I asked Kaneda to do it. As Rezel Cross was being made, if Kaneda didn't focus on the characters he wouldn't have been able to keep up with the volume and the pace, so I had someone else do the monster design. But most of that came from drawing a lot of animals.

–As a producer, what do you think of Kaneda?

Yoshizawa:Kaneda has a unique style. His drawings themselves reflect his unique world view, but as a video game manufacturer I find him to be very flexible and open to requests for this or that in the game. He gives me the impression that he's not limited to drawing his own one world view, but can adapt his character design to match each job, and he can change his work style too. The look of our Rezel Cross is steampunk, but in anime he can draw SF, and he can do card illustrations as well. He can draw a huge variety of pictures, so his drawings have depth and variety as well.

–How about as a producer? Any advice you would give to aspiring character designers?

Yoshizawa:Just look at Kaneda's work! Or start drawing noses! (Laughs) I'm often called the creator's big brother, but just have a dream. Just have a vision of what you want to do. I think that's all it boils down to.

–Is there any advice you would give to aspiring character designers?

Kaneda:Recently, when I see drawings from young people, I think they're trying to fit too much into the drawing. I can't help but think it'd be better if they just narrowed their focus and just draw that. It's like they have so much they want to do, and so they're cramming too much into it. I'm sure that the more they draw, the more ideas come into their heads and the more they want to fit these in. That's fine, and I'm jealous too, but you have to hold yourself back. I think it's best to simply focus on what you think is best and feature that strongly. But recently even high schoolers are putting out superb drawings. When I look at pixiv I see how good everyone is and I just want to stop looking. (Laughs)

–Is there any kind of work that you would like to do in the future?

Kaneda:As I mentioned, I'd like to take another stab at some of the manga that I gave up on back in school. I'd like to draw something completely original.

作品インデックス

018 『AKIBA'S TRIP』
ハード PSP「プレイステーション・ポータブル」
発売日 2011年5月19日
開発／発売 アクワイア

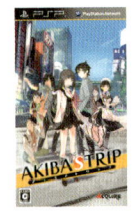

©2011 ACQUIRE Corp All Rights Reserved.

020 『あの日見た花の名前を僕達はまだ知らない。』
テレビ放送期間　2011年4月～2011年6月
DVD・BD　1巻～6巻発売中
発売　アニプレックス
販売　ソニー・ミュージックディストリビューション

©ANOHANA PROJECT

026 『Aチャンネル』
原作　「Aチャンネル」(芳文社刊) 黒田bb 著
テレビ放送期間　2011年4月～2011年6月
DVD・BD　1巻～6巻発売中
発売　アニプレックス
販売　ソニー・ミュージックディストリビューション

©黒田bb・芳文社/Aチャンネル委員会・MBS

028 『エルシャダイ』
ハード　PlayStation 3/Xbox 360
発売日　2011年4月28日
発売　イグニッション・エンターテインメント・リミテッド

©2011 Ignition Entertainment Ltd. All Rights Reserved.

032 『オトメディウスX（エクセレント!）』
ハード　Xbox 360
発売日　2011年4月21日
発売　KONAMI

©2011 Konami Digital Entertainment

034 『俺の妹がこんなに可愛いわけがない』
原作　「俺の妹がこんなに可愛いわけがない」(アスキー・メディアワークス刊) 伏見つかさ著　かんざきひろイラスト
テレビ放送期間　2010年10月～2010年12月
DVD・BD　1巻～8巻発売中
発売　アニプレックス
販売　ソニー・ミュージックディストリビューション

©伏見つかさ／アスキー・メディアワークス／OIP

036

『ガチトラ！ ～暴れん坊教師 in High School ～』

ハード　PSP「プレイステーション・ポータブル」
発売日　2011年4月21日
発売　スパイク

©Spike All Rights Reserved.

038

『逆転検事2』

ハード　ニンテンドーDS
発売日　2011年2月3日
発売　CAPCOM

©CAPCOM CO., LTD. 2011 ALL RIGHTS RESERVED.

044

『キャサリン』

ハード　PlayStation 3/Xbox 360
発売日　2011年2月17日
発売　アトラス

©ATLUS CO.,LTD. 2010

046

『Persona3 Portable』

ハード　PSP「プレイステーション・ポータブル」
発売日　2009年11月1日
発売　アトラス

©ATLUS CO.,LTD. 1996.2009

049

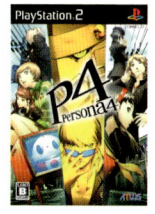

『Persona4』

ハード　PlayStation 2
発売日　2008年7月10日
発売　アトラス

©ATLUS CO.,LTD. 1996.2008

050

『Persona4 The GOLDEN』

ハード　PlayStation Vita
発売日　2012年春発売予定
発売　アトラス

©Index Corporation 1996,2011 Produced by ATLUS

051

『Persona4 The ULTIMATE in MAYONAKA ARENA』

ハード　PlayStation 3/Xbox 360
発売日　2012年夏発売予定
開発　アトラス＆アークシステムワークス
発売　アトラス

©Index Corporation 1996,2011 Produced by ATLUS

054 TVアニメ『ペルソナ4』

テレビ放送期間　2011年10月〜
DVD・BD　1巻
2011年11月23日発売

©Index Corporation/「ペルソナ4」アニメーション製作委員会

056 『極限脱出 9時間9人9の扉』

ハード　ニンテンドーDS
発売日　2009年12月10日
開発　CHUNSOFT
発売　スパイク

©2009 CHUNSOFT

058 『ギルティクラウン』

テレビ放送期間　2011年10月〜

©GUILTY CROWN COMMITTEE

064 『グロリア・ユニオン -Twin fates in blue ocean-』

ハード　PSP「プレイステーション・ポータブル」
発売日　2011年6月23日
開発　STING
発売　インデックス

©Index Corporation 2011 Developed by STING

066 『グングニル - 魔槍の軍神と英雄戦争 -』

ハード　PSP「プレイステーション・ポータブル」
発売日　2011年5月19日
開発　STING
発売　インデックス

©Index Corporation 2011 Developed by STING

068 『月華繚乱ROMANCE』

ハード　PSP「プレイステーション・ポータブル」
発売日　2011年9月15日
企画・開発　Rejet・オトメイト
発売　アイディアファクトリー

©2011 Rejet / IDEA FACTORY

070 『剣と魔法と学園モノ。Final 〜新入生はお姫様！〜』

ハード　PSP「プレイステーション・ポータブル」
発売日　2011年10月13日
開発　ゼロディブ
発売　アクワイア

©2011 ACQUIRE Corp. All Rights Reserved.

072 『Shining Force Feather』

ハード　ニンテンドーＤＳ
発売日　2009年2月19日
開発　フライト・プラン
発売　セガ

©SEGA

078 『Shining Force EXA』

ハード　PlayStation 2
発売日　2007年1月18日
開発　ネバーランドカンパニー
発売　セガ

©SEGA

082 『STEINS;GATE』

ハード　Xbox 360/PSP「プレイステーション・ポータブル」
発売日　2009年10月15日（Xbox 360版）
　　　　2011年6月23日（PSP版）
開発　5pb.
発売　5pb.

©2011 5pb./Nitroplus

085 『STEINS;GATE 比翼恋理のだーりん』

ハード　Xbox 360
発売日　2011年6月16日
開発　5pb.
発売　5pb.

©2011 5pb./Nitroplus

086 『世紀末オカルト学院』

テレビ放送期間　2010年7月～2010年9月
DVD・ＢＤ　1巻～6巻発売中
発売　アニプレックス
販売　ソニー・ミュージックディストリビューション

©A-1 Pictures/Aniplex・テレビ東京

088 『世界樹の迷宮』

ハード　ニンテンドーＤＳ
発売日　2007年1月18日
発売　アトラス

©ATLUS CO.,LTD.2007 ALL RIGHTS RESERVED.

088 『世界樹の迷宮 II 諸王の聖杯』

ハード　ニンテンドーＤＳ
発売日　2008年2月21日
発売　アトラス

©ATLUS CO.,LTD 2007

088 『世界樹の迷宮Ⅲ 星海の来訪者』

ハード　ニンテンドーDS
発売日　2010年4月1日発売
発売　アトラス

©ATLUS CO.,LTD 2007,2009

091 『ノーラと刻の工房 霧の森の魔女』

ハード　ニンテンドーDS
発売日　2011年7月21日
発売　アトラス

©Index Corporation 2011 Published by ATLUS

092 『セブンスドラゴン2020』

ハード　PSP「プレイステーション・ポータブル」
発売日　2011年11月23日
開発　イメージエポック
製作　SEGA

©SEGA
Licensed by TOKYO TOWER

094 『閃光のナイトレイド』

テレビ放送期間　2010年4月〜2010年6月
DVD・BD　1巻〜7巻発売中
発売　アニプレックス
販売　ソニー・ミュージックディストリビューション

©A-1 Pictures/ 閃光のナイトレイド製作委員会

096 『青の祓魔師』

原作　「青の祓魔師」（集英社刊）加藤和恵著
テレビ放送期間　2011年4月〜2011年10月
DVD・BD　1巻〜6巻発売中（2011年12月10日現在）
　　　　　7〜10巻発売予定
発売　アニプレックス
販売　ソニー・ミュージックディストリビューション

© 加藤和恵/集英社・「青の祓魔師」製作委員会・MBS

098 『戦国乙女〜桃色パラドックス〜』

原作　（株）平和（CR戦国乙女より）
テレビ放送期間　2011年4月〜2011年6月
DVD・BD　1巻〜6巻発売中（2011年12月10日現在）
　　　　　7巻 2012年1月4日発売予定
アニメーション制作　トムス・エンタテインメント
販売　ポニーキャニオン

©HEIWA／天下統一くらぶ

100 『戦国BASARA3』

ハード　PlayStation 3 / ニンテンドーWii
発売日　2011年7月29日
発売　CAPCOM

©CAPCOM CO., LTD. 2010 ALL RIGHTS RESERVED.

102 『戦律のストラタス』

ハード　PSP「プレイステーション・ポータブル」
発売日　2011 年 10 月 27 日
発売　KONAMI

©Konami Digital Entertainment

104 『ソニコミ』

ハード　日本語版 Windows XP Home/XP Pro/Vista/7
発売日　2011 年 11 月 25 日
発売　ニトロプラス

©Nitroplus

106 『それでも町は廻っている』

原作　「それでも町は廻っている」（少年画報社刊）石黒正数著
テレビ放送期間　2010 年 10 月～ 2010 年 12 月
DVD・BD　1 巻～ 6 巻発売中
販売　ポニーキャニオン

© 石黒正数・少年画報社／それ町製作委員会

108 『ダンガンロンパ 希望の学園と絶望の高校生』

ハード　PSP「プレイステーション・ポータブル」
発売日　2010 年 11 月 25 日
発売　スパイク

©Spike All Rights Reserved.

110 『超次元ゲイム ネプテューヌmk2』

ハード　PlayStation 3
発売日　2011 年 8 月 18 日
発売　コンパイルハート

©GUST CO.,LTD. ©Nippon Ichi Software, Inc.
©2011 5pb. ©KI/comcept Inc. ©2011 IDEA FACTORY
©2011 COMPILE HEART

112 『デビルサバイバー オーバークロック』

ハード　ニンテンドー 3DS
発売日　2011 年 9 月 1 日
開発　アトラス
発売　インデックス

©Index Corporation 2008,2011 Published by ATLUS

115 『デビルサバイバー2』

ハード　ニンテンドーDS
発売日　2011 年 7 月 28 日
開発　アトラス
発売　インデックス

©Index Corporation 2008,2011 Published by ATLUS

118	『DUNAMIS15』
	ハード　PlayStation 3/Xbox 360
	発売日　2011年9月15日
	発売　5pb.
	©2011 5pb.

120	『とある飛空士への追憶』
	原作　犬村小六（小学館「ガガガ文庫」刊）
	制作　トムス・エンタテインメント
	アニメーション制作　マッドハウス
	発売日　DVD・BD 2012年2月24日
	発売元　小学館／販売元：バンダイビジュアル
	©2011 犬村小六・小学館／「とある飛空士への追憶」製作委員会

122	『NO.6』
	原作　「NO.6」（講談社刊）あさのあつこ著
	テレビ放送期間　2011年7月～2011年9月
	DVD・BD 1巻～3巻発売中（2011年12月5日現在）
	4～6巻発売予定
	発売　アニプレックス
	販売　ソニー・ミュージックディストリビューション
	© あさのあつこ・講談社／No.6製作委員会

126	『NEWラブプラス』
	ハード　ニンテンドー3DS
	発売日　2012年2月14日
	発売　KONAMI
	©Konami Digital Entertainment

128	『NO MORE HEROES 2 DESPERATE STRUGGLE』
	ハード　ニンテンドーWii
	発売日　2010年10月21日
	発売　マーベラスエンタテイメント
	開発　グラスホッパー・マニファクチュア
	©Marvelous Entertainment Inc. ©GRASSHOPPER MANUFACTURE INC.

130	『花咲くいろは』
	テレビ放送期間　2011年4月～2011年9月
	DVD・BD　1巻～5巻発売中（2011年12月5日現在）
	6～9巻発売予定
	販売　ポニーキャニオン
	© 花いろ旅館組合

134	『華ヤカ哉、我ガ一族』
	ハード　PSP「プレイステーション・ポータブル」
	発売日　2010年7月1日
	開発　ヴァンテアンシステムズ
	販売　アイディアファクトリー
	©2010 IDEA FACTORY / Vingt et un Systems Corporation

136 『バレットソウル -弾魂-』

ハード　Xbox 360
発売日　2011年4月7日
　　　　Xbox LIVE ゲーム オン デマンド 配信 2011年4月7日
発売　5pb.

©2011 5pb.

138 『東のエデン』

テレビ放送期間　2009年4月～2009年6月
DVD・BD　1巻～6巻発売中
映画　東のエデン 劇場版 I The King of Eden
映画　東のエデン 劇場版 II Paradise Lost

© 東のエデン製作委員会

140 『BEYOND THE FUTURE -FIX THE TIME ARROWS-』

ハード　PlayStation 3
　　　　PSP「プレイステーション・ポータブル」
発売日　2011年12月8日
開発　5pb./Rejet
発売　5pb.

©2011 5pb.

144 『ファントムブレイカー』

ハード　Xbox 360
発売日　2011年6月2日
発売　5pb.

©2011 5pb.

146 『Fate/Zero』

原作　虚淵玄（ニトロプラス）/ TYPE-MOON
キャラクター原案　武内崇
テレビ放送期間　TOKYO MX・MBS・チバテレビ・tvk・テレ玉・
とちぎテレビ・群馬テレビ・BS-11 他にて 2011年10月～

©Nitroplus／TYPE-MOON・ufotable・FZPC

148 『武装神姫 BATTLE MASTERS Mk.2』

ハード　PSP「プレイステーション・ポータブル」
発売日　2011年9月22日
発売　KONAMI

©Konami Digital Entertainment

150 『フラクタル』

テレビ放送期間　2011年1月～2011年3月
DVD・BD　1巻～4巻発売中

© フラクタル製作委員会

Heroes & Heroines

156 『BAYONETTTA』

ハード　PlayStation 3/Xbox 360
発売日　2010年9月2日
開発　プラチナゲームズ
PS3版移植開発　セガ

©SEGA

160 『ボーダーブレイク　エアバースト』

ハード　アーケードゲーム
発売日　2010年10月21日
発売　SEGA
ボーダーブレイク　エアバースト　Ver.2.5
全国ゲームセンターで稼働中

©SEGA

162 『真剣で私に恋しなさい！』

ハード　ＰＣゲーム（18禁）
ジャンル　武士娘恋愛ＡＤＶ
発売日　2009年8月28日発売
企画・シナリオ　タカヒロ
原画　wagi

©みなとそふと 2009

162 『真剣で私に恋しなさい！S』

ハード　ＰＣゲーム（18禁）
ジャンル　武士娘恋愛ＡＤＶ
発売日　2012年1月27日発売
企画・シナリオ　タカヒロ
原画　wagi

©みなとそふと

164 TVアニメ『真剣で私に恋しなさい！！』

原作　みなとそふと
キャラクター原案　wagi
テレビ放送期間　2011年10月〜
ＢＤ・DVD　第1巻　2011年11月25日発売予定

©みなとそふと／まじこい製作委員会

166 『魔法少女まどか☆マギカ』

テレビ放送期間　2011年1月〜2011年4月
DVD・ＢＤ　1巻〜6巻発売中
発売　アニプレックス
販売　ソニー・ミュージックディストリビューション

©Magica Quartet / Aniplex・Madoka Partners・MBS

168 『宮本武蔵―双剣に馳せる夢―』

公開日　2009年6月13日
DVD・ＢＤ　発売中
発売・販売　ポニーキャニオン

©2009 Production I.G／宮本武蔵製作委員会

170 『METAL GEAR SOLID PEACE WALKER HD EDITION』

ハード　PlayStation 3／Xbox 360
発売日　2011年11月10日
発売　KONAMI

©Konami Digital Entertainment

---

172 『メモリーズオフ ゆびきりの記憶』

ハード　Xbox 360／PSP「プレイステーション・ポータブル」
発売日　2010年7月29日（Xbox 360版）
　　　　2011年5月26日（PSP版）
発売　5pb.

©2010-11 5pb./CYBERFRONT

---

174 『四畳半神話大系』

テレビ放送期間　2010年4月〜2010年7月
DVD・BD　1巻〜4巻発売中

© 四畳半主義者の会

---

176 『REZELCROSS』

ハード　PSP「プレイステーション・ポータブル」
発売日　2007年9月6日
発売　ソニー・コンピュータエンタテインメント

©2007 Sony Computer Entertainment Inc.

---

178 『Lucian Bee's RESURRECTION SUPERNOVA』

ハード　PlayStation 2／PSP「プレイステーション・ポータブル」
発売日　2009年7月30日（PlayStation 2版）
　　　　2010年10月28日（PSP版）
開発　ヒューネックス
発売　5pb.

©2009 5pb. ／ Hunex ／ HirotakaMaeda
©2010 5pb. ／ Hunex ／ HirotakaMaeda

---

181 『Lucian Bee's JUSTICE YELLOW』

ハード　PlayStation 2／PSP「プレイステーション・ポータブル」
発売日　2010年5月20日（PlayStation 2版）
　　　　2010年10月28日（PSP版）
製作　5pb.Inc.

©2009 5pb. ／ Hunex ／ HirotakaMaeda ©2010 5pb. ／ Rejet
©2010 5pb. ／ Hunex ／ HirotakaMaeda ©2010 5pb. ／ Rejet

---

182 『Lucian Bee's EVIL VIOLET』

ハード　PlayStation 2／PSP「プレイステーション・ポータブル」
発売日　2010年5月20日（PlayStation 2版）
　　　　2010年10月28日（PSP版）
製作　5pb.Inc.
開発　5pb. Games／Rejet

©2009 5pb. ／ Hunex ／ HirotakaMaeda ©2010 5pb. ／ Rejet
©2010 5pb. ／ Hunex ／ HirotakaMaeda ©2010 5pb. ／ Rejet

184 『ROBOTICS;NOTES』

ハード　PlayStation 3/Xbox 360
発売日　2012年春発売予定
発売　5pb.

©MAGES./5pb./Nitroplus

186 『ロリポップチェーンソー』

ハード　PlayStation 3/Xbox 360
発売日　2012年発売予定
開発　グラスホッパー・マニファクチュア
発売・製作　角川ゲームス

©KADOKAWA GAMES/GRASSHOPPER MANUFACTURE

188 『WORKING!!』

原作　「WORKING!!」（スクウェア・エニックス刊）高津カリノ著
テレビ放送期間　2010年4月～6月
DVD・BD　1巻～6巻発売中
発売　アニプレックス
販売　ソニー・ミュージックディストリビューション
※第2期は2011年10月より放映中

© 高津カリノ/スクウェアエニックス・「WORKING!!」製作委員会（第1期）

帯　掲載イラスト

『NO MORE HEROES 2 DESPERATE STRUGGLE』
コザキユースケ
©Marvelous Entertainment Inc. ©GRASSHOPPER MANUFACTURE INC.
『Shining Force Feather』
pako・いとうのいぢ　©SEGA
『ギルティクラウン』
redjuice・加藤裕美　©GUILTY CROWN COMMITTEE
『あの日見た花の名前を僕達はまだ知らない。』
田中将賀　©ANOHANA PROJECT
『セブンスドラゴン 2020』
三輪士郎　©SEGA
Licensed by TOKYO TOWER
『NEW ラブプラス』
ミノ☆タロー　©2011 Konami Digital Entertainment
『ソニコミ』
津路参汰　©Nitroplus
『超次元ゲイム　ネプテューヌ mk2』
つなこ
©GUST CO.,LTD. ©Nippon Ichi Software, Inc.
©2011 5pb. ©KI/comcept Inc. ©2011 IDEA FACTORY
©2011 COMPILE HEART
『STEINS;GATE』
huke　©2011 5pb./Nitroplus
『デビルサバイバー 2』
ヤスダスズヒト
©Index Corporation 2008,2011 Published by ATLUS
『WORKING!!』
足立慎吾
© 高津カリノ/スクウェアエニックス・「WORKING!!」製作委員会(第 1 期)
『魔法少女まどか☆マギカ』
蒼樹うめ・岸田隆宏
©Magica Quartet / Aniplex・Madoka Partners・MBS
『Persona4』
副島成記　©ATLUS CO.,LTD. 1996.2008
『Fate/Zero』
須藤友徳・碇谷敦　©Nitroplus／TYPE-MOON・ufotable・FZPC
『A チャンネル』
© 黒田 bb・芳文社 /A チャンネル委員会・MBS
『BAYONETTTA』
島崎麻里　©SEGA

ゲーム&アニメ
キャラクターデザインブック

2011年12月5日 初版第1刷発行
2012年2月20日 　　第2刷発行

編集	大場義行
編集協力	
テキスト製作	ヒヨコ舎
本文デザイン	サトウセーイチ
ジャケットデザイン	草野剛

発行元　　パイ インターナショナル
〒170-0005　東京都豊島区南大塚 2-32-4
TEL 03-3944-3981
FAX 03-5395-4830
e-mail : sales@pie.co.jp

印刷・製本　　図書印刷株式会社
制作協力　　PIE BOOKS

©2011 PIE International/PIE BOOKS
ISBN978-4-7562-4169-6 C0079
Printed in Japan

本書の収録内容の無断転載・複写・複製等を禁じます。
ご注文、乱丁・落丁本の交換等に関するお問い合わせは、
小社までご連絡ください。
内容に関するお問い合わせは下記までご連絡ください。
PIE BOOKS　TEL : 03-5395-4819

Heroes & Heroines
Japanese Video Game + Animation Illustration

Editor Oba Yoshiyuki
Editor
Text Hiyokosha
Design Satoh Seiichi
Jacket Design Kusano Tsuyoshi

Publishing Company PIE International
2-32-4, Minami-Otsuka,Toshima-ku,
Tokyo 170-0005 JAPAN
Tel:+81-3-3944-3981
Fax:+81-3-5395-4830
e-mai:sales@pie.co.jp

©2011 PIE International / PIE BOOKS
All rights reserved. No part of this publication
may be reproduced in any form or by any means,graphic,
electronic or mechanical, including
photocopying and recording by an information storage and retrieval
system, without prior permission in writing from the publisher.